GRACE OF MONACO

also by Jeffrey Robinson

GRACE OF MONACO

Jeffrey Robinson

Da Capo Press
A Member of the Perseus Books Group

First published as *Ranier and Grace: An Intimate Portrait* in Great Britain 1989 in the United States of America 1989

Editorial production by *Marrathon* Production Services. www.marathon.net

Book design by Jane Raese Set in 12-point Goudy Old Style by Jane Raese

Cataloging-in-Publication data for this book is available from the Library of Congress.

ISBN 978-1-60286-241-8 (paperback) ISBN 978-1-60286-242-5 (e-book) ISBN 978-1-60286-258-6 (international paperback)

First Da Capo Press edition 2014

Published by Da Capo Press A Member of the Perseus Books Group www.dacapopress.com

Da Capo Press books are available at special discounts for bulk purchases in the U.S. by corporations, institutions, and other organizations. For more information, please contact the Special Markets Department at the Perseus Books Group, 2300 Chestnut Street, Suite 200, Philadelphia, PA 19103, or call (800) 810-4145, ext. 5000, or e-mail special.markets@perseusbooks.com.

10 9 8 7 6 5 4 3 2 1

Author's Note

At Princess Grace's funeral in 1982, one of her old Hollywood buddies, Jimmy Stewart, summed up what so many people in the church that day, already knew: "I just love Grace Kelly. Not because she was a princess, not because she was an actress, not because she was my friend, but because she was just about the nicest lady I ever met. Grace brought into my life, as she brought into yours, a soft, warm light every time I saw her. And every time I saw her was a holiday of its own."

Years before, when Frank Sinatra sang to her in *High Society*, "You're Sensational," he got that right. Years later, after her death, he was right again when he told friends, "She was one helluva special broad."

Princess Grace of Monaco, nee Grace Patricia Kelly in Philadelphia, Pennsylvania, is lovingly remembered by everyone who knew her.

This book was originally written in 1989, with the full and unprecedented cooperation of the four people who loved her best: Prince Rainier III, Prince Albert, Princess Caroline and Princess Stephanie.

Over the years I have revised it for various editions. *Grace of Monaco* is the latest incarnation. Understandably, then, this book will forever be dedicated to

Grace (1929–1982)
and to Rainier (1923–2005)
And to Albert, Caroline, and Stephanie, too.
Your parents were sensational.

Foreword

by Nicole Kidman

I knew Grace Kelly, the actress, from films such as *Rear Window* and *To Catch a Thief*, but I only knew Princess Grace from her very public image, the fairy tale we all witnessed from afar. I didn't know anything about her childhood. Or about her struggles as an actress, as a young artist trying to find herself, to find her place in the world. I knew even less about her marriage to Prince Rainier, and what her family life was like.

For me, approaching this role, there was a disconnect between the public Grace—the actress and the Princess—and the private Grace, the mother, the wife, the daughter. For me, the central question became, what lies beneath the fairy tale? Grace was very private, deliberately so, and I wanted to honor that. But I also wanted to be true to her life and experiences.

The problem is that any time an artist or performer is asked to portray a real person, especially someone as famous as Princess Grace, there is the risk of impersonation or imitation. That's not what I wanted. So I started by reading everything about her I could find. I studied her interviews. And I watched her films. My goal was to absorb the essence of her, so that I could honor with integrity the person she was, while also bringing a sense of expression to the part.

From experience, I knew that by taking it all in, letting everything sink in, the Grace I would portray would emerge, almost subconsciously.

At the same time, I have always been fascinated by the blurry line between art and reality. But there is also an overlap. And that's where an artist can find expression to translate into the fictionalized world of film. I'll show you what I mean. There is a moment in the film when Grace is struggling to succeed as a royal figure, when she is told by her confidante, Father Tucker, that she needs to approach her royal duties as if she is acting the role of a lifetime. It's a key moment, because that's how Grace discovers who she is in Monaco. That became one of my keys to understanding her. It stayed with me because I could imagine how complex and difficult that was. As a head of state, you have to act, you have to perform, and yet, it is not an act or a performance, it is your life. In real life, you don't have the walls of the movie set, the frame of the camera, to tell you who to be. Grace survived a tremendous challenge of identity: finding the right balance between actress, mother, wife, and princess.

That's impressive.

As I got to know her, I was also very impressed how deeply dedicated she was to her children and to her husband—to providing for her family. Her early years had been spent amidst the wealth of old money Philadelphia. Then came the struggle to succeed as an artist, and the fame of Hollywood stardom. After that came ever greater fame, plus the glamor of Monaco. And yet, she stayed true to her convictions, to her belief that love is the most important thing of all.

It was love, compassion, and sensitivity that served as her compass as she navigated her way through life. We all know that fame and wealth can be deceptively misleading. And Grace knew that more than most. But she knew what mattered, set her compass true and often referred to it for guidance. It told her, listen to your heart.

Staying true to her heart is why, I think, people connect so strongly with her. And nowhere is that connection greater than in Monaco. She arrived in 1956 as Grace Kelly, the actress, but by 1962, around the time that Alfred Hitchcock asked her to return to acting and star in his film *Marnie*—which is one of the central themes of the film—she was no longer Grace Kelly, she had become Princess Grace.

It was a unique transformation, something the world had never seen before. Even today, you can feel Grace's presence in Monaco. It's something that Olivier Dahan, the director of the film, kept saying—that Grace became Monaco and Monaco became Grace. That the two were inseparable then. That they are inseparable now.

I find something beautiful about that—a person, a moment of existence, and a place being aligned so clearly.

But I also came to feel a certain emptiness.

I got to know Grace by reading about her and studying her and seeing her films, and with that familiarity came a sense of loss.

I feel deeply that, when she died in 1982, the world lost a really special woman.

What remains is the film version of her life, which has taken gentle liberties with her story for the sake of the cinema, and this biography, which tells it like it really was. For my part, I have tried to keep alive in the film the true magic that was Grace. And Jeffrey has kept that same magic alive in this book.

I hope you enjoy both.

Dawn

There is a slight chill in the air as the sun starts to climb its way over the edge of the horizon, far out to sea.

The water goes from pale gray, a mirror of the sky, to a stunning bluish green as the morning steadily sneaks into the corners of the port and lights up a building there that is strawberry pink.

It lights *Le Roche,* the rock overlooking the harbor the juts into the sea where the Prince's Palace sits guarded by its ancient ramparts. It lights the high-rise apartment houses that line the Avenue Princess Grace, along the fabulously expensive stretch of seafront called Monte Carlo Beach. It lights the old villas, piled almost one on top of the other, along the face of the hill the stares down at the casino and the Hotel de Paris and the Café de Paris and the Mediterranean behind them.

At first everything seems flat.

All the colors seem washed out.

But the early morning sun casts a special light that you only see in the south of France, especially after the nighttime Mistral has swept away the clouds. It's intense, dustless, crystal-clear light which brings colors alive in such a way that you think to yourself—nowhere else on the earth does it color everything quite like this.

The sun catches the buildings almost unawares. For a second it turns them all a pale pinkish orange. But almost before you notice it, that's gone. Now you see red and yellow and some of the buildings are a soft, rich Assam tea golden shade—gold in this case being an appropriate color considering the price of real estate here.

Now you also see awnings opening across thousands of balconies—blue awnings and pink awnings, and faded red awnings that have lived through too many summers, and bright yellow awnings that have just been bought.

The night train from Barcelona pulls into the station on its way to the Italian border town of Ventimiglia. A voice with a marked accent announces over the loud speaker, "Monte Carlo, Monte Carlo ... deux minutes d'arret ... Monte Carlo."

On the other side of the tracks, the morning train from Ventimiglia pulls into the station on its way to Nice and Antibes and Cannes, and the man with the marked accent makes the same announcement. "Monte Carlo, Monte Carlo ... deux minutes d'arret ... Monte Carlo."

The first room-service shift has already begun at the Hermitage and the Hotel de Paris where the smallest croissants on earth arrive promptly, in a basket with coffee and orange juice, at a cost of $40.

A lone helicopter flies the length of the beach.

At La Vigie restaurant on the cliff behind the pink stucco 1930s style Old Beach Hotel, they're already setting up the buffet lunch tables. While an old man in a boat with an outboard engine sails by. And two women take an early morning swim together, dog-paddling and talking all the way out to the far buoy.

Gardeners are trimming rose bushes on the road up to *Le Rocher*.

A very large yacht leaves the port, ever so slowly.

A police officer in his well-starched red and white uniform directs traffic at the *Place d'Armes*.

A sometimes-famous tennis player poses next to a swimming pool for a spread before going up to the Tennis Club to spend the next three hours working on his once devastating backhand.

Two rather pretty German girls walk back to their tiny studio apartment after a night at Jimmyz.

A teenaged Italian boy stands behind the service bar at the Moana, washing glasses and listening to music on a portable radio while a teenaged French boy piles chairs on top of tables so that the dance floor can be buffed.

A middle-aged man in a blue work smock runs a vacuum cleaner over the carpets in the casino.

An old woman dressed in black makes her way through the narrow streets of *Le Rocher* towards the Cathedral of Our Lady of the Immaculate Conception, which the locals call, St. Nicholas.

The *quartier* is empty, except for a single policeman walking slowly past the Oceanographic Museum, and a black-robed priest taking some fresh air on the steps of the church before the morning mass.

The old woman dressed in black gives the priest a simple nod and moves into the darkened church, crossing herself and mumbling under her breath, hurrying past the altar to a pair of marble slabs.

One says, RAINIERIVS III.

The other says GRATIA PATRICIA.

She crosses herself, pauses for only a second, then leaves the church and hurries towards the large open place in front of the Palace.

Two *Carabiniers* are guarding the entrance, another is standing near the smaller side door and a fourth is walking casually through the street where a thick black chain prevents cars from parking just there.

The old woman dressed in black stops at the end of the street and looks at the Palace, to see the Prince's ensign flying there, then nods and crosses herself again.

Prologue

From where Grace sat at her desk in her fair-sized office on the top floor of the Palace tower, she had a view from two windows looking at the yacht laden harbor below, and the tiny hill behind it that is Monte Carlo.

She'd decorated the room in pale greens and pale yellows, and placed a big couch in the middle of it—she'd brought that couch with her from Philadelphia—and on either side of it were tables covered in magazines.

There were silver-framed photographs of her family scattered around, on her desk, on tables and on shelves, and on the walls she'd hung paintings and drawings, her favorite being a large oil of New York City.

Now, staring down at the blank piece of paper, thinking about this letter she never wanted to write, the woman who'd given up Hollywood fame as Grace Kelly to become Princess Grace of Monaco, took her fountain pen and in her very deliberate and very neat handwriting, put ***"June 18th, 1962"*** at the top.

It was a start.

Then she wrote, *"Dear Hitch—"*

Had it been 12 years already?

In 1950, as an aspiring actress living in New York, she was offered a black and white screen test by Twentieth Century Fox, for a role she didn't get.

But the director Fred Zinneman had seen that test and two years later cast her opposite Gary Cooper in *High Noon*.

It was her first major screen role.

And while the public found her beautiful, and Cooper won the Academy Award for best actor, Grace didn't even figure on the original poster. The *New York Times* review only gave her passing mention.

The director John Ford had seen that screen test, too. He decided she had, "breeding, quality and class," and convinced MGM to fly her out to Los Angeles to audition for *Mogambo*, a picture he was going to make in Africa with Clark Gable and Ava Gardner.

The part was hers if she wanted it, which she did, but MGM insisted that she sign a seven-year contract to get it. The studio was going to pay her $850 a week, which might have seemed like a lot of money at the time to many people, but by Hollywood standards, was paltry.

Holding out as long as she could, she managed to get two important concessions from the studio. They wouldn't up the money, but they agreed she could have time off every two years to work in the theater, and that she wouldn't have to move to California, that she could stay in New York.

"The studios are tenacious," she had to admit, "when they want someone or something, they always get it"—signing her name with a borrowed pen, standing at the airport counter with the engines of the plane that would take her to Africa, already turning.

In the meantime, Alfred Hitchcock had also seen that 1950 screen test. He decided she was, "a snow-covered volcano."

She wrote, *"It was heartbreaking for me to have to leave the picture—"*

This was the first time she'd confessed that to anyone, besides her husband.

The British born Hitchcock had moved to Hollywood in 1939 and had just become a US citizen. In his mid-50s, he was bald, shaped like an egg, had a very distinctive voice, and was right at the top of the A-List of Hollywood directors, making films that are now considered classics: *Spellbound* with Ingrid Bergman and Gregory Peck; John Steinbeck's *Lifeboat*; *Suspicion* with Cary Grant and Joan Fontaine; and *Notorious*, again with Cary Grant but this time with Ingrid Bergman and Claude Rains.

When he cast Grace to play alongside Ray Milland in a thriller called *Dial M for Murder*, he did what no previous director had done—put her on a pedestal and turned her into a movie star.

Now she wrote, **"I was so excited about doing it and particularly about working with you again—"** using dashes instead of commas or periods, which she often did.

Throughout the filming of *Dial M*, he kept talking to her about his next picture, this one with Jimmy Stewart called *Rear Window*. He'd been so enthusiastic about it, that when the time came, she turned down the chance to work with Marlon Brando in *On the Waterfront*—her replacement, Eva Marie Saint, won the Best Actress Oscar for that role—and opted for Hitch's new film.

She wrote, **"When we meet I would like to explain to you myself all of the reasons which is difficult to do by letter or through a third-party—"**

After that, she teamed up with Hitch again, for *To Catch a Thief*, working alongside Cary Grant, which they filmed on the French Riviera. It was on the success of that film that she returned to France the following year, to the Cannes Film Festival, which is when she met Prince Rainier.

That was 1955.

"When I married Prince Rainier," she told people at the time, "I married the man and not what he represented or what he was. I fell in love with him without giving a thought to anything else."

But that "anything else" was something very unique and seven years later, the fairy tale that had begun with that first meeting in Monaco, was alive and well.

She came to the office every day, but did not keep banker's hours. Sometimes she'd come in early, sometimes she'd come in late. She'd stay as long as she had to, depending on her appointment schedule. But even when she wasn't in the office, her days were busy because Rainier had given her a lot of responsibilities. She'd already redecorated the Palace, a huge task, airing the musty place out, repainting and redecorating, then dividing the children's room in two, putting a partition down the middle, so that each of them would have their own space. Long before that was finished, she'd become President of the Monegasque Red Cross, President of the local Garden Club and oversaw almost all of the official cultural activities in Monaco. She also had the household to run, which meant administering a sizeable staff and also supervising the marketing. She personally planned every menu for the family, paying special attention to Rainier's weight, and her own, and making sure that her children ate well-balanced meals.

"You know what my husband calls me?" she would confide to friends. "He says I'm his Domestic Affairs Coordinator. Makes me sound like a member of the cabinet."

She was dedicated to what she was doing and wanted everything to be perfect because—as people had quickly discovered soon after she'd arrived—Grace was a perfectionist.

Arriving as she did in Monaco, knowing no one except Rainier, being that far away from home at a time when telephones didn't work so well, and not speaking the language, was difficult. But by now she'd grown comfortable in her role as Princess Grace.

And the year had begin so promisingly.

Her daughter Caroline was five and her son Albert—everyone in the family called him Albie—was four. Her husband, whom she called Ray, had just turned 39. They were a handsome, happy and healthy family. Rainier spoke French to the children and she spoke

English to them, so Caroline and Albie were growing up completely bilingual. And her own French had improved so much that she happily spoke the language in public, although she never lost her American accent.

But then she'd suffered a miscarriage.

And there would be a second one that year.

At the same time, France's President Charles de Gaulle was making threatening noises, again, about tax evaders in Monaco. He was threatening Rainier that he was going to clamp down.

De Gaulle and Rainier had been through this before. Rainier always maintained Monaco's sovereignty from France, which had been written into official treaties. But, this time, de Gaulle wasn't having it and, official treaty or no, he was determined to do something about it.

Grace could see, up close, the pressure her husband was under.

And now there was this with Hitchcock.

The two had stayed in touch ever since she'd left Hollywood. And she never hesitated to credit him with making her a star.

"Hitch taught me everything about the cinema," she would say. "It's thanks to him that I understood that murder scenes should be shot like love scenes and love scenes like murder scenes."

Towards the end of 1961, while working on a new picture called *Marnie*—which would star a handsome Scots actor named Sean Connery, who'd just broken all the box office records playing James Bond in *Dr. No*—Hitchcock decided Grace would be perfect for the title role.

He often cast actors he'd worked with in previous films. He'd hired Cary Grant and Jimmy Stewart four times, and Ingrid Bergman three times. Now he wanted to hire Grace for the fourth time.

For her, it would mark a return to her film career and doing that with Alfred Hitchcock seemed to her, and to Rainier, as well, the best choice.

Except this time different. Hitch liked her for what he called her "sexual elegance," and wanted her to make a comeback as a sexually frustrated kleptomaniac who is raped by her controlling husband.

No one doubted that actress Grace Kelly could do that, but could Princess Grace?

She and Rainier had discussed it. He had some doubts and, frankly, so did she. But once she convinced herself it would be right, and once he agreed, she told Hitch yes.

So Hitch announced in March that Grace Kelly would be returning to acting, and that's when the furor began.

First, MGM said she couldn't, because she was still under contract to them.

The way they saw it, when she walked out on Hollywood to marry Rainier and live in Monaco, the studio had suspended her without pay. They were now claiming that the suspension extended the termination date of her contract and that, therefore, it was still in force. If she were going to make a movie, she'd either have to make it with MGM, or Hitchcock would have to buy her out of the contract.

That was only the beginning.

While her lawyers in the States and Hitchcock's lawyers, too, decided that MGM was blowing smoke—the studio responded that it was taking this seriously and "considering our position"—the people of Monaco had their own ideas.

The 26-year-old who had arrived in 1956 as movie star Grace Kelly, was now a 32-year-old mother of two and First Lady of the Principality.

Hollywood actresses made movies, Monaco's Princess did not.

She wrote, **"It is unfortunate that it had to happen this way and I am deeply sorry—"**

By the end of her Hollywood career, she didn't even try to hide her feelings that she was ready to leave.

"When I first came to Hollywood five years ago," she told a reporter during the filming of *High Society*, "my makeup call was at eight in the morning. On this movie, it's been put back to seven thirty. Every day I see Joan Crawford, who's been in makeup since five, and Loretta Young, who's been there since four in the morning. I'll be God-damned if I'm going to stay in a business where I have to get up earlier and earlier and it takes longer and longer for me to get in front of a camera."

That wasn't her only problem with "Tinself Town."

At times she'd say she hated the place. "I have many acquaintances there, but few friends." Other times, she'd call it, "A town without pity. I know of no other place in the world where so many people suffer from nervous breakdowns, where there are so many alcoholics, neurotics, and so much unhappiness."

Then again, there were times when Hollywood amused her. "It's holier than thou for the public and unholier-than-the devil in reality."

No one who knew her doubted that somewhere, in the back of her mind, she'd always hoped, one day, she could return to acting.

But now that she had the chance . . .

She wrote, *"Thank you dear Hitch for being so understanding and helpful—I hate disappointing you—"*

It was well known around Hollywood that Hitch thought of actors as "cattle."

So now she added, *"I also hate the fact that there are probably many other "cattle" who could play the part equally as well— Despite that I hope to remain one of your "sacred cows—"*

She stopped there to re-read the letter.

Then she wrote, *"With deep affection—"* underlines the word "deep," and signs it, *"Grace."*

And with that, her career as Grace Kelly was, undeniably, over.

Chapter 1

Becoming Grace

There was never any mistaking them.

Not those two.

No matter how hard they tried to remain anonymous, there was always someone who'd spot them, who'd know their names.

One night in London, after dining at a Japanese restaurant with friends, Grace asked the waiter to get a taxi. When it arrived, she and Rainier and another couple piled in. But as soon as they did, the driver started laughing. He chuckled all the way to Connaught Hotel where Grace and Rainier got out. And he kept on chuckling all the way to the other couple's flat in Chelsea.

Finally the other couple simply had to know, "What's so funny?"

"It was the little Japanese fellow who hailed me," the driver said. "I couldn't figure out what he wanted. I couldn't figure out what he was talking about because he kept saying over and over again, 'Glazed cherries, glazed cherries.' So who gets into my cab? Grace Kelly."

John Brendon Kelly, the ninth in a family of ten children, was a tough, two-fisted, hard-drinking man with an eye for the ladies who, like so many sons of immigrants to the United States, battled his way from poverty to riches to live the American dream.

His parents came from County Mayo, Ireland, to the New World with nothing more in their pockets than a thick brogue and a lot of hope. John B., who was usually referred to as Jack, was born in 1890 in East Falls, one of Philadelphia's Irish working-class neighborhoods. From the age of nine, to help support his family, he worked after school in the local carpet mills. He quit school three years later for full-time employment as a hod carrier and apprentice brick-layer with one of his older brothers who had, by then, started his own construction firm.

But Jack was destined for better things. He had the drive to succeed and somehow discovered he also had a talent for rowing. With his back and arms strengthened by construction work, he took to sculling on the nearby Schulkill River and quickly developed into a champion oarsman.

Returning from the Army after World War I in 1918, he and his Vesper Boat Club teammates spent the next two years preparing to race, first at England's world-famous Henley Regatta, then at the Olympics in Antwerp. But two days before Kelly planned to leave Philadelphia for Europe, a telegram arrived from the Henley organizers saying, "Entry rejected."

The official explanation has always been that Kelly was banned because the Vesper Club had violated their "amateur" status in 1905 when they solicited donations to cover the costs of going to Henley. And the ban on Vesper was still in effect in 1920.

But Kelly saw it differently.

He took the ban personally, maintaining throughout his life that his entry was refused because he'd once been a common laborer and therefore not welcome to compete with "gentlemen" at class-conscious Henley.

The revenge he took on them has become the stuff of American sports mythology.

Not only did Jack go on to defeat the best of the British a couple of months later in the Olympics—he came home with two gold medals—he then spent several years training his son John Jr. who, in 1947 and again in 1949, reminded the British of the earlier insult and twice took Henley's first prize.

Once described by his chum Franklin Roosevelt as, "the handsomest man I've ever seen," Jack Kelly was heavy on charm and humor, graced till the day he died with an athletic physique, driven by a fearless enthusiasm to get what he wanted, predisposed to womanizing and consumed by a passion for politics.

In 1919 he borrowed $2,500 from two of his brothers to start a company called Kelly For Brickwork, which, by 1935, had become so successful that he used it as a springboard to run for mayor. Although he was defeated and never put his name on another ballot, he flirted briefly with the idea of running for the US Senate in 1936, was head of the Philadelphia Democratic Committee until 1940 and remained, for the rest of his life, a dominant backroom force in Philadelphia politics.

Perhaps not surprisingly, as Kelly was so well connected in the City of Brotherly Love, not one single building was erected in Center City between the mid-1920s and the mid-1950s without Kelly For Brickwork getting the contract.

In 1924 Jack married Margaret Majer, a woman he'd known for nearly nine years. The daughter of German immigrants, she'd been raised a Lutheran in the Strawberry Mansion area of Philadelphia.

She grew up speaking German at home and stressed with her children the same strong sense of Prussian discipline that had been such an important part of her own youth. Everyone obeyed her. Not even Jack dared go up against her.

Although when she insisted her children learn to speak fluent German, they hid the grammar books because they hated the language and feared that, late in the 1930s, speaking German was an unpatriotic thing for Americans to do.

A former magazine cover girl, she studied at Temple University for two years to get herself an Associate's Degree in Physical Education. That quickly led her to a job as the first woman to teach P.E. at the University of Pennsylvania.

She converted to Catholicism to marry Jack and their first child, Peggy, was born within a year. John Jr.—always known as Kell—followed two years later in 1927. Grace was born two years after that, on November 12, 1929. Their fourth and last child, Lizanne, was born in 1933.

Being a stickler for routine, Ma Kelly programmed every part of the day to a tight schedule. There was just so much time for breakfast, just so much time for listening to the radio, a specific time for piano lessons, a specific time for bed. She ran her household with an iron hand and, when she laid down the law, that's the way it was.

Years later, Caroline, Albert, and Stephanie would get to see Ma Kelly at her best when they spent summers with her at the Kelly family beach house, at 26th and Wesley Avenues, in Ocean City, New Jersey.

Grace and Rainier would bring the kids to visit their grandmother and their American cousins. At dinner time, it was Ma Kelly who sat at the head of the table. On more than one occasion, when she spotted Rainier leaning comfortably forward, she'd grab her fork and jab him with it, shrieking, "elbows," until he took them off her table.

As a family, the Kellys lived in a 15-room house built with Kelly bricks at 3901 Henry Avenue in the then upwardly mobile part of Philadelphia called Germantown.

Grace was born there.

Her mother described her as a happy child, even though she was asthmatic and suffered ear and throat infections throughout childhood. As those bouts with illnesses often kept her home in bed,

Grace discovered the joys of reading. And reading remained one of her great pleasures throughout life.

For Jack and Ma, athletics came a close third behind religion and schoolwork. Kell, very much his father's son, was not only victorious at Henley, he also took a bronze medal in sculling at the 1956 Olympics. Peggy, her father's favorite, was a competitive swimmer. Lizanne, the baby of the family who could usually get away with anything, was clearly the most athletic of the three girls and a champion swimmer. Grace played tennis, was captain of her school field hockey team, swam and could dive, but she was never the athlete her brother and sisters were. She wasn't as pretty as Peggy and Lizanne, nor as extroverted as her brother. Very much a middle child, she tended to retreat into her protective shell.

But she was "Fordie's" favorite and years later she'd say memories of her friendship with him were among her fondest of childhood.

Godfrey Ford worked for the Kellys as a general handyman and all-round "Mr. Fixit." A kind and gentle black man from North Philadelphia, he spent his life with the Kellys, was totally dedicated to them, and watched the children grow up as they watched him grow old. Grace loved to tell stories about him, like how when the family moved to Ocean City for the summer all the other kids would have to ride with their parents except her. She got to ride in the old pick-up truck with Fordie. Ma Kelly worried they'd never arrive safely but that didn't stop Grace from piling into the front seat next to Fordie, with their luggage and some of the family furniture pouring off the back, taking twice as long to get to the beach as anyone else, making up stories, singing and laughing all the way.

Though Ma Kelly never knew it, sometimes Fordie would even let Grace steer the truck.

Fordie might have been the first person in Grace's life to say it didn't really matter if she wasn't the athlete her brother and sisters were.

Because Ma Kelly was such a disciplinarian, Grace was enrolled at the Ravenhill Academy in East Falls, a parochial school run by nuns who rigorously stressed discipline and correct manners. But by the time she was 12, Grace had convinced her mother that the less severe Stevens School would be better for her and she was allowed to transfer there.

It was at about that time she started wishing she'd been a boy.

As she later explained, her father's influence on her had been formidable. He used to lecture all of his children, "Nothing is given for nothing," so Grace grew up believing that everything worth having had to be earned and the way you earned anything was through hard work.

The problem with being a teenage girl in the 1940s was that real opportunities were reserved for boys.

"My father was a leader of men," she said. "Whatever the cost, one had to follow him. And to follow in his footsteps it was easier to be a boy than a girl." Still, she added, "An enthusiastic father is a marvelous start in life."

Having inherited some of her dad's enthusiasm, after seeing a performance of the Ballet Russes, she took to studying ballet and classical piano. There was even a time when she thought she might like to become a professional dancer.

Then she discovered the dramatic stage.

She was 12 when she made her debut with the East Falls' Old Academy Players in a production called *Don't Feed the Animals*. She next appeared in a production of *Cry Havoc* and, much to her delight, was cast by the group in their version of *The Torch Bearers*, a play written by her father's brother, George.

She graduated from Stevens in June 1947 and applied to Bennington College in Vermont. But she'd never been too keen on math and science and didn't have the academic qualifications they wanted. Bennington turned her down.

While trying to decide where her future lay, she attended a few courses at Temple University. However, she soon made up her mind to take a serious stab at acting, moved to New York, installed herself at the Barbizon—a residential hotel for well-bred young women—and enrolled at the American Academy of Dramatic Arts.

Watching Grace, barely 18, go off to seek fame and fortune in the big city was not something that Jack Kelly found easy to accept.

His own sister Grace, for whom his daughter was named, had expressed an interest in acting many years before. But her career was stopped by her parents before it ever began because proper young ladies in those days did not do such things.

As Grace herself would later say, "Aunt Grace made the mistake of being born just one generation too soon. I had better luck."

She also had a pair of uncles on her father's side who made her dream of a career in the theatre a genuine possibility. Walter Kelly, much older than her father, was an itinerant actor who had moderate stage success in his youth playing a vaudeville character known as "The Virginia Judge." He went to Hollywood in the early days of the American cinema, but his career never got much further than vaudeville and he died in 1938 when Grace was nine.

Still, she grew up knowing that one of her uncles had been "on the boards" and Uncle Walter stories were a common topic at the family dinner table.

Uncle George was infinitely more successful.

He was John's immediate elder brother, although the two were totally different. Whereas John was physical, George was a dreamer, a delicate man of moods and intellect who started in the theatre as an actor, then evolved into writing plays. He was Grace's godfather and perhaps one of her most important early influences.

In 1926, George Kelly won a Pulitzer Prize for his play *Craig's Wife*, the success of which eventually took him to Hollywood where he was on the writing staff at MGM. Even though his years there never came close to equaling his earlier Broadway promise, being able to say that she was George Kelly's niece opened some early doors for Grace.

It didn't hurt, for instance, at the American Academy where her audition for admission included a speech from *The Torch Bearers.*

Over the next two years she studied diction and posture and learned how to walk on a stage. She gradually overcame her shyness and learned how to create a character. She studied improvisation and Constantin Stanislavski's famous "Method," and found herself doing all sorts of things that would have horrified her parents. For instance, she trekked down to the Bowery to watch bums stumble around so she could improvise a drunk, and spent afternoons at the Bronx Zoo studying the way animals moved.

Acting school was, she would always claim, "the only place I was ever called on to play a llama."

While living at the Barbizon—which more often than not was referred to by the hoards of young men who hung out in the lobby as "The Amazon" because very few of the residents were anywhere near as beautiful as Grace Kelly—a friend suggested she might be able to earn some extra money by modeling. She refused at first, knowing what her parents would think, then let herself get talked into it.

Just before her 19th birthday she signed with a small agency, which managed to get her work at $7.50 an hour. That was a fairly good salary in those days when you consider that most of the rest of the world was struggling to make $1 an hour.

And her parents weren't pleased.

But before long, her blonde, "girl-next-door" looks—as they were then described—found their way into national advertising campaigns. She sold Ipana toothpaste, Old Gold cigarettes, dandruff shampoo, overnight beauty creams, insecticide, and several different kinds of beer. Her fee was quickly upped to $25 an hour and by the time she graduated from the American Academy of Dramatic Arts in 1949, she was doing fashion spreads for newsreels at $400 a week.

Whether or not she could have gone on to be one of the great New York models is another matter. The problem with modeling, as she saw it, was that modeling wasn't acting and she wanted to be an actress.

So now she made the rounds of Broadway casting calls. Time and time again she was told, "Don't call us, we'll call you." She was subjected to the humiliation that all actors and actresses suffer when they're first starting out: of standing around for hours in long lines, being asked to read a dozen lines but getting stopped after just one or two by a voice at the rear of the darkened theatre saying, "Thank you, next please."

Being George Kelly's niece did not save her from paying her dues, from learning the hard way about rejection. No matter what her last name was, at nearly 5' 7" she was too tall to play the innocent little girl that her pretty face and bright blue eyes suggested. Still, she stuck it out and persevered until Uncle George stepped in and helped her land her first professional acting job.

It was 1949, at the Bucks County Playhouse in New Hope, Pennsylvania, for their summer-stock production of *The Torch Bearers*.

He'd put her name forward for the part, but insisted that she shouldn't get it just because she was his niece. Later, he always claimed that she got hired because the director believed she'd be "okay." And while she might not have been particularly remarkable in the role, she worked hard and was good enough to be invited back for their second production of the summer, *The Heiress*.

And this time she was very good.

Flattering notices at Bucks County led to a screen test.

It was 1950 and director Gregory Ratoff was making a film called *Taxi*. He thought she might be right to play the young Irish immigrant. So she took that screen test in New York but failed to get the role.

Little did she know, then, how that screen test would change her life.

Undaunted by the rejection, she continued auditioning until she won the part of Raymond Massey's daughter in a Broadway revival of August Strindberg's *The Father*.

He was a majestically tall actor so this time the problem wasn't her height.

It was the *New York Times*.

They gave her a passable review—noting that her performance was charming and pliable, but panned him. The power of the *Times* being what it was on Broadway in those days, the show closed in nine weeks.

Grace spent the rest of that winter and spring on the audition circuit, modeling to earn money but, as an actress, otherwise out of work.

Of course, timing and luck are important in all careers and Grace's timing, combined with her Kelly-green Irish luck, was near perfect. She was in the right place at the right time because New York in the early 1950s was where television was happening and television in the early 1950s was fast becoming America's most important arena for aspiring actors and actresses.

Unable to land another role on Broadway, she plugged herself into the weekly television drama circuit. She started appearing regularly in dramas presented on the Philco-Goodyear Playhouse. That led to appearances in all the other major "playhouse" productions, such as the Kraft Television Theatre, the Nash Airflyte Theatre, and the Prudential Family Playhouse.

Over the course of 30 months, Grace worked in no less than 60 live television productions.

Then in 1951, just as she was starting to make a name for herself in television, she was offered her first movie, a minor part in a film called *Fourteen Hours*.

Based on a true incident, it's the story of a man standing on the ledge of a building for 14 hours, threatening to jump. It featured Richard Basehart, Barbara Bel Geddes, Paul Douglas, Debra Paget, Agnes Moorehead, Jeffrey Hunter, and Howard Da Silva. The film was not a success at the box office and didn't do much for Grace's career.

Enter again, Uncle George.

The summer she'd appeared at the Bucks County Playhouse, George had phoned his friend, producer Gant Gaither, suggesting that he see her work. And while Gaither liked what he saw—at least he thought she was okay—he also knew he'd be doing George a favor if he hired her. So he gave her a job in an out-of-town preview of a play called *Alexander*. Her role was sexy and, even though the Albany, New York, critics wrote, "Grace Kelly was too cool to be sexy," it was that very quality which would one day make her a major movie star.

Recognizing her promise, while they were still in Albany, Gaither told her, "You've got the part when we come to New York."

Years later he recalled affectionately, "She was a lovely young girl who became a magnificent woman. The thing that amazed me most about her was that her judgment was always so good. She had such wonderful common sense. Long before she got married, if I was working on a show that needed help, I'd ask her to come see it. If she was critical of something she'd offer something else in its place. She had a wonderful sense of construction."

Just before Gaither's play traveled down the Hudson to Broadway, Grace received a phone call out of the blue saying that Hollywood producer Stanley Kramer wanted her for a Western called *High Noon*, to be directed by Fred Zinnemann.

It was Zinnemann who'd seen that 1950 screen test. She auditioned, won the part, spent much of the summer of 1951 doing stock in Colorado, and made *High Noon* that autumn.

Despite the film's classic big-movie reputation these days, her portrayal of Amy Kane opposite Gary Cooper's Oscar-winning tin-star sheriff did not make her a movie star. When she was finished, Hollywood merely said thank you and handed her a ticket back to New York.

Grace returned to the apartment she now called home at 200 East 66th Street, worked some more in television, and kept pounding the pavement looking for a part on Broadway.

Then, again, seemingly out of the blue, a call came from producer Sam Zimbalist and director John Ford. They wanted her for the second female lead in a picture they were going to shoot in Africa called *Mogambo*.

She assumed at the time it was her work on *High Noon* that had earned her the call. It wasn't. Quite by chance Zimbalist and Ford had also seen her 1950 screen test and hired her on the strength of that.

Grace wanted to do the picture and years later, explained why. "Three things that interested me. John Ford, Clark Gable and a trip to Africa with expenses paid. If *Mogambo* had been made in Arizona, I wouldn't have done it."

The only stumbling block was the contract that MGM demanded she sign.

Once that was done, she offed to Kenya with Clark Gable who was re-creating the white hunter role he'd first played in *Red Dust*, and with Ava Gardner, who was the female lead.

Grace's performance as the ice-cool "other woman" earned her an Oscar nomination that year as Best Supporting Actress.

With her characteristic charm, she always credited Ford for her success in that picture and, also, with having taught her a lot about acting on screen. She used to say that he knew just how far he could push his actors without forcing them to overstep the limits of their potential.

And though she lost the Oscar to Donna Reed, now when Grace Kelly's name was mentioned, so were the words "movie star."

Except she wasn't yet a big enough movie star to carry a picture on her own.

Enter here, Alfred Hitchcock.

Although he'd found her "mousy" in *High Noon*, he remembered her screen test and he could see her "potential for restraint." So he hired her to play opposite Ray Milland in *Dial M for Murder*.

It was the beginning of her most successful working partnership because Hitchcock understood how to direct her better than anyone else.

It was also the beginning of a love affair with Milland, which hit the headlines and nearly saw him walk away from his wife for her.

Hitchcock immediately cast her a second time, putting her opposite Jimmy Stewart in *Rear Window*.

She followed that with *The Country Girl*, starring alongside Bing Crosby and William Holden.

Ironically, a few years before, the producer who brought *The Country Girl* to Broadway had turned Grace down for the same role for which she now won the Oscar as Best Actress.

Just a few short years away from selling bug spray and toothpaste, Grace Kelly had become a household name in America.

She was the role model for half a generation of young American girls in the mid-1950s. They dressed like her and wore their hair like her and tried to speak like her. If you were a young girl growing up in America in those days and you were beautiful, what you wanted to hear most was someone saying, "You're as pretty as Grace Kelly."

To the utter delight of MGM, who'd locked her into that contract for *Mogambo*, Grace Kelly was suddenly worth a fortune. They used her in *Green Fire* with Stewart Granger, but once that was done they realized they could keep their books in the black by renting her out to other studios.

They loaned her out to Paramount for *The Bridges at Toko-Ri* with Bill Holden and Fredric March and, for the third time, to Alfred Hitchcock for *To Catch a Thief* with Cary Grant.

After filming that in the south of France—where she could see Monaco far below as she and Grant drove in that famous scene along the Grande Corniche—MGM announced that she was going to do a picture called *The Adventures of Quentin Outward* with Robert Taylor.

But when Grace read the script, she hated it.

As far as she was concerned the role the studio had in mind for her gave her nothing more to do than walk around wearing a tall hat and watch Robert Taylor joust.

She told MGM she wouldn't make the picture.

They said she had to do it and reminded her that she was under contract.

She stood her ground and refused.

So MGM put her on suspension.

If she wouldn't work for them, MGM was going to teach her a lesson—now she wouldn't work for anybody.

Her career had run headfirst into a "Kelly brick" wall.

Chapter 2

A Shy Man

For a period of about ten years, from the end of the war until the end of 1955, Prince Rainier III of Monaco was considered the world's most eligible bachelor.

Everybody could see he was handsome. Everybody knew he owned a country. And everybody also reckoned he must therefore be very rich. The woman he would eventually choose to marry would become a princess. Not surprisingly, he was forever being invited to dinner parties only to find that an extra lady had been seated beside him.

By his own admission, it wasn't too long before he stopped going to dinner parties.

After having fallen out with his grandfather at the end of World War II, Rainier purchased a small villa in St. Jean-Cap-Ferrat, on the side of the peninsula facing Villefranche. It had been going for a good price because it was on an inside cove and, although it didn't have a large garden, he could swim in the cove off a little dock.

He lived there as a bachelor, although once he ascended the throne he tended to spend the week at the Palace and go to the villa for weekends.

The villa was all the more special because he lived there for nearly six years with his friend, Gisele Pascal.

The two met when he was a student at Montpellier. She was an actress who'd come down from Paris to do a play there. They were the same age. She was born in Cannes, so they also had the Mediterranean in common. They sailed together in the summer and skied together in the winter, and, as time wore on, speculation mounted that they would soon marry.

When it didn't happen, the press decided the two couldn't marry because the Monegasques would never stand for their prince wedding an actress.

Next came the story that the National Council wouldn't allow the Prince to marry because Mlle. Pascal was the daughter of a florist and therefore a commoner.

That had no bearing on anything, either. Neither did the report that Grace Kelly was the daughter of a bricklayer.

Finally the story ran that Rainier and Gisele had been forbidden to marry because she couldn't have children.

Rumor had it that the National Council badgered Rainier, fearing that unless he produced an heir the principality would revert to France.

That, too, was nonsense.

"There was no reason for us to get married," Rainier admitted many years later. "We were together six years and it was fine while it lasted but I think we both felt it was long enough. It was a love affair that had come to its own end. I don't think there was any real intention on either side to get married. As long as things were good they were fine just as they were. Then it simply ended."

Both of them were obviously affected by the breakup. Years later, Gisele would marry and have a child, scotching the gossip that her inability to bear children kept her from becoming Monaco's Princess.

But for now, needing time to be by himself, and to get away from Monaco for a while, Rainier climbed on board his boat and set sail for Conakry, in what was then French Guinea, on the west coast of Africa.

"I had a little Citroen 2CV that I tied down to the deck," he said, "so that when we docked I could take a long drive inside the country. My manservant in those days, Coki, was from a village called Kankan, about 350 or 400 miles due east of the coast. One of our objectives was to get him home to buy a wife. He didn't have enough money so I staked him. I bought half his wife. Well, we got there and he chose the woman he wanted. He gave her parents enough goats, sheep and beads and made arrangements for her to arrive in Monaco around Christmas. When she didn't show up we both got anxious about it. A few months later we learned that her mother had sold her to somebody else. Someone made a better offer and we got cut out of the deal. He and I were both very sad."

Rainier spent several months in Africa—he referred to it the way the French do as, "a change of air"—and when he was ready to come home, he played Noah and filled his ark. "I bought a couple of ostriches and three chimps, a few baboons and some crocodiles which we packed in crates but had to water every day in order to keep their skin from cracking. I had my chaps build a shack on the aft of the boat and we kept the animals there. I was happy to feed them every day but none of the crew would clean [it] out, so for the whole trip back, a friend and I did that every day, too."

He was just starting to get to know the animals when they stopped to refuel at Dakar. "Two of the baboons got loose. You can imagine what we must have looked like chasing them all over the port. We attracted quite a crowd with this weird boat full of animals."

As soon as Rainier returned to Monaco, he was again a prime target for the matchmakers. Even Aristotle Onassis tried to find a bride for him.

Convinced that only someone very special would do, Onassis looked around and decided the perfect match would be Marilyn

Monroe. He plotted their engagement and leaked stories to the press hoping to force the issue. But Rainier and Marilyn weren't to be.

In fact, they never even met.

"You must understand how shy he was in those days," noted Khalil el Khoury, a Sydney Greenstreet look-alike whose father had been the first president of Lebanon. El Khoury originally came to Monaco in the spring of 1950 and as was the custom, went up to the Palace to sign his name in the official guest book. A few hours later the chief of protocol rang to say that the Prince would like him to come for tea the following afternoon.

"I went to the Palace and there we sat, Prince Rainier and I, two very young and very shy characters, neither of us terribly relaxed with the other. We were making small talk when the Prince asked my age. I told him. He said, 'Me, too.' He asked me when I was born. I told him and it turned out we were not only the exact same age, we were born within four or five hours of each other. That broke down the barriers."

Their friendship endured a lifetime, but was built gradually and, at least in the early stages, through letters.

El Khoury again: "We kept up a very important correspondence. I think it must be a way of communicating meaningfully with people while still being able to hide behind one's own timidity. I'm sure that was the case when he was young because he really was painfully shy."

Another man who knew firsthand just how shy Rainier was turned out to be the Irish-American leprechaun priest who changed Rainier's life forever.

Francis Tucker, formerly of Wilmington, Delaware, was in his 60s and spoke with a thick brogue. He served Rainier as father confessor and had witnessed, perhaps more clearly than anyone else, not simply how the end of Rainier's love affair with Pascal had affected him but how, in turn, it had added to the pressure of finding a suitable bride.

So the priest vowed to do something about it.

"Father Tucker was definitely an enthusiast," Rainier recalled tenderly. "He never hesitated to get involved with things he believed in. I remember he once tried to group the kids from his parish into a marching band. He bought uniforms and instruments for everybody. But most of the kids only showed up for rehearsals once or twice and then never came again. Well, at least he tried. When he wanted to do something he did it. He took an efficient and lively approach to everything. That didn't always please the Bishop but he'd been assigned to me directly by the Vatican whereas the Bishop of Monaco is assigned by the Cardinal of France. So he knew what he could get away with."

By the mid-1950s, the decidedly conniving, witty, and thoroughly loyal Father Tucker had taken it upon himself to play cupid. The only problem was that he didn't know how to stage-manage a romance.

With no experience in this sort of thing at all, he sought divine guidance. And to the day he died, he was convinced that his prayers were answered by MGM when they suspended Grace Kelly.

Chapter 3

A Public Romance

A Monegasque was traveling in South America, crossing from Argentina into Paraguay at a small checkpoint, when the border guard saw his passport and said, *"No esta bueno"*—It's no good.

The Monegasque demanded to know, "What do you mean it's no good?" He insisted, "There's nothing wrong with my passport."

The border guard made signs to suggest that he'd never heard of anyplace called *La Principaute de Monaco.*

The Monegasque tried to explain where it was.

The border guard didn't seem to care. "No *esta bueno!"*

The Monegasque did everything he could think of to convince the border guard that such a country existed. "Monaco. You know, Monaco." He said it louder each time. "MON-A-CO!"

Then, suddenly, as if a light deep inside his head had flicked on, the border guard's face lit up. "Ah, yes, Grace Kelly."

Rupert Allan first met Grace in the spring of 1952 in an elevator at the Savoy Hotel in London. As *Look* magazine's west coast editor, Allan had been in the UK throughout that winter to coordinate a massive lead story on Queen Elizabeth's coronation.

Returning to the hotel one afternoon, he stepped into the lift and literally bumped into an old friend who'd just flown in from Kenya. Allan asked what he was doing in London. The friend explained he'd been MGM's publicity director on *Mogambo*. Standing next to that man was an unobtrusive but pretty young blonde woman wearing dark-rimmed glasses.

Allan smiled politely at her.

The MGM publicist announced, "I'd like you to meet the star of our film, Grace Kelly."

Dressed in a beige sweater, a tweed skirt, flat shoes, and a string of small pearls, and with no makeup on at all, she struck Allan as, "a kind of Peck and Peck girl," a reference to a well-scrubbed young woman straight out of a magazine like *Country Life*.

Of course, he'd heard about her and seen all the press she'd been getting, but couldn't understand how this woman in the elevator could be the same woman who'd created such a stir in films like *High Noon*.

Allan bumped into Grace again a few days later at a Sunday afternoon party given by Ava Gardner.

The *Mogambo* company had switched from Africa to London to shoot interiors, and Gardner had rented a house near Marble Arch. But the place didn't have any chairs so everyone wound up sitting on the floor, eating and drinking, while Gardner's secretary told a story that became the hit of the party.

One evening in Nairobi, Gardner and her secretary heard there was going to be a pantomime at a private club near their hotel. With nothing else to do, the two women walked over to the club, only to be told by the maitre d' that unescorted ladies were not permitted. Flushed with anger, they returned to the hotel where

Gardner proceeded to ring the club and introduce herself as Clark Gable's secretary. She said that Mr. Gable wished to attend the pantomime that night with six guests. The maitre d' said that Mr. Gable would be most welcome. Gardner said that Mr. Gable was dining with his guests and would come by as soon as dinner was finished. The maitre d' said he would reserve front-row seats for the Gable party and added that they would hold the curtain for him. Ava Gardner and her secretary promptly went to sleep. When Gable heard about it, he was furious.

But Grace thought it was hysterical, and she and Allan laughed about it all afternoon.

Returning to California, Allan mentioned to his editor at *Look* that he'd met Grace Kelly. So he assigned Allan to do a story on her.

A far cry from the average Hollywood reporter, Allan's natural southern charm and his gentle demeanor quickly put Grace at ease.

When the article ran as a cover story, she told Allan it was the best piece yet written about her. What's more, it proved to be so popular with *Look's* readership that Allan was asked to do a second interview with Grace. The readers loved it, his editors assigned a third story with her and out of that, a lifelong friendship took hold.

Because Grace only came to California to work, she didn't have much free time there. But what little time she did have she often spent with Allan, a reliable escort and soon her chief confidant.

In the meantime, Allan had established himself as the Cannes Film Festival's unofficial liaison with Hollywood. Not only had he been educated in France and spoke the language, but he'd once worked in Paris for the Motion Picture Association of America where one of his jobs had been to handle the American participation at Cannes.

However, by the mid-1950s American participation at Cannes wasn't what you might call overwhelming. At the 1953 festival the paparazzi cornered Robert Mitchum and convinced him to pose with some young starlet. Not suspecting anything, Mitchum agreed. He and the starlet walked to the beach together, followed by the photographers. She took her place in front of him and, as soon as she saw that the photographers were ready, she promptly dropped her dress. Without thinking, Mitchum tried to cover her by throwing his hands across her chest. The photos were distributed worldwide.

Then it was learned that the Mayor of Cannes happened to be a member of the French Communist Party and, with the McCarthy witch-hunt days still fresh in most Hollywood minds, no one in the US film world wanted to be associated with anything that could in any way be construed as un-American.

The festival organizers, desperate for American stars, turned to Rupert Allan to get them some. He said he'd try. They said the star they wanted most for the 1955 festival was Grace Kelly.

She was still on suspension, so Allan called her in New York to ask if she'd like to go to Cannes.

But Grace said no.

She'd just moved into a new apartment at 880 Fifth Avenue, near the Metropolitan Museum, had hired a new secretary, and told Allan she needed time away from Hollywood to put her own life in order.

Allan chided her, "You sound like an old lady."

She eventually confessed to him that there were other, more personal reasons for not wanting to go to Cannes.

The summer before, while filming *To Catch a Thief*, she'd been in love with fashion designer Oleg Cassini. At one point, they were even engaged. But that romance ended. There had also been a romance in France once upon a time with actor Jean-Pierre Aumont.

She said she felt that returning to that part of the world would only serve to resurrect a lot of old memories that might be best left to fade away on their own. "I'd rather not go anywhere just now."

But he wasn't going to give up. "Spring in Cannes will do you some good. Anyway, I'll be there so you won't have to worry about anything. I know everybody. I'll translate for you. I'll take care of everything."

Again she said no.

He told her, "They'll send you a round-trip, first-class ticket. The return portion can be left open so that you can have as much time as you want to spend in Europe."

She wasn't easily swayed, but the more he persisted the more he wore her down.

Finally, just to be polite, she promised, "I'll think about it."

The next thing that happened, unbeknownst to Allan, was that Paramount rang Grace, suggesting it would be useful if she went to Cannes because it had just been announced that *The Country Girl* was being screened at the festival.

That tipped the balance, and Grace phoned Allan to say, okay.

She flew to Paris where she met her friend Gladys de Segonzac, who'd been costume mistress on *To Catch a Thief*, spent a few days there and, on the evening of May 4, 1955, the two of them took the ultra-posh, overnight "Blue Train" to Cannes.

Also on that train was Olivia de Havilland and her husband Pierre Galante, an editor with *Paris Match* magazine.

Allan met Grace and Gladys the next morning at the station, and that night over dinner, Grace mentioned to him that she'd bumped into de Havilland and Galante. She'd never met de Havilland before but, as they were in neighboring compartments, the four of them spent some time talking, especially after breakfast early the next morning as the train swung eastward along the Mediterranean coast.

They were all standing in the narrow corridor looking out of the window at the sea when Galante mentioned that *Paris Match* might like to do a cover story on her. He suggested he take her to Monaco, to photograph her there in a royal setting with the young bachelor Prince Rainier.

What Grace didn't know at the time was that the photo session was not exactly Galante's spontaneous early morning idea. Having heard that she'd be coming to Cannes, the idea had been discussed the week before in a *Paris Match* editorial meeting.

Anyway, contrary to most reports of the incident, she never actually said yes to Galante.

The truth is, she wasn't terribly interested in being photographed with Rainier. She'd hardly even heard of him. And anyway, Monaco was 90 minutes away.

So when Galante asked if she would do it, Grace gave him a polite, non-committal answer. She said it sounded like a good idea but first she'd have to see how it fit in with her schedule.

In fact, she hadn't so much as given it a second thought until later that morning in Cannes when Galante told her that the Prince had agreed to meet her at the Palace the next day, Friday, 6 April, at 4 P.M.

Grace answered that she couldn't make it. She explained that she had to be at an official reception for the American delegation at Cannes. As the reception began at 5:30, a 4 o'clock appointment with the Prince was absolutely out of the question. She apologized to Galante and explained that the trip to Monaco would have to be cancelled.

A few hours later, Galante informed her that the Prince had kindly agreed to advance their meeting to 3 o'clock.

He kept saying to Grace how excited he was about the photo session and promised her several times that it would make a terrific cover story.

Except Grace still didn't want to go.

When she told Rupert Allan about it that night over dinner, he asked "Do you want to do it?" and she answered, flatly, "No." She said she didn't care about the photo session, that Monaco was too far away, and that she had too many things to do in Cannes.

Allan, shaking his head as if to suggest this was her own fault, reminded her of his promise to handle everything for her while she was in Cannes, then rubbed a little salt into the wound by saying that he could easily have gotten her out of the *Paris Match* commitment if she'd told him about it when she first got off the train.

She nodded, knowing that he was right.

So he said, "All right, I'll cancel Monaco for you."

But now she announced, "I just don't know if I can. The Prince changed his schedule to accommodate mine. I'm not sure how I can get out of this politely."

Allan said, "I'll try to find a way."

"I don't..." Grace shook her head. "It may be too late."

Interestingly enough, throughout her life that would be Grace's attitude towards most things. If someone asked her to make an appearance or to do an interview, she always had trouble saying no.

By the time Grace went to bed that night, she'd resigned herself to the trip to Monaco.

But in the middle of the night, one of the French labor unions called a strike. To reinforce their position, they turned off all of the electricity in Cannes.

The next morning Grace got up, washed her hair, plugged in her portable drier, and nothing happened. She tried another socket. It didn't work there either. Nothing worked. None of the lights came on in her room, so she phoned the front desk.

They gave her the bad news.

In a mild panic, she rang Allan. "Have you noticed there's no electricity? What am I supposed to do?"

By this time, the *Paris Match* people were waiting with a car downstairs.

Also, MGM's new publicity man from Paris had just called in a fury to say that she had no right to be in Cannes because she was still under suspension by the studio and that her appearance there could cost her a lot of money.

Allan rushed to her room.

Grace's soaking wet hair was wrapped in a towel. She was also struggling to find something to wear that hadn't been wrinkled in her suitcase because, with no electricity, there was no way she could iron any of her clothes.

The only thing she had that didn't need pressing was a black silk dress with large pink and green print flowers. It was a beautiful dress. But it was not a good one for pictures. And she didn't want to wear it.

Allan convinced her she didn't have a lot of choice.

Grace put it on, then parted her wet hair in the middle and put some flowers in it, hoping it would dry in the car.

As they left the room she cried, "This is terrible."

Allan kept saying, "If you'd told me, I never would have let you agree to this. Anyway, I should have gotten you out of it last night. This is precisely the kind of thing that will happen tomorrow and the next day and the day after that unless you have them call me first."

She nodded several times, "Yes, you're right," not only because she didn't have time to discuss it with him but because she was angry at herself for having gotten into this.

Allan tried to console her. He said as long as she couldn't get out of it, he'd come along too.

They went downstairs to meet the *Paris Match* people.

Winding their way through the crowded lobby of the Carlton, past movie executives and fans and a hoard of photographers, they stepped outside to the waiting car in the middle of the driveway.

Grace stopped short.

She couldn't believe how many people were planning to come with her. There was Galante, two *Paris Match* photographers, the MGM guy from Paris, and Gladys de Segonzac.

She muttered, "How am I supposed to get into this car with all these people?"

Allan gave her a kind of "I hate to say I told you so" shrug and begged out of the trip.

Grace crammed into the back seat of a Studebaker with Galante, de Segonzac, and the fellow from MGM.

The photographers followed on their heels in a Peugeot.

But they followed so closely that, just as they reached the city limits of Cannes, the Studebaker braked sharply and the Peugeot ran into them.

The damage was minimal yet it kept them from getting to Monaco on time.

By now Grace was starving. So, before heading up to *Le Rocher*—where the Palace is—they made a fast detour to the Hotel de Paris where Galante dashed into the bar and bought her a ham sandwich.

They arrived at the Palace just after 3 o'clock, having already rehearsed their excuses, only to be informed that the Prince wasn't yet there.

Grace just couldn't believe how this whole episode had run away from her.

The group stood around for a while, until one of the Palace officers volunteered to give them a conducted tour.

Annoyed at being made to wait, Grace and her party went haplessly from state room to state room.

Everyone kept glancing at their watches.

The photographers occasionally took photos of Grace against the superbly furnished background.

It was 4 o'clock when a valet announced that the Prince had just arrived.

Now Grace seemed nervous. She checked herself in a mirror and asked Galante, "What do I call the Prince? Does he speak English? How old is he?"

Suddenly, Rainier walked into the room wearing a dark blue, two button suit and went straight to Grace. He offered his hand.

She gave a little curtsy, as she'd been told to do.

In perfect English, he apologized for being late and asked if she'd like to see the Palace.

She said they'd already done the tour.

He then offered to show her the animals in his private zoo.

She said she would.

So now they walked together through the gardens, the two of them followed by the entourage from *Paris Match* and the Palace.

He introduced her to his two young lions, a bunch of monkeys, and a baby tiger.

Grace kept her distance from the cages but Rainier put his arms past the bars and rubbed the back of the tiger's neck.

Grace later admitted that she was suitably impressed.

And all the time the *Paris Match* photographers kept snapping away.

On the trip back to Cannes, Galante asked her what she'd thought of Rainier.

All she'd say was, "He is charming, charming."

At the Carlton she told Allan how the Prince had kept her waiting, how the whole thing had taken too much time, and how, if she was going to do that sort of thing, she wanted to do it right. She said she was embarrassed that her dress was terrible for photographs, that her hair was wet, and how the whole thing had been wrong.

Allan asked how she'd liked the Prince. And she told him, too, "He is very charming."

Later that week Grace wrote Rainier a thank-you note.

Then she left Cannes.

Had she not been suspended from MGM she wouldn't have been free to go to Cannes. Had she taken another train down from Paris and not bumped into Galante and Olivia de Havilland, Galante might not have been able to talk her into the photo session. Had she listened to Allan and channeled all her press requests through him, he could have easily cancelled the trip to Monaco.

But fate can be an odd bedfellow.

The *Paris Match* story ran and immediately everyone started talking about a possible romance.

Most people realized it was hype, that such stories sold newspapers, but the idea of the fairy-tale prince and the beautiful movie star was so romantic that, even if it wasn't true, people wished it was.

That autumn, Grace was reinstated by MGM and started work on her tenth film, *The Swan*, based on a play by Ferenc Molnár. It starred Alec Guinness and Louis Jourdan.

They shot exteriors near Asheville, North Carolina, then moved to Hollywood for the studio work.

Towards the end of the year, Allan received a call from Bill Atwood, an editor at *Look* who was doing a piece on Prince Rainier. He said that during one of the interviews, he'd discovered that the Prince was very pro-American, although he'd never been to the States. When Atwood wondered why, Rainier told him that, as a matter of fact, he was now planning his first trip there. He said he'd be traveling in December with a priest friend, Father Tucker, and a young French doctor friend, Robert Donat, who was, by coincidence, going anyway to do some work at Johns Hopkins University in Baltimore. Rainier said he'd like to go to Florida to fish and maybe also go to California. Atwood asked if there was anybody on the west coast he'd like to meet.

Rainier answered, "Yes. That young actress I met in Monaco. Her name is Grace Kelly. I'd like to see her again."

The Prince's comment came as a total surprise to Rupert Allan. Because, as far as he knew, Grace had never heard from him after their photo session at the Palace.

Rupert later explained, "Bill Atwood phoned me and asked if I could arrange for Grace to see Prince Rainier on the set of her film and get some photos. I said I was sure I could because as far as I knew she'd liked him. When I asked her if she'd let us take some photos with Prince Rainier on the set she said, yes, of course, any time. But then she made a point of saying, 'Listen Rupert, this is no romance.' She said, 'I'm so damned tired of hearing about a romance between him and me in all the European papers. I haven't heard a thing from him since I was in Cannes.'"

The photo session was arranged but shooting on *The Swan* ran overtime. Grace was annoyed because she was due back in Philadelphia for a family Christmas party. The director finally broke for the holidays just in time for her to catch her plane.

Allan continued, "She was living then on the west side of Los Angeles. I went home with her to help her pack. She was one suitcase short so I ran to my place to get her an extra suitcase. There were a few splits of champagne in the fridge so we wished each other Merry Christmas and drank them. She loved champagne. That's all I ever saw her drink. I never saw her drink liquor. I never saw her touch a drop of whiskey. She also loved caviar. Anyway, I took her to the airport early the next morning and put her on a flight for New York. She arrived home in Philadelphia just in time for the party. When I mentioned Prince Rainier to her in the car on the way to the airport she told me again, 'Rupert, really, there is no romance.'"

It wasn't true.

Chapter 4

The Last Secret
Treasure Garden

The official version of their love story had always been told like this:

Grace and Rainier met during the 1955 Cannes Film Festival, spent one afternoon together, enjoyed each other's company—both of them used the word "charming" to describe the other—didn't meet again until Christmas and, sometime between Cannes and Christmas, Father Tucker did his best to make a match.

The old priest appreciated the fact that Grace Kelly was beautiful and didn't mind that she was a movie star. Nor did it hurt that she was a fellow American. Best of all he liked the idea that she was a good Catholic girl with a good reputation.

Having once served in Philadelphia, he used his connections there to check out Grace. It was simple for him to contact the Archdiocese and ask the Cardinal's office to tell him about the Kellys.

Within a few days of the photo session at the Palace, Father Tucker had gleaned a wealth of information about Grace and the Kellys from his priestly intelligence network.

Although he wasn't present that Friday afternoon when Grace and Rainier met, Father Tucker soon took it upon himself to write Grace a note saying, "I want to thank you for showing the Prince what an American Catholic girl can be and for the very deep impression this has left on him."

Rainier recalled the event with a large smile. "I spoke to Father Tucker about Grace. He knew she was coming to visit that afternoon and after she left, he asked how we got along. It's only natural that we would have discussed it because he and I always talked about lots of things. And yes, of course, I was impressed with her when I met her. Who wouldn't have been?"

A few months later, and really just by coincidence, old friends of the Kellys arrived in the south of France.

Russell and Edith Austin were "uncle and aunt" to Grace when she was growing up. He was a Philadelphia dentist who had a summer house near the Kellys' place in Ocean City. The Austins were staying in Cannes, heard about the Red Cross Ball in Monaco—the social event of the Riviera season—and inquired about tickets. When their hotel concierge reported that it was impossible to get tickets as the evening had long since been sold out, they showed some typical American moxie and phoned Prince Rainier's office. They explained that Grace was their niece and wondered if, all things considered, they could somehow impose on her friendship with the Prince to buy a pair of tickets to the ball. The message wound up on Father Tucker's desk.

Whether this was sheer coincidence or something of his own design, he personally delivered the tickets to the Austins with the Prince's compliments, then maneuvered the conversation around to the Kellys and, in particular, to Grace.

In his laughing, friendly way, he got the Austins to tell him everything they knew about Grace.

When he returned to the Palace he just happened to mention the subject to Rainier.

Later that week, at Father Tucker's suggestion, the Austins were invited to tea with the Prince. Once again Father Tucker steered the topic of conversation to Grace.

At the end of the afternoon, the Austins suggested, as Americans are wont to do, that if the Prince should ever find himself in the States he might enjoy coming to Ocean City where they would be pleased to repay his hospitality.

Rainier politely agreed to consider it.

Thanks to Father Tucker, the Austins returned to Philadelphia not merely thinking that the Prince was interested in Grace, but with the clear impression that a love match might be on. It's possible, and highly probable, that the Austins—like everyone else involved in this tale of old-fashioned matchmaking—have, with the years, exaggerated their own role just a bit. But at least Father Tucker had planted the idea in their minds.

The next thing anyone knew, Prince Rainier announced that he would go to America in December 1955.

As soon as Father Tucker got wind of this, he contacted the Austins and they seemingly persuaded the Kellys to invite the Prince to their home for dinner on Christmas Day.

Late in the afternoon on December 25, the Austins arrived at 3901 Henry Avenue with Prince Rainier, Father Tucker, and Dr. Donat.

It was the first time since the film festival that Rainier had seen Grace.

They spent Christmas afternoon and early evening talking.

The Kellys liked Rainier from the moment they met him, although, at least in the beginning, not everybody knew who he was or what to call him.

Ma Kelly thought he was the Prince of Morocco.

Grace had to explain to her mother that wasn't quite right.

Jack Kelly then pulled Father Tucker aside to ask what the proper form of address was. "Do I call him Your Majesty?"

"No," Father Tucker said, "he's referred to as Your Highness." So Jack played along and called the Prince, "Your Highness," even though he later explained to Rainier, "Royalty doesn't mean any-thing to us."

After dinner, Kelly drove Father Tucker to the station to catch a train to Wilmington while Grace and Rainier, with Dr. Donat in tow, went to Grace's sister's house to dance and talk until 3 A.M.

Rainier and Donat spent the night in the Kelly's guest room which meant Grace and Rainier had the chance to spend part of the next day together as well.

Supposedly unbeknownst to anyone, while being driven to the station on Christmas night, Father Tucker confided in Kelly that the Prince was considering asking Grace to marry him.

If Jack was surprised, he hid it well.

He told the priest that he suspected something like this might be on the cards and gave Father Tucker permission to tell the Prince that as long as Grace was willing, he'd have the Kellys' blessing.

Rainier waited a few days before proposing, Grace accepted and the engagement of the decade was announced to the world.

For most people, including Rupert Allan, news of the engage-ment came totally out of the blue.

He remembered, "I was driving back to Los Angeles from a photo session for *Look* magazine at Squaw Valley when I heard on the ra-dio that Prince Rainier of Monaco had just announced his engage-ment to Grace Kelly. I couldn't believe it. I kept saying, that can't be. I kept saying, they don't even know each other."

Except they did.

The official version of their love story—that Grace and Rainier had no contact whatsoever between their first meeting in the spring of 1955 and his trip to Philadelphia that December—is not the way it really happened.

The true story of how they fell in love had never been revealed until Rainier spoke about it for this book.

Acknowledging that their first meeting had been less than pri-vate, he said that once they got past the formalities of shaking hands and posing for pictures, once they started to walk together in the garden with the entourage far enough behind them that they could relax a bit and talk, they started to realize they had some things in common.

They'd both been lonely children.

She told him she'd come from a family where success was based on sporting achievements, except she wasn't terribly interested in sports.

He told her that he'd come from a broken home where his future responsibilities were impressed on him at an early age, where he was often reminded that he wasn't the same as other little boys and couldn't behave the same way they did.

They were both shy.

She told him she was only just learning what it was like to be a public figure, to be deprived of her privacy by the press.

He told her he'd suffered that all his life and could sympathize with her.

She didn't necessarily care for the sea in the same the way he did but she shared his love of animals and felt comfortable with him as he led her around his private zoo.

She also couldn't get over the way he put his arms through the bars of the tiger's cage and played with the cat as if it were nothing more than a house pet.

She appreciated the old world charm and sophistication of European men.

He liked the freshness and spontaneity of American women.

And they were both Catholic with a fundamental belief in their faith.

Rainier couldn't recall exactly what he expected when he was told that Grace Kelly was coming to visit. He knew who she was but the idea of posing for publicity photos with a movie star didn't particularly excite him.

When she confessed to him that she hadn't wanted to do the photo session either, he realized they had that in common as well.

He said he found her gentle, naturally elegant, and was captivated by her aura of purity.

She eventually admitted that she found him totally engaging, not in the least stuffy or pretentious, the way she'd expected.

He liked the way she laughed.

She discovered he was a sensitive man who, when he relaxed, had a good sense of humor. And she loved to laugh.

Back at the Carlton in Cannes, she wrote him a letter to say thank you and included her address in New York.

He answered her, saying how glad he was that they'd met.

She answered that letter, saying that she, too, was pleased to have met him.

He wrote to her again.

And then she wrote back to him.

A regular correspondence began and they gradually got to know each other as pen pals.

The Prince said it was easy that way. It was comfortable. He said they could hide behind their own letters and could give each other time.

Slowly at first, step by step, he said, they revealed more and more with each letter. They wrote about the world and they wrote about life. They wrote about themselves, explained a feeling, wondered if it was shared, and confessed a secret.

By the end of that summer, Rainier knew he'd found someone very special.

He'd often said how difficult it was for him to get to know a woman. The frequently quoted remark from his bachelor days was, "My greatest difficulty is knowing a girl long enough and intimately enough to find out if we are really soul mates as well as lovers."

Like any wealthy, handsome young man, it was easy for him to find a lover. All too often that came first and there was no time left, once word leaked out, to discover if she might be a soul mate.

This time, perhaps for the first time, he was doing it the other way around.

Long before they ever held hands, he said, they both knew they were friends.

He couldn't recall how many letters there were. He wasn't even sure they still existed. At least, he said, he didn't have the ones she sent to him. "I didn't save them. Maybe I should have but that's not the way I am. I don't keep things like that."

As for the ones he sent to her, he shook his head, "I don't know. Maybe she kept them. I suppose women do save letters. But if she did keep them I don't know where they are."

He was asked, "Would you look for them?"

Taking a deep breath and pausing for a moment, he shook his head. "No one has ever seen them. Not even my children." There was an even longer silence. "Those letters..." His voice grew very quiet... "To be honest, I wouldn't want anyone to see them. Even if I could find them." He shook his head again. "Please understand, I simply couldn't let anyone trespass on that. After having lived such a public life..." He stopped, looked away and in an even quieter voice said, "Those letters may be the last secret treasure garden I have left."

Chapter 5

The Private Story

The Paris Match *photos had created such interest in the possibility of a* romance between Grace and Rainier that, on October 11, 1955, Rainier went on Radio Monte Carlo to tell the people of Monaco, "Any rumors you might hear of my impending marriage are just that, rumors. The question of my marriage, which rightly preoccupies you, interests me, believe me, just as much, and more."

After insisting that certain sections of the press had been making all sorts of speculations that were simply not true, he told his people, "Just give me another three years and then we shall see."

Still, before the month was out he'd already secretly arranged to meet Grace at Christmas and to ask her to be his wife.

"I knew what I wanted to do," Rainier said, then confessed, "But I couldn't just assume she'd marry me. I had to ask her. So I went to the States to see her. But I couldn't ask her to marry me if I wasn't absolutely sure she'd accept. I couldn't ask her to marry me if there was any chance she'd say no."

He sailed from France on December 8, arriving in New York one week later.

Ostensibly, the reason for Rainier's visit was to go with Donat to Johns Hopkins for a checkup at the university hospital. There was also talk of visiting friends on the east coast and some fishing in Florida.

While Father Tucker was let in on the secret before they sailed, the only other people wise to Rainier's marriage plans—besides Grace who, by this time, had good reason to believe from their correspondence that Rainier's intentions were serious—were his closest advisers at home.

After all, the possible marriage of the Prince of Monaco was an affair of state.

According to the Franco-Monegasque treaty of 1918, the engagement announcement of anyone in line for the Monegasque throne must be preceded by a formal request for permission from the French government. Of course, French government consent is nothing more than a rubber stamp. But in 1920, when Princess Charlotte announced her engagement to Count Pierre de Polignac without first seeking such permission—even though her grandfather was sovereign prince, her father was hereditary prince, and she was only number three in the line—a strong letter was promptly sent from the French Foreign Minister to the Minister of State that rules of protocol had to be observed.

And Rainier would, of course, observe them now.

Some time in early November, he discussed his plans with the Minister of State who then spoke to the French Consul General in Monaco.

On November 30, 1955, eight days before Rainier sailed from Le Havre, the French Consul General wrote to the Minister of State, "On the eve of SAS Prince Rainier's departure for the United States where he intends to propose marriage to *une Americaine*"—the fiancée to be is not named—"my government suggests that this is perhaps a good opportunity to bring your attention to the 1920 precedent."

The Minister of State duly passed that letter on to the Prince.

Grace's name does not appear on any official correspondence at this point because Rainier had not yet revealed it, even to his Minister of State.

He'd decided that no one should know her identity for a couple of reasons. It would be extremely embarrassing to both Grace and himself if word leaked out before he had the opportunity to propose. And, if she accepted, protocol again dictated that a formal announcement would have to be made in Monaco before, or at least at the very same time, that it was made in the US.

So, right up to the point where he arrived at her front door on Christmas Day, it was only Grace and Father Tucker who knew precisely what Rainier had in mind.

As the week after Christmas wore on, as Grace and Rainier were seen together in Philadelphia and on December 27 in New York, the press began adding one and one and coming up with two.

The official version of the story is that he proposed to her on New Year's Eve.

The truth is that he did it a few days after Christmas.

He asked her quite simply, "Will you marry me?"

And she answered quite simply, "Yes."

But they couldn't tell anybody because this was not just an ordinary marriage, this was a Prince, and head of state, asking her to become his Princess.

Before the world could be told there were all sorts of hurdles to clear.

First, there was her father. A man known for usually speaking his mind, Jack Kelly pulled Rainier aside and said he hoped the Prince's intentions were serious.

Rainier answered, "I want to marry her," without explaining that Grace had already said yes.

Kelly gave Rainier his permission right away, but then cautioned him, "I hope you won't run around the way some princes do because if you do you'll lose a mighty fine girl. Don't forget, she's got Irish blood in her veins and she knows what she wants."

Next came Ma Kelly, who intended that Grace and Rainier should be married in Philadelphia. "That's how it is in America. The girl's parents arrange the wedding and Grace always promised me she wanted that."

Rainier had to explain that this would not be just an ordinary wedding, that Grace would become the Princess of Monaco and, in that regard, she now had responsibilities to the Monegasques.

It took some time but Ma Kelly eventually gave in.

Then there were the negotiations for the marriage contract. A multi-paged legal document was drawn up over the next few weeks by lawyers in Monaco acting for the Prince and attorneys in New York acting for Grace. Conforming to European custom, it specifically outlined the rules that would govern the material side of their marriage.

In France and in Monaco, contractual agreements to establish rights to property, as defined by the Napoleonic Codes, are a traditional part of any marriage. There are three basic types: communal property, a specific division of property, and a total separation of property. Most people marry under the first clause. In fact, in France, unless you specifically request otherwise, you automatically get a communal property agreement. The second arrangement is one wherein all the material things that each party brings to the marriage remain their own, but everything acquired after the marriage is shared. The third is simply an agreement that everything brought to the marriage plus everything acquired during the marriage will belong to one partner or the other.

It was this third clause, known in French as *separation des biens*, under which Grace and Rainier were wed.

"It was the right thing for both of us," Rainier explained. "But it was absolutely a normal standard marriage contract and there was nothing out of the ordinary about it."

If not out of the ordinary for a certain class of European—most of France's wealthiest people are married under this clause—it must have seemed quite odd to the Kellys of Philadelphia, especially because the contract stipulated that Grace would have certain responsibilities towards household costs.

In other words, she would have to pay some of their bills.

But again, that's a normal practice under such a contract.

Finally, there was the matter of a dowry.

According to the contract, it would be paid by the Kellys to the Prince for his taking Grace as his wife. Dowries are also the norm among older European families, not just French or Monegasque, although they were hardly an everyday occurrence in East Falls in 1956.

Some years ago a book intending to do nothing more than sensationalize Grace and Rainier's life together made the claim that Rainier forced an otherwise reluctant Jack Kelly to pay $2 million for the right to see Grace married to the Prince of Monaco. That is not true. Having seen the marriage contract, which is in Prince Rainier's private files, I can state categorically that, while certain financial arrangements were made, a $2 million dowry was not involved.

For the sake of accuracy, the author of that particular book acknowledged assistance from various people who now say they've never spoken to him or that when he contacted them they refused to cooperate. Some of the most startling quotes in that book are attributed to dead people. And, if that isn't enough to cast serious doubt on the accuracy of the author's reporting, there are also gross errors of fact. Among them, the statement that the only reason Dr. Donat went to the States with Rainier was to personally administer a fertility test to Grace before a marriage could be planned. After all, the argument went, if she could not bear children he could not marry her.

Rainier wrote off this utter nonsense as total fiction. "It was very much the fad in the mid-1950s for Europeans to have a thorough medical check-up in the United States. Lots of people I knew were going to places like the Mayo Clinic. My friend Robert Donat, who was a surgeon in Nice and had taken out my appendix, suggested that as long as I was going to the States anyway, why didn't I take a few days and get a check-up. He wanted me to go to Johns Hopkins. I decided, why not, as I'd never had a general health check-up before. So I went with him to Baltimore. I spent three very boring days sitting in the hospital there getting poked and prodded."

Just as quickly, he dismissed any discussion of Grace's fertility.

To begin with, he rightly pointed out, there is no such thing as a simple fertility test for women.

According to a noted gynecologist contacted in London through the Royal College of Obstetricians and Gynaecologists, you never know for sure if the equipment works until you give it a try. A doctor can check to see that a woman ovulates, and can take X-rays to see that her Fallopian tubes are clear, and that there are no obstructions to fertilization. But that's about it. So any scene that describes Grace with her feet in the stirrups while two doctors poke and probe to make certain that she can bear the heir to Rainier's throne is not only extremely tacky, but pure invention.

All the more so because no physical examination of any kind was required of her.

Many years later, in the case of Princess Diana, it's known that a physical was demanded by the British crown before she could marry the heir to the throne. A gynecologist certainly checked to see that everything was in order. Equally important, doctors also traced her family medical history to make sure that there were no genetic diseases, such as epilepsy or hemophilia, which might be passed on.

Yet, where Grace was concerned, Rainier was frank. "She didn't go through any special medical tests whatsoever. As far as I know she didn't even have a simple check-up before we got married. And there definitely was no fertility test."

What's more, Rainier said, the excuse that she needed to be capable of bearing children or the wedding was off, is just as ludicrous. "Had she not been able to bear children there was another option available to us. We could have adopted a child. The law is quite clear. According to the treaty with France, should there be no natural heir to the throne, the ruling sovereign may adopt a child to perpetuate the reign."

On Tuesday night, January 3, 1956, Grace and Rainier went to the Stork Club in New York with some friends.

Jack O'Brian, the theatre critic for the *Journal-American* newspaper, spotted them across the room and sent a note to their table with the waiter. It read, "Dear Grace, I understand you're planning to announce your engagement on Thursday or Friday. Answer here please." At the bottom he drew two boxes, one marked for each day.

After showing it to Rainier, Grace went to O'Brian's table. She told him, "I can't answer your question tonight."

He asked, "When can you answer it?"

After a short pause she said, "Friday."

The official announcement was made on Thursday, January 5, first in Monaco and then a few minutes later at a luncheon Jack Kelly hosted for Philadelphia dignitaries at a local country club.

On Friday morning, as she'd hinted to O'Brian, it was front-page news.

"I've been in love before," Grace told the press, "but never in love like this."

Later she would confess, "By getting married I was stepping straight into a new, unknown world and that was, I have to say, a little frightening. But I was ready for making a change in my life. And so was the Prince. I think we were lucky enough to meet at the right moment. I've always thought that a man who marries a famous woman, a woman more famous than him, can lose his own identity. I didn't want a future Mr. Kelly, if you see what I mean. I didn't want to take a husband. I wanted to become someone's wife."

The magic of their engagement captured the public's imagination to such an extent that even today theirs is still considered one of the greatest love stories of the 20th century.

"We were both old enough to know what we wanted," Rainier said. "And once we saw each other again in Philadelphia I think we both realized that what we wanted to do was make our lives together. Neither of us were children. We both understood what marriage meant. Both of us had gone through difficult times but both of us had learned from those difficult times that what we were each looking for was marriage. We discussed it and we thought about it and we decided to go ahead with it. We fell in love. A lot of people couldn't believe that. A lot of people never thought it would last. I guess we fooled them."

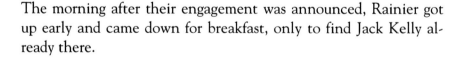

They also fooled the supposed "Curse of the Grimaldis."

Around the end of the 13th century, Prince Rainier I gained the reputation among the Grimaldi clan as a great sailor and lover. He was awarded the title, Admiral General of France for his naval exploits. But in his amorous conquests he fared less well. After one of his battles he's said to have kidnapped a beautiful Flemish woman whom he took as his lover and then betrayed. Shortly thereafter she is said to have turned herself into a witch. To repay her unhappiness, she cursed him and all those who followed with the prophesy, "Never will a Grimaldi find true happiness in marriage."

It's possible that Charles III wasn't happy in his marriage. Or that Albert I wasn't happy in either of his. Perhaps Louis II and Charlotte were equally unhappy in wedlock.

But when the curse was mentioned to Rainier, he grinned broadly and said, emphatically and without any hesitation, "Yes, we beat the curse too."

The morning after their engagement was announced, Rainier got up early and came down for breakfast, only to find Jack Kelly already there.

His future father-in-law jumped up to give Rainier a hearty slap on the back. "Sleep well, sonny?"

Rainier understood what Kelly was telling him. He smiled, "Very well, Dad."

And their friendship was secured.

Chapter 6

Making Plans

Rainier returned to a joyous Monaco to prepare for the wedding while
Grace headed west to Hollywood to make her final motion picture,
the Cole Porter musical version of *The Philadelphia Story*, called
High Society.

But within a few months, Rainier returned to the States, renting
a small villa in Hollywood so that he could be with her.

The diamond engagement ring she wears in the film is the
"friendship" ring Rainier gave her when he asked her to be his
Princess.

Over the next few months the press never let up. They followed
him wherever he went, peeked over his shoulder as he planned
every stage of their wedding, and followed her wherever she went,
as she bought what must have been the most written-about
trousseau of the century.

She started at Neiman Marcus in Dallas, the Texas oil millionaires' favorite store. They made suits for her, several gowns, an as-
sortment of street clothes, an entire wardrobe of sports clothes, and

even a yachting outfit, although she ordered it without the traditional pair of sailor's shorts. The bridesmaids' dresses, in yellow silk organdie over taffeta, were also made at Neiman Marcus. Lingerie came from Los Angeles, where one press report vividly described her purchase as, "wispy thin silk, lace edged nightgowns, negligee and foundation garments in pink, peach or black."

Other undergarments, including nylon stockings, came from New York.

So did her everyday dresses, purchased from an unnamed Manhattan wholesaler.

Her shoes were bought at Delman's on Fifth Avenue. "Not too high in the heel," the papers said. At one point, a story appeared that they were flats, so as not to make her look taller than Rainier. Actually, they had 2½" heels.

One of the shoes in that pair, the right one, also had a copper penny hidden in it for good luck.

Her hats—a travel turban of white silk jersey, a delicate yellow straw toque plus a white tulle creation cut in baby tucks for the crown and veiling for the brim—were made by Mr. John, a well-known New York designer.

But the best frock of all came straight from MGM. As a gift, the studio not only gave her all the clothes she wore in *High Society*, they also asked their Academy Award–winning chief costume designer, Helen Rose, to create her wedding dress.

On the night of April 3, 1956, Grace Kelly dined with her parents at the Ambassador Hotel in New York. She had to go out for dinner because her Fifth Avenue fridge was empty. She couldn't even make a cup of coffee for herself early the next morning before she left for Pier 84 on West 44th Street.

There was a light drizzle that morning.

Still, a good-sized crowd of well-wishers were waiting at the pier when she arrived in a limousine to board the USS *Constitution*.

The press also came out in force. She'd previously agreed to meet them for 20 minutes inside the ship's Pool Café. The idea was that reporters would be allotted some time with her, then a session with photographers would take place. Then, just before the ship sailed, she'd agree to appear on deck for television and newsreel cameras.

But because of the weather, all three groups jammed into the room at the same time.

Nearly 250 people fought for space in a bar that was meant to hold 50.

"This is frightening," she gasped as microphones were shoved into her face and flashbulbs went off, non-stop. "I'm flattered at all this attention, but I wish all of you would be more considerate of one another."

Questions were hurled at her from all sides of the room, rapid-fire, one right after another.

Q: Miss Kelly, Miss Kelly, will you now give up your career?
A: I feel I am starting a new one.
Q: Miss Kelly, does that mean you won't make any more movies?
A: Right now I'm too interested in my marriage career to think about the movies.
Q: Miss Kelly, will you love, honor, and obey?
A: Whatever His Highness wishes is fine with me.
Q: Miss Kelly, what will it be like to be a princess?
A: I intend to take each day just as it comes.
Q: Miss Kelly, Miss Kelly, please, will you wear something old, something new, something borrowed, and something blue?
A: Yes, I hope so. But I haven't figured out exactly what, yet.
Q: Miss Kelly, has the Prince called to wish you a bon voyage?
A: We haven't talked by telephone but we hear from each other every day by letter.

Grace of Monaco

At precisely 11 A.M., with a blast of the ship's horn and the tug boat's sirens, with a ton of yellow confetti and a thousand colored streamers thrown from the upper decks, and with the sound of a band playing Dixieland jazz on the promenade deck, the USS *Constitution* slipped out of her berth into the Hudson River, swung downstream and sailed for Monaco.

Grace had booked the bridal suite.

A combination living room and bedroom with a veranda on the high sun deck, it was the ship's most luxurious accommodation.

A party of 70 friends and relatives were sailing with her. So was her French poodle, Oliver.

The only thing she inadvertently left behind was the key to one of her large steamer trunks. The ship's carpenter had to chisel off the hinges.

However, almost as soon as the *Constitution* left New York, with the Statue of Liberty in her wake, Grace discovered she had a lot more shipmates than she'd originally bargained for.

It was when the captain called a lifeboat drill. An announcement came over the public address system instructing everyone on board to don a lifejacket and proceed immediately to the designated station nearest their cabin. Each lifeboat on the *Constitution* was intended to accommodate 150 people. But this was the cruise taking Grace Kelly to Monaco to marry Prince Rainier and there wasn't a single person on board who didn't want to meet her.

When she got to her lifeboat she found nearly 300 people also claiming it as their own.

A whole slew of reporters also sailed with her, although they were in tourist class and rules forbid tourist-class passengers to enter first-class territory. Nevertheless, they wired daily reports back to their papers.

She even broadcast a short speech by ship's radio to the people of Monaco, in French, saying how much she was looking forward to meeting them, promising that she would try her best to be a worthy princess.

Meanwhile, in Monaco, the Prince was frantically busy with all of the last-minute preparations. He didn't have much time for the press so the reporters gathering there had to find something else to write about.

And it didn't take them long to discover the best interview in town was the leprechaun priest from Delaware.

"She knows that she's making history," Father Tucker told reporters, "and that she has a tremendous duty to these people here. She will not, I am sure, interfere politically, not more than any American girl would whose husband were a Republican and she a Democrat."

When asked how the Prince was taking the wait for his fiancée, Father Tucker assured them, "He's as nervous as any bridegroom. He's pretending to be calm but underneath he's just like a jubilant boy."

And when they questioned him about his own role in arranging this, the self-proclaimed matchmaker insisted, "Grace was really the Prince's choice. I was just a kind of consultant."

Eight days after she left New York, the *Constitution* slipped into the Bay of Hercules off the coast of Monaco.

Rainier was waiting for her on the deck of the couple's new motor yacht, *Deo Juvante II*.

Built in England in 1928, the 298-ton, 147-foot ship was a wedding gift to the couple from Aristotle Onassis.

The sky was dull and overcast and the seas were slightly choppy as the *Deo Juvante II* came up alongside the ocean liner. Surrounded by a flotilla of small boats with photographers and cameramen at the ready—plus a helicopter hovering overhead—Rainier waited for Grace to appear.

He admitted that his heart was pounding.

She never hid the fact that hers was, too.

Smiling and waving, carrying a bouquet of roses, she came down the gangplank. He helped her step onto his boat. Sirens and ships' horns blasted their welcome.

More than 20,000 people lined the streets surrounding the port, waving flags and cheering and applauding as the *Deo Juvante II* brought her ashore.

Now there were more horns and more sirens. Cannons boomed. Planes flew overhead and parachutes appeared. Flares went up.

It was her greatest entrance.

Only one thing marred it. She'd worn the wrong hat. It was too big and the brim hid her face. The entire population of Monaco had come out to see her but all most of them saw was the brim of her hat. What they missed was the joy, wonderment, excitement, and tears of happiness in what were then the most famous blue eyes in the world.

Chapter 7

The Wedding

The wedding was a complicated affair.

Because this romance had so captured the imagination of the world—the movie star and the fairytale prince—over 1,600 reporters and photographers showed up, nearly three times the number of journalists, photographers, and broadcast crew members who'd later report on the marriage of Prince Charles and Lady Diana.

As if that's not statistic enough, consider the fact that there weren't 1,600 reporters and photographers at any one time covering the entire European Theatre during all of World War II.

The problem was that no one in Monaco had the experience to deal with so much press. The principality had never known anything so grand. For that matter, few countries had.

There were lunches and dinners and parades and appearances and great galas where everyone danced on into the night.

There were eight days of festivities that both Grace and Rainier agreed were not quite the way they would have wanted it had they been given a choice.

Rainier could only chuckle when he recalled what he and his bride had to go through. "It wasn't fun and in the middle of the turmoil, Grace kept saying, maybe we should run off to a small chapel somewhere in the mountains and finish getting married there. I wish we had because there was no way either she or I could really enjoy what was happening."

Thinking back, he decided, it was simply too big an event for its time. "There's no doubt about that. It was very over-publicized. The press showed up *en masse* and because so many of the events were private, they had nothing much to do. One day we went to have lunch at my sister's villa at Eze. Afterwards we were driving back to Monaco and one of the photographers who'd followed us lay down across the road. He actually lay down, flat on his back. I wasn't driving quickly and saw him from far away so when I got close I stopped. That was my mistake. All his friends started shooting pictures. The next morning in the papers it looked as if I'd knocked him down. They'd have done anything for a photo."

In describing the mayhem that had overtaken Monaco, Grace once told her daughter Caroline that those eight days were so awful, and that she and Rainier felt so uncomfortable, they couldn't look at the home movies of the event for more than a year afterwards.

Everything turned out to be a major hassle. Even the guest list had to be compiled with several thoughts in mind.

Of course, Grace and Rainier both wanted their friends and family to be present. But there were also European royals who had to be invited and political protocol to be considered.

Queen Elizabeth was invited, not just because she was Queen of England, but also because she and Rainier were, to be precise, 15th cousins. Their common line was traced through Monaco's Prince Albert who married Scotland's Lady Mary Victoria Douglas Hamilton, who in turn was related to Henry VII and Elizabeth of York.

In fact, most of the ruling houses of Europe are related through that same line to the Grimaldis of Monaco. It ties them to the Swedish, Norwegian, Danish, Belgian, Dutch, Luxumbourger, and

Greek royals. It also tied them to Elizabeth the Queen Mother and to Winston Churchill.

Anyway, while most of the other royals accepted, the Queen of England declined. Whatever her personal reasons were, the public version was a matter of protocol. As she'd never met Rainier or Grace, neither she nor any member of her family could attend the ceremony. She did, however, send the couple a gift of a gold serving tray.

Cary Grant gave them an antique writing desk. The Societe de Bains de Mer, the company that runs the casino and the fanciest hotels and restaurants in Monte Carlo, gave her a diamond and ruby necklace. Friends in Philadelphia gave Grace a Cinemascope screen and two 35mm projectors to create a movie room in the Palace so that she wouldn't have to miss any American films. The local American community presented the couple with a solid gold picture frame, the local German community offered them a fine porcelain table service and the French government presented them with a matching pair of decorated helmsman wheels for their honeymoon yacht. Grace's fellow cast members on *High Society* sent her home with a loaded roulette wheel.

A wedding list was not posted, so there were duplicates. There was plenty of gold, silver, glass, paintings, antique picture frames, and jewelry, although the couple only received one baby lion, for the Prince's zoo.

Perhaps most touching of all, were the gifts that flowed in from people who didn't know either Rainier or Grace, but simply wanted to send a little something, people who somehow wanted to feel a part of this wedding. There were dozens of objects people made themselves, whole cheeses and cured hams. There were cookbooks, potholders, shamrocks, wall plaques, knitted goods, and all sorts of ash trays, ceramic animals, and plaster-of-Paris angels.

Many of those gifts are still today scattered around Palace shelves.

Each gift was logged by Grace in a white satin bride's book and, by the time all of the gifts were accounted for, she'd filled a dozen volumes.

The press, somewhat indelicately, estimated the value of the wedding gifts at well over $1 million.

If putting a price tag on the gifts wasn't embarrassing enough, the story of the gift from Monaco's National Council's certainly was.

A few weeks before the wedding the Council sent one of their elders to a jeweler in Paris, where he selected a necklace worth 39 million francs—then about $72,000. He advanced the jeweler 12 million francs and brought the gift back to Monaco. As far as he was concerned it was wonderful.

Unfortunately, it was awful, a heavy, multi-jeweled, absolutely grotesque object.

There was no way that anyone with taste could imagine this might be suitable for a modern, 26-year-old woman.

When the Prince saw it he supposedly found it so hideous that he doubted it would even be worthy of the Dowager Empress of China.

Adding insult to injury, it turned out that the National Council's representative had lined his own pocket with a five million franc commission from the jeweler.

To cover themselves, the Council immediately rushed over to the local Cartier's and bought Grace an even more expensive matching necklace, bracelet, ring, and earrings set. They then tried to return the original necklace to the Parisian jeweler. But he said no, refused to refund their money and demanded that they pay the remaining 27 million francs. The Council said that such a payment was out of the question and threatened the jeweler with a court action. Immune to their threats, the jeweler would not take the monstrous necklace back—it was really so terrible, who could blame him— and instructed his attorneys to block the Prince's assets in Monaco and in the United States in order to force payment.

To no one's surprise, that failed.

The Council, in fact, did take the jeweler to court and won. But they lost in the press as the papers turned the affair into a front-page scandal.

Describing the jewelry fiasco as, "sordid," Rainier admitted it was very embarrassing but out of his control. "The National Council chose the jeweler, they settled on the price with him and that was their gift to Grace for the wedding. We couldn't interfere at all. Grace wasn't asked, nor did she ever volunteer to them, or to anyone else, that she might have preferred pearls to diamonds or emeralds to rubies."

The way marriage has worked since Napoleon in France, and consequently in Monaco, too, is that a bride and groom must go through two ceremonies.

The law requires that a civil marriage take place first, at the local city hall—where either the bride or groom has been resident for at least 40 days—and is usually performed by the local mayor, a deputy mayor, or a city councilor. Even then, before any civil marriage can take place, banns must be posted. This "official announcement" must be displayed in City Hall, for all the public to see, no fewer than 10 days preceding the date of marriage.

The religious ceremony can only be performed after the civil ceremony.

These requirements cannot be waived.

Unless you happen to be a ruling prince.

Unlike other marriages in Monaco, no banns were posted for this one, presumably so that no one could object to it.

Not that anyone would have objected.

Although, as the wedding day approached, signs of nervousness and tension began to get the best of everybody. Rainier grew especially short-tempered with the photographers and cancelled a photo session that was supposed to re-enact the couple's signing of the marriage register. During the rehearsal, Grace looked strained and Rainier bit his fingernails.

The civil ceremony took place on April 18, in the Palace throne room, with only the immediate family and a few very close friends present. But television cameras were permitted in, so that all of Europe could watch, too.

Grace wore a pale pink gown and carried a bridal bouquet. Her hair was done by MGM's own celebrity stylist, Sydney Guilaroff, whom Grace had flown over from Hollywood for the occasion. Her perfume was from the House of Creed and called *Fleurissimo*, which Rainier had commissioned exclusively for her on her wedding day.

Rainier wore a black morning suit with gray striped trousers. Both were obviously suffering from stage fright and neither of them smiled.

The room was hot, filled with powerful television lights for television and also for MGM's cameras who had the exclusive film rights to the ceremony.

The bride and groom sat a few feet apart on a pair of red velvet chairs, Grace with her gloved hands in her lap, Rainier nervously fingering his moustache.

As a member of the sovereign family may marry only with permission of the ruling prince, the senior judge who conducted the ceremony in French began by asking for the prince's authorization to hold the marriage. Rainier gave himself permission to get married and 40 minutes later Grace and Rainier were legally man and wife.

Most couples only have to suffer such an ordeal once. But this wasn't most couples. Grace and Rainier had to do the whole thing a second time, re-staging it for the sake of MGM.

Later Father Tucker told reporters, "They wouldn't go through this again for the world."

That afternoon, the entire Monegasque population, all 3,000 of them, were invited to a gala to celebrate the marriage. That night, Grace and Rainier attended the opera. She wore a Lanvin gown made of hand-embroidered white silk organdy. It featured a V-shaped décolleté, with a high waistline and a bustle. It was decorated with several thousand pearls and rhinestones, and hundreds of thousands of sequins. Across the front of the dress, she wore a sash, marking her first formal public appearance as Princess Grace.

But because that night was not their official wedding night, the official version of the story is that they slept in separate rooms.

The next morning, the religious ceremony was viewed by 30 million people in nine European countries and a full house in Monaco's Cathedral.

A very crowded, strictly white tie event, Rupert Allan found himself seated next to Ava Gardner. On the other side of him there was an empty seat, the only empty seat in the Cathedral. Puzzled, Allan one day got around to asking Grace, "Who didn't show up?"

She told him, "Frank Sinatra."

Allan was shocked. "You put me in the middle of Ava Gardner and Frank Sinatra?"

The couple's publicly turbulent marriage had gone sour a few years before and Allan couldn't believe that, had Sinatra shown, he would have found himself literally at the center of their first meeting since the breakup.

"You wanted me to sit between them?" he said to Grace. "Who knows how they would have gotten on?"

She smiled, "I knew you could handle it."

Actually the reason Sinatra stayed away had less to do with Ava Gardner than it did with his affection for Grace.

He'd flown to London from Los Angeles a few days before the wedding to have final fittings for his white tie and tails. One of the first things he saw in London was that the newspapers were filled with Gardner's arrival in Monaco. She was attracting a lot of publicity. He knew that once he arrived the press would be on him, too, because of their bitter divorce.

So he phoned Grace to say, "I won't be there."

She wanted to know why.

He told her, "I'm not coming, because this is your day."

Grace later confided to Allan that she always thought Sinatra was the only man Ava Gardner ever loved. "They were right for each other. I put them on either side of you because it seemed like a good way of trying to rekindle the flame."

The religious ceremony was held with great dignity.

White lilacs and lilies-of-the-valley filled the ancient Cathedral, contrasting with the red silk drapes and a red carpet that stretched from the altar to the front steps.

Bright late morning sunshine poured through the stained glass windows.

Men in morning suits and women with colorful hats took their places.

Then there was an organ chord and all heads turned and Grace appeared.

It was a breathtaking moment.

Helen Rose, the MGM designer who'd created Grace's wedding dress, had outdone herself.

Six weeks of work by three dozen seamstresses went into the ivory, Renaissance style regal gown made up of 25 yards of heavy taffeta, 25 yards of silk taffeta, 100 yards of silk net, and 300 yards of Valenciennes lace for the petticoats.

Grace's wedding gown was the single most expensive item of clothing that Rose had ever made.

The train was three and a half yards long. The long-sleeved, rose point-lace bodice was re-embroidered to hide the seams. The gown fastened down the front with tiny lace buttons and fit over a silk soufflé, flesh-tone under-bodice. The overskirt was bell-shaped without any folds in front. The fullness at the back was laid in pleats at the waist, flaring into a fan shape at the bottom. The underskirt was actually three petticoats in crepe and taffeta.

The veil, which Rose specifically designed to keep Grace's face on view, was embroidered with 125-year-old rose point-lace which was purchased by MGM from a museum, and had several thousand tiny pearls hand-sewn into it. It was paired with a Juliet cap of matching lace with a wreath of small orange blossoms and leaves fashioned from seed pearls. Appliquéd onto the rear of the veil were two miniature lace love birds. Grace also carried with her a prayer book covered in taffeta to match her gown, with the cross on the prayer book embroidered in pearls.

Later, fashion designer Oscar de la Renta would say, "On her wedding day, Grace Kelly gave new meaning to the word *icon*. Her whole look, from the regal veil to the feminine lace details and the conservative gown, made her an ageless bride."

Protocol had it that she would wait at the altar for Rainier to arrive. The way the script was written, she was to wait there alone, but her father wouldn't have it and Jack stood near by.

As the story goes, during the rehearsal, Grace expressed some concern about a bride waiting at the altar for the groom to make his appearance. In the States, it's always the other way around.

Rainier is said to have joked, "Don't wait more than half an hour."

That quip may or may not be true. But it sounds exactly like his sense of humor.

In any case, she didn't have to wait long. He joined her at the altar wearing a uniform he'd designed himself, based on the uniform of Napoleon's marshals. The trousers were sky blue with a gold stripe down the sides. The jacket was black with gold oak leaves on the lapels and gold braid over his right shoulder.

As they took their seats, he gave her a fleeting smile. Then the two of them looked straight ahead, unable to hide their nerves.

The choir sang Bach's "Uxor Tua" and Purcell's "Alleluia."

There was an awkward moment as Rainier had trouble getting the ring on Grace's finger—she had to help—and both were still so nervous that their vows were only loud enough for the Bishop to hear.

He asked her in French if she took the prince to be her lawfully wedded husband, and she whispered, "*Oui.*"

They kneeled and prayed, he gave them his blessing, and then it was over. The Bishop declared them man and wife.

And now there wasn't a dry eye in the house.

As Rainier kissed his bride, the Cathedral's bells rang out to signal that they were, in the eyes of God, one.

Six hours of parades, receptions, and balcony appearances later—which included a ride through the streets of Monaco in the brand-new black and tan Rolls Royce convertible that was a gift from the citizens of Monaco—they boarded his boat and left for a one-month honeymoon cruise around the Mediterranean.

They literally sailed off into the sunset.

Hollywood couldn't have ended the day better.

Six thousand miles away, the show-business newspaper *Variety* announced the wedding with the headline, "Marriages—Grace Kelly to Prince Rainier III. Bride is film star, groom is non-pro."

Chapter 8

Rainier Reminiscing

Shortly after Grace and Rainier married, the couple bought a farm called Roc Agel in the French hills, 3,000 feet above the sea, overlooking the Principality of Monaco, a crab-shaped pocket that stretches no more than two miles along the eastern corner of the French Riviera, and never more than a few hundred yards inland.

The property is not huge, but behind the always-guarded gates, and surrounded by the Prince's trees, there's a medium-sized, modern stone house at the end of a long asphalt driveway. There's a swimming pool and three tiny cottages on the property, which he later turned into playrooms for his grandchildren. There are swings and a merry-go-round and a lot of dogs.

Now, just after dawn, wearing slacks, a golf shirt, and a comfortable pair of old loafers, Rainier pointed out with great pride how he'd personally worked so much of the land here. "I put in about 400 trees here. I also made all the paths around the property. I drove the bulldozer myself."

The 26-year-old, dark-haired, dark-moustached, slightly awkward man who had ascended to his country's throne in May 1949, had slipped into his latter years a handsome, self-assured man, whose hair and moustache were snow-white, but whose natural shyness was always evident, only barely hidden by a well-practiced reserve.

"It's very satisfying to do that," he said, "to work with your hands. I have a workshop here where I can weld iron and metal or make things with bits of iron and bolts. It gets me away from reading official papers. That's one of the reasons I don't read a lot of books any more. After three or four hours a day of reading papers I just want to get away and do something manual."

There's a fair-sized vegetable patch for lettuce and tomatoes and a large group of apricot, apple, cherry, and plum trees. He kept poultry for eggs and a couple of Jersey cows for fresh milk. For many years there were also four llamas, a hippopotamus named Pollux, and a rhinoceros he bought in England that was already called Margaret.

"They both weigh about two tons. But you can go up to the rhino and walk around and she'll follow you like a dog. The hippo is also quite domestic." He paused for a moment, then added, "I love animals," as if there could have been any doubt about someone who kept a rhino and a hippo at home. "I believe I understand them. When you show them you're the boss, that you're not afraid, that you mean them no harm, you can have a real communication with them."

Returning to Monaco from that trip to Africa with his "Rainier's Ark" of animals, he installed them in the gardens below his Palace. When word got out about his collection, friends started giving him gifts to help it along. The King of Morocco sent a couple of lions and the King of Siam offered a small baby elephant, although the elephant quickly outgrew the place and Rainier had to give it to a safari park where they could keep it better.

His collection became the Monaco Zoo. "I run it myself. It's very popular because visitors can get as close as is safely possible to the animals. But these days there are so many safari parks, both good ones and bad ones, that people have gotten a little tired of zoos."

Even if the public had tired of zoos, he never did.

In the mid-1980s, when he heard about a circus going bust and realized they had some good animals that had all been born in captivity, he couldn't resist. "I bought an entire herd of big Manchurian camels, some dromedaries, an African buffalo, two guanacos and a couple of ponies. I had them delivered to Marchais, my family estate between Paris and Brussels, and put them out in the pasture with the cows."

That property, the Chateau de Marchais, lies at the foot of the Ardennes and is no less than six times the size of Monaco. It includes a pair of working farms and some very fine shooting. But as soon as the camels moved in, it became something of an unexpected local attraction.

He grinned broadly. "It's very funny to see people drive by in a car. I can almost hear the wife say, 'Look at the camels over there,' and the husband says, 'What do you mean, camels?' Then you hear the brakes jammed on and you see the car back up. Come to think of it, I guess it is a little strange to see camels grazing with cows in the French countryside."

In addition to animals, he was also fond of automobiles. "I have cars but I can't say that I am a serious collector. If a car comes up in a sale and appeals to me because it's a special model, I may buy it. I enjoy cars but I'm not terribly passionate about them. I've got cars ranging from a 1903 Dion up to a 1938 Packard eight cylinder."

By the time he'd acquired 45 cars, he couldn't help but notice that the Palace garage was cramped for space. Instead of selling off some of the cars to make room, he asked the state for space to create a museum.

"The cars are all in driving order," he said, "but I'm not sure driving them is always a good idea. The Packard, for instance, is a very heavy car with no power steering. People must have been terribly strong in 1938. I drove the car for an afternoon and had to stay in bed for three days afterwards."

The 225-room Palace overlooking the Port of Monaco, with its small private apartments and large, formal halls was where Grace and Rainier and their three children had their official residence. But *Roc Agel* was where Mr. and Mrs. Grimaldi and their three children were often happiest to spend their time.

The main house is a mixture of chintz and rustic. The living room is comfortable, with every sign of being lived in. There are bedrooms enough for their children and a few extra for grandchildren, too. The kitchen is modern, much of it having been shipped from America when Grace complained that she didn't see anything at all romantic about preparing meals in what was originally a typically cramped, badly equipped European kitchen.

"Grace was pretty good at doing barbecues," he said. "She also used to like to cook breakfast for the family."

While they always maintained a full household staff at *Roc Agel,* at the Palace, and at Marchais, too, Rainier occasionally showed his hand in the kitchen. "But only for fun. I'm not a great cook by any means although I can do a terrific crêpe suzette. I used to do pancakes with maple syrup in the morning for the children and was very good with Aunt Jemima mix."

For him, and for Grace, too, *Roc Agel* was where they could get away from phone calls and official appointments, and listen, uninterrupted, to music.

"Grace loved classical music," he said, "especially Bach, enjoyed opera and of course loved ballet. But she wasn't very fond of Wagner. She liked jazz and so do I. Music has always played a role in our family life and there was always music playing. Grace would play music when she painted or pressed flowers. She even did gymnastics to music. And this, I'll have you know, was long before Jane Fonda and aerobics."

As for himself, "I once tried to learn to play the saxophone but didn't get very far because it's a difficult instrument and especially painful for people around you while you're learning. So I stopped that and took up the drums. I still sometimes play them for fun. I like music immensely although I'm by no means a great musician. I happen to love Tchaikovsky. I guess I'm a great fan of romantic music. On the other hand I'm not that fond of Mozart because I find it repetitious and I don't like Wagner because it's too clashy, too Teutonic. I don't like any of the Wagnerian operas because I don't like the sound of the voices. But I like Italian opera, which I think is the best."

Perhaps not surprisingly, Grace and Rainier at *Roc Agel*—but especially Rainier—were not the same people one saw in Monaco. When he was at the Palace, he was the prince. At *Roc Agel*, he was a husband, Grace was a wife, and together they were parents. Later, he would also be a grandfather.

Throughout his life he'd maintained a certain reserve, was always a man very aware of his position and conscious of the image that went along with that. But when he was at *Roc Agel* he showed himself to be a simple man. It was only when you saw the difference that you could start to understand that his role was not an easy one.

At the end of the 19th century, a play was written about one of Rainier's ancestors, Prince Florestan. It was called *Rabagas* and was advertised as a political comedy. The most touching part of the piece is Florestan's monologue on the weight of his responsibilities.

"If I go for a walk, it is found that I have too much idle time. If I don't go for a walk then I am afraid of showing myself. If I give a ball I am accused of wild extravagance. If I do not give a ball then I am mean and avaricious. If I hold a review I am attempting military intimidation. If I do not hold a review I am afraid I cannot trust the troops. When fireworks are let off on my birthday, I am wasting the people's money. When I suppress the fireworks, then I do nothing for the people's amusement. If I am in good health it is because I am idle and take no trouble over public matters. If I am in bad health, that is the result of debauchery. If I build, I am wasteful. If I do not build, then what about the working classes? Everything I do is proclaimed detestable and what I do not do gives even greater offence."

More than a century later, Rainier claimed, that speech touched close to home. "It's as true today as it was then. It's a very thin line to walk. And it took me quite some time to figure out where that line is because it's not something you can just learn. You have to feel your way. My grandfather would say to me, 'Don't go to too many things. You must choose where to be seen, otherwise the Prince's presence doesn't means as much.' But no one ever told me if ten events were too many or if five were not enough. In the beginning I had a tendency to go whenever I was asked, to shake hands, to give away cups and prizes, to be seen. It took awhile to know how much is the right amount. That's something I've tried to teach my son, Albert, who will one day succeed me. He's got to be seen around in the beginning and he should go to a lot of things. But then he must start choosing so that his participation, his presence, is something of value, something people will look forward to."

In other words, the job required a talent for aloofness. "At times I must be aloof because aloofness gains respect. Otherwise people see you everywhere and it doesn't mean anything when you give your patronage to something. I'm not saying to my son that he shouldn't walk around and be accessible, but part of my job and the job he will inherit from me is in learning where to draw the line between being accessible and being over familiar. That might not be a difficult thing to do for say, the President of the United States or the Prime Minister of England or even the Mayor of Paris. But it's especially difficult here because the place is so very small."

Did that mean, he was asked, there's no question of ever strolling out of the Palace in a pair of Bermudas and heading to a pizza joint at the port for a beer?

He thought about that for a moment. "I guess nowadays I could but I wouldn't be inclined to. Albert can. He's younger and that's more the trend these days. But he mustn't do it every day. He goes out with friends and plays tennis at the Country Club and goes to the stadium to workout. That's good. However he'll have to draw the line when he succeeds because he can't then have fellows coming up to him on the street saying, 'Hey Al, let's go jogging.' The rules change when he becomes the sovereign. Nowadays it's even more difficult than it was when I was his age. Sure, going down to the port for a pizza with some friends might be fun. But I'm very aware of the fact that, with the press as active as they are, a picture might be taken of me there and who knows what the caption under it will say."

Rank may have its privileges, he knew, but he'd learned the hard way that it never comes without a price. And this was, he said, a lesson that Albert had had to struggle with, too.

He explained that when Albert was five or six, he was sitting with a group of children who were each in turn asked by an old lady, "What would you like to do when you grow up?" One little boy said he wanted to be a fireman and another said he wanted to be a policeman, the way children always answer that question. Then she turned to Albert and asked him. He answered, "I don't have any choice."

Rainier shook his head. "I'm not sure he understood until now just what that really means. He's discovering, as I did, that it's not always easy knowing who to trust. Albert's had to learn the hard way that some fellows who've been seen around with him were really only interested in what he could do for them. That it was a one-way street. Now he's much wiser about that sort of thing and tries to find out who people are before he allows them to get close. He has to protect himself, especially here, again, because it's so small. We live under a microscope."

The Principality of Monaco is a city-state of 30,000 people. As only about 6,000 are actually Monegasque, it is unique as a country because the natives are so outnumbered by foreigners. The majority of those foreigners are French, with Italians, British, and Americans well accounted for. Altogether Monaco can boast residents from nearly 100 other countries.

Less than half the size of New York's Central Park, or just about the same as London's Hyde Park, it was once described by Somerset Maugham as "a sunny spot for shady people" because its 480 acres were made famous by bright sunshine, mild winters, the most glamorous casino in the world, millionaires, movie stars, courtesans, wannabes, yachts, expensive restaurants, expensive hotels, expensive apartments, jewelry stores, banks, Formula One race cars, stamps, high-priced black tie suppers straight out of a Scott Fitzgerald novel, and no income tax.

Monaco's residents have the highest per capita net worth of any state in the world, plus the highest ratio of automobiles: 30,000 people own more than 15,000 cars. There is no poverty to speak of, the state is extremely benevolent when any of its citizens suffer social problems, and the standard of living is, even by French Riviera criteria, impressive.

Two-thirds of the way between city of Nice and the Italian market town of Ventimiglia, the principality is surrounded by France, the border is made of flowers. French is the official spoken language, although English and Italian are close runners-up. There's a tongue called Monegasque, which sounds more like Italian than French, but the only time you ever really hear it these days—except in a local high school class—is at weddings. Still, the Monegasques are not French, and they staunchly defend their right never to become French.

For nearly 2,000 years *Le Rocher* was ruled by a succession of peoples: Phoenicians, Ligurians, Romans, Barbarians, Saracens, the Counts of Provence, the Church, the Genoese, and the Ghibellines. Towards the end of the 13th century, the Grimaldis were just another clan of wealthy ship owners and merchants from Genoa. When the Guelphs went to war with the Ghibellines, the Grimaldis weighed in on the side of the Guelphs. But they were backing the wrong Godfather. The Ghibellines took the upper hand and the Grimaldis decided they would stay healthier if they were living somewhere else.

They might well have been destined for historical obscurity as a family in exile except for the Grimaldi known as Francois "Le Malizia"—Frank the Spiteful. He wanted revenge. The Phoenicians and the Greeks had both constructed temples on a slice of rock jutting out to sea some 100 miles east of Genoa that came to be called Monoecus, after the local name for the god Heracles. But neither of them could hold onto it and by the year 1162, it had been claimed by the Ghibellines. They valued it so highly that they built an almost impenetrable, four-turreted, 37-sided, high-walled fortress there. Sitting above a tiny, natural harbor, the rock protected the eastern approach by land and sea to the Bay of Genoa.

The garrison would be a big prize for anyone who could claim it. So on the night of January 8, 1297, Francois donned the heavy brown robes of a wandering Franciscan monk and banged on the wooden gate begging refuge. The unsuspecting guards allowed him to enter. Before they could shut the gates, he'd pulled a sword from under his robes, his henchmen had rushed in, and the massacre had begun. Within hours, the Grimaldis had declared the rock to be their own.

Significantly, Monaco's coat of arms boasts a pair of friars wielding swords.

Over the next 100 years, the Grimaldis lost Monaco twice and regained it twice, although by the first quarter of the 15th century they'd pretty well established their feudal rights over Monaco and the two neighboring towns of Roquebrune and Menton. They were officially allied with France until 1524 when the ruling prince made a deal with Spain for "rights to the sea." That meant he could levy a tax of two percent on the value of merchandise in the hold of any ships passing within sight of the rock. Taxing ships like that was a decent family business until the middle of the 17th century when a later ruling prince realigned Monaco with France. Then the French

Revolution got in the way. The Grimaldis were removed from their throne and Monaco was annexed to France. In 1814, the family's claim was restored by the Treaty of Paris. The following year the Treaty of Vienna placed Monaco under the protection of the Kings of Sardinia. It wasn't until 1861 that Monaco was once and for all recognized to be an independent state.

As the 33rd ruler of Monaco, Rainier III not only represented the oldest ruling family in Europe but, following the death of Japan's Emperor Hirohito in 1989, he became the longest-serving monarch in the world.

Chapter 9

Growing Up Monegasque

On December 18, 1933, the Principality of Monaco declared war on the United States of America.

Well, not exactly the entire US of A, just Mississippi.

A series of bearer bonds issued by Mississippi in the 1830s had been stashed in bank vaults and forgotten about for more than 90 years, until the heirs of the original owners discovered them and tried to secure the monies due. With interest, the nominal $100,000 value of the bonds had turned into $574,300. But Mississippi had defaulted on the loans in 1841.

They tried to sue Mississippi, only to learn that American law prohibited such an action, as an individual state may only be sued by another state, by the US Government, or by a foreign government. So they looked around for a foreign state, approached Prince Louis II of Monaco and offered him 45 percent of the action if the principality would assume ownership of the bonds and press the court case.

Monaco applied to the United States Supreme Court for permission to file the suit. However, because Mississippi had amended its own constitution in 1875 specifically barring all claims against those bonds, the principality first had to prove that the amendment was unconstitutional. Attorneys for Monaco argued that they were giving the State of Mississippi, "An opportunity to erase this stigma from her reputation."

Even the *New York Times* came out in favor of the Monegasques.

In an editorial on December 19, 1933, the paper suggested, "Surely Mississippians should think kindly of a foreign state which owes the United States nothing." Two days later the same newspaper wondered, "How would it be if Mississippi proposed to Monaco to roll dice for the money?"

The United States Supreme Court heard the arguments in January 1934 and immediately ordered Mississippi to show cause why the principality should not be permitted to file suit.

Attorneys for Mississippi now claimed that Monaco was not an independent state. They cited the 1918 treaty with France where Monaco undertook to exercise its rights of sovereignty "in accord with the political, naval and economic interests of France." But the French Foreign Office testified that the treaty did not imply that Monaco had surrendered its rights as a foreign entity.

Unfortunately for Monaco, Chief Justice Charles Evans Hughes rendered the opinion that the principality, like the original holders of the bonds, did not, in fact, have the right to sue the State of Mississippi without consent of the state and that consent would not be forthcoming.

The war was over, Mississippi declared victory, and the Principality of Monaco has been at peace with the United States of America ever since.

Prince Charles III, for whom Monte Carlo had been named, was succeeded to the throne by his son, Albert I, a tall, handsome man with a well-groomed black beard whose first love was marine research. Under his reign, the casino brought to the principality an era of unparalleled prosperity. But certain influential Monegasque families resented the fact that prosperity had turned Monte Carlo into a company town.

The Societe des Bains de Mer et Du Cercle des Etrangers (SBM)—the Sea Bathing Society and Foreigners' Club—was the publicly quoted company that controlled Monaco's gambling franchise. As Monaco's largest employer and by far the nation's largest source of revenue, SBM wielded a grossly disproportionate amount of political power. Certain influential Monegasque families soon began to feel that Albert had sold them out by allowing SBM to wedge itself in between the prince and his people. A plot was hatched to force Albert's abdication and put his son on the throne. Recognizing that it was best to offer radical change before it was forced upon him, Albert relinquished his powers of absolute rule.

His constitution of 1911 separated the Prince's household from the government. The prince remained chief executive but the government was now composed of a Minister of State plus three counselors. Legislative power was to be split between the prince and the newly formed National Council, whose members would be elected by the people.

Immediately following World War I, Albert negotiated a long-awaited, vitally important pact with France, which was incorporated into the Treaty of Versailles. He agreed to exercise his rights in conformity with the political, military, and economic interests of France.

The French, in turn, agreed to defend the principality's independence and sovereignty. They were worried about a distant German branch of the Grimaldi family that could possibly one day make a claim. From this came the accord that, should there be no heir to maintain the line, Monaco would be formed into a French protectorate. However, the ruling prince would always have the option of adopting an heir should he not be able to produce one, thus forever assuring the Grimaldi line.

Ironically, Albert's son was born and raised in Germany.

In 1869, at the age of 20, Albert had married 18-year-old Lady Mary Victoria Douglas Hamilton, daughter of the late Duke of Hamilton, Scotland's premier peer. The alliance had been arranged by Napoleon III. But within five months she'd walked out on him and had gone to live with her mother in Baden-Baden, where their son, Louis, was born. Albert requested and received a church annulment, then dissolved the civil marriage by decree.

Despite his official status as hereditary prince, the young Louis didn't set foot in Monaco or even meet his father until he was 11. When they did meet, they didn't get along. The pair lived together, mainly in Paris, for five years, until Louis escaped to serve with the French Foreign Legion.

While posted in North Africa, Louis fell in love with a young laundress named Marie Juliette Louvet. Albert refused to grant them permission to marry, either because she'd once been married or because she came from working-class family. Their love-child, Charlotte, was born in 1898. Now Albert refused to recognize either their alliance or his granddaughter's legal rights. Louis and Marie Juliette separated when Charlotte was very young. While Louis always acknowledged Charlotte to be his rightful heir, it wasn't until her 21st birthday that Albert finally conceded that her accession to the throne was the only sensible option to perpetuate the family's grip on Monaco. He insisted Louis officially name her as his successor and, just in case there might be any lingering doubt, ordered Louis to legally adopt her.

A tiny, feisty woman who always spoke her mind, Charlotte was an eccentric in the wonderful way that some women from the 19th century were natural eccentrics. Married at the age of 22 to a distinguished and cultured French nobleman, Count Pierre de Polignac, she was revered by her family, especially her grandchildren who always called her "Mamou."

Rainier characterized her as a woman with a kind heart who'd been a nurse during World War I and who spent her later years helping less fortunate people, among them prisoners.

"My mother lived most of her life in Paris and at Marchais," he explained. "But it was sad, really, because she was unhappy almost from the start of her marriage. She never had very good memories of Monaco. I think she was always lonely here. She didn't have any friends here. She didn't have anyone around her. Being an only daughter, I'm afraid there were times in her life when she was badly torn between her husband and her father."

To keep the family name alive, Albert required Pierre to change his name to Grimaldi, becoming Prince Pierre Grimaldi Count of Polignac, the day before his wedding.

Rainier described his father as a man of old-fashioned elegance with a pencil-thin moustache who was interested in music, art and literature, and also fluent in several languages. "He was a very delicate, very sensitive man. Although, looking back, he might not have been very accessible where the younger generation was concerned. I regret maybe not having listened and spoken to him more. But that might be the problem with all young people. When you're young you don't listen enough."

Pierre and Charlotte's first child, Antoinette, was born in 1920. Two years later, when Albert passed away, Louis became ruling prince. Then, on May 3, 1923, Charlotte's second child—Rainier Louis Henri Maxence Bertrand Grimaldi—was born in the Palace in Monaco. He was the only grandson and eventual heir of a ruling monarch, so his home was wherever the sovereign held court.

Rainier continued, "We'd only come to Monaco for about three months of the year. It was usually in the spring around Easter when the weather was good. I liked that because there was always a lot to do and the people were very welcoming. We wintered at Marchais. The Palace of Monaco was closed. My family, my grandfather's entire staff, the cooks, valets, footmen, maids, everybody would go to Marchais for five or six months. Except the government. They stayed in Monaco. I remember my grandfather installed a telegraph at Marchais so he could keep in touch with them. It was very exciting, something brand-new for us. I can still see a secretary tapping out messages all day long. There were also a couple of months every year when the family went shooting in Scotland. But I hated that. It never stopped raining. It was very boring."

Claiming that his childhood was "basically a contented one," Rainier acknowledged that his parents' divorce in 1929 left him feeling insecure. "Insecure in the sense that children of divorced parents are always getting shuffled around and are never quite certain where they belong. There are times when you doubt your parents' love."

It had been agreed that Rainier and Antoinette would spend part of each year with their mother and grandfather and part of the time with their father. "When we were with mother we were always being told, when you see your father don't say anything to him about me or your grandfather. When we were with father we were always being told, don't say anything to your mother or your grandfather about me. That wasn't easy. Like any child who is the product of divorced parents, I felt hurt by it."

Nor was his childhood made any easier by political tension at home. Louis found himself under severe pressure, which began just as the "Roaring 20s" drew to a close. The National Council tried to force a showdown. Under the constitution they could only make recommendations to the prince. They had no real power. This was the first of many things they wanted changed. For example, they were unhappy with the way SBM operated as a state unto itself, contending that the company somehow threatened the independence of the country. They also wanted the prince to hold SBM to its contractual responsibility of supplying Monte Carlo with basic services such as water, gas and road maintenance. They claimed SBM had neglected its obligations by investing instead in new tennis courts and a beach.

At the same time Princess Charlotte asked her father for permission to divorce Prince Pierre. Louis agreed to his daughter's divorce and effectively banished Pierre from the principality.

A newspaper report of the day described Monaco as, "a box of toys in which everything is brilliant and artificial and a little fragile and must be kept carefully fitted into its place if it is not to be broken."

Louis's problem was that he never really understood just how fragile that box of toys was.

Chapter 10

The Birth of
Modern Monaco

It had been agreed at the time of Pierre's divorce from Charlotte that he would take charge of Rainier's education. "My father wanted me to have an absolutely superior education so he sent me to England in 1934. I started at the Summer Fields School at St Leonard's-on-Sea. It was a horrible place. Short pants, cold showers, and canings. The only good time I had there was boxing. I won the school title in my weight class. Other than that, I hated it."

From there Rainier went to the equally British, Stowe. "It was a beautiful setting, but I remember arriving there with my father, not knowing any of the house masters or any of the students. I found the old castle atmosphere very dreary. It rained all the time so as soon as you went out to play any games you were knee-deep in mud. Then I had to learn about things like fagging, which meant doing menial chores for the older boys. Happily they were nice fellows but the whole thing always struck me as being stupid. I wasn't very happy at Stowe either."

So unhappy, in fact, that he ran away. "On my third day I escaped. It turned out to be much easier than I thought it would be. I left the grounds and headed for the railway station. My plan was to buy myself a ticket to London and then make my way home from there. But I guess I wasn't very good at that kind of thing. I never thought there was anything unusual about going to the railway station with my school cap still on my head."

The moment the school authorities realized he was gone, the police were notified. And as soon as the station-master noticed a lad with a school cap on his head trying to get to London, he rang the school.

"I was picked up and promptly brought back to Stowe," Rainier said. "The head master, an ex-military man, came to fetch me in his enormous car. I thought I was in for trouble and would be severely caned. But he took me back to his study and welcomed me home with a gigantic high tea. He didn't reprimand me at all. He said, 'You must be hungry so here's something to eat.' It was the first meal I'd had all day. I thought to myself, finally someone understands. But then I was put in the school infirmary because they couldn't figure out why any child wanted to run away from this heaven."

The young Rainier was officially "under observation" for two entire weeks, confined to doing absolutely nothing, until the staff gave up trying to figure him out and returned him to his dorm and his classes.

All those years later, he felt, the problem should have been obvious to them. Even though he spoke perfect English—"We had a British nanny so I spoke English before I spoke French"—he was a chubby, timid child, and the only foreigner among 500 boys. He'd withdrawn into his shell. Yes, he could handle himself very competently with a pair of boxing gloves strapped onto his hands but his innate shyness outside the ring was a red flag for the school bullies.

Rainier said he told his father how unhappy he was and that his father must have mentioned it to someone because, before long, Louis began to fear that Pierre might try to take him out of England, might somehow prevent the child from returning to Monaco or otherwise come between Rainier and his grandfather.

So in August 1936, Louis filed a petition in London for custody of Rainier, seeking to restrain Pierre from removing the 13-year-old from Great Britain.

During the March 1937 High Court hearing, it came out that Louis had made similar appeals in Monaco and France and had won both times. Among the intriguing possibilities actually considered in the London action was making an heir to Monaco's throne a ward of the British courts. In the end, the judge ruled in favor of Louis but not before the affair hit the front pages and generally served to embarrass everyone concerned.

From England, Rainier was sent to Le Rosey, one of the finest of the Swiss boarding schools.

And there, he said, he was very happy. "I adored it. I was there until 1939, until the first bombing of Lyons. It was a wonderful place to go to school. There were only about 100 boys at Le Rosey in those days and the girls' school was just across the way. It was the sort of place where, if you wanted to learn, everything was possible. If you wanted to work, it was great. If you didn't, they simply didn't worry about you. We even spent part of the winter in Gstaad."

After graduation from Le Rosey, he attended the University of Montpellier where he received his BA, then spent a year in Paris studying Political Science. His mother formally resigned her position on May 30, 1943, the day before Rainier's 21st birthday. Three days later Louis officially proclaimed Rainier as heir to the throne.

It was not an especially joyous moment, he said. "It was, in some ways, very sad. My mother renounced because she felt incapable. She was unhappy. I felt sorry for her. At the same time it meant a severe change of style in my life. I suddenly had to assume a lot of responsibilities."

A few months later, as soon as he finished school, Rainier was commissioned as a second lieutenant and assigned to the headquarters' intelligence staff of the 2nd Corps, 1st French Army.

The young prince suffered through the winter campaign in Alsace and saw some action.

"But not as much," he said, "as I wanted to. I had a pretty useless job posting notices on factories. It would have been more fun if we could have blown the damn things up. Because I spoke English I was sectored off to the 36th Infantry Division in Strasbourg, the Texas Rangers, and acted as a liaison on the general staff."

Decorated for gallantry in areas under fire, he was promoted to first lieutenant and transferred to the economics section of the French Military Mission in Berlin. He served just over 17 months before returning to Monaco to see firsthand how the war had taken its toll.

His grandfather was ailing and the Nazis were in charge.

World War II was not one of Monaco's more glorious moments.

Although the Monegasques did not capitulate the way the French did, they remained officially neutral.

But because the French had come into Monaco at the start of the war to build defense installations along the coast, the moment France fell the Italians took the principality on the pretext that it had been previously occupied by France.

The next wave of soldiers came from Germany.

In 1943, Berlin sent a Consul General and a military commandant to Monaco. A Gestapo unit took up residence at the Hotel de Paris and a Panzer division moved into the Hotel Metropole.

The Germans weren't in Monaco long before the tide started to turn in the Allies' favor. Increasingly short supplied, Berlin ordered that the copper roof of Monte Carlo's casino be removed so that the metal could be used in the war effort. The Panzer general, himself a frequent visitor to the casino, refused to comply. He even used his influence to have the casino listed by the Nazis as "a cultural and historic monument," thereby saving it from the war.

The Americans landed way down the beach at St. Raphael in August 1944, and walked into the principality five weeks later.

The Nazis had already left.

Once the GIs had secured the region, barbed wire was taken down, work began to de-mine the port, gun emplacements were dismantled, and collaborators were arrested.

The American general in charge of the region decided Monte Carlo would be the ideal R&R spot for his troops.

But Louis said no.

The prince claimed there wasn't enough room in the country for so many soldiers plus the regular visitors who, now that the war was over, would soon be coming back.

Insulted by Louis's attitude towards the liberators, the US Army placed Monaco off-limits to all US service personnel. Even General Eisenhower, who toured the region in the summer of 1945, refused to set foot in Monaco, staying instead on Cap d'Antibes.

Not only was Rainier's sense of honor offended by Louis's conciliations—he felt that his grandfather, under the influence of several people in his entourage, had failed in not taking a forceful position against the Germans—but he now found Monaco desperately bleak.

The entire country needed to have the Nazi occupation washed and painted and wallpapered away.

Rainier was also concerned that SBM maintained a stranglehold on the nation's economic power and tried to explain to his grandfather that changes were necessary. But Louis had other things on his mind.

In 1946, and in failing health, he married his longtime companion, a Parisian actress named Ghislaine Marie Dommanget, and altered his will accordingly to provide for her. His only interest was in spending his remaining years with her. He simply didn't care what Rainier thought.

So, in great frustration, Rainier walked out of Monaco.

He bought that small villa at St. Jean-Cap-Ferrat and lived there, spending the years between the end of the war and his accession to the throne racing cars in the Tour de France Rally, skin-diving, fishing, sailing, occasionally writing poetry, going to exhibitions and otherwise quietly meeting his obligations to the principality.

It was May 9, 1949 when Louis II passed away.

Rainier was three weeks short of his 26th birthday.

But now, finally in charge, Rainier found himself alone.

He set about trying to put his own stamp of authority on the ruling Prince's office and one of the first things he did was to bring his father back from exile.

There were then renewed mutterings from that cousin who'd once tried to claim the throne.

At 79, the pretender reasserted his protest that Charlotte's adoption and later admission to full hereditary rights contravened the constitution. The best Rainier could do was ignore him, secure in the knowledge that this particular annoyance couldn't go on forever.

Next he struck a deal with Princess Ghislaine, Louis's widow.

In his will, the late sovereign left 50 percent of his estate to Rainier, 25 percent to his granddaughter Antoinette, and 25 percent to Ghislaine. But included in the estate was property that Rainier claimed belonged to the crown, property that was not Louis's to give away.

The case was heard by the specially convened Court of Revision, a secretive tribunal created specifically to settle Monaco's dynastic disputes. Consisting of ten attorneys chosen by the French Foreign Office and whose names are never disclosed, they were flown clandestinely to Monaco where they ruled in Rainier's favor.

Ghislaine appealed but, in the end, there was nothing she could do except refuse to leave her one room at the Palace.

Rainier's accession to the throne had been welcomed by the Monegasques, but his honeymoon with the otherwise cantankerous National Council was short lived. They picked up with him where they'd left off with his grandfather and made demands that Rainier found unacceptable.

Led in part by a local lawyer named Jean Charles Rey, the Council regularly tried to compete with Rainier's authority. Rey later married Princess Antoinette and together they claimed that because the law did not limit succession to males, Princess Charlotte's first born was therefore Monaco's rightful heir.

Years later, Rainier insisted they never actually posed a serious threat, that it was just vague talk, that everything was "up in the air."

Be that as it may, the two were quickly rebuked and, if nothing else, the affair was an embarrassment.

In the summer of 1955, the heavily government-subsidized Monaco Banking and Precious Metals Society went bankrupt. The Council pointed a finger at four close aides of the Prince and demanded their resignations. Questions of mismanagement and conflicts of interest were raised. At first Rainier stayed loyal to his aides. Then, faced with a mass walk-out by the Council, he accepted the resignations.

A few months later he reappointed the four to other posts and almost immediately eleven members of the Council quit in protest.

Rainier made little effort to appease the Council. Legally, he held the power. All they could do, all they were supposed to do, was advise.

But they were undeterred in their opposition. Rey, especially, sought confrontation wherever possible, like in the Council's bizarre stance against Rainier's plan for covering the railroad.

Running straight through the center of Monte Carlo, with tracks sunk into an open ditch, trains from Nice to Italy literally sliced the country in half. Rainier proposed to cover the tracks and build on top of them. The council said no and tried to withhold the money that was required.

It was idiotic because the plans were not only sound, they were paramount to the further development of Monte Carlo.

But then Rey and the Council also fought him on making funds available for the Oceanographic Institute to afford its newly appointed director, Jacques Cousteau. There's no doubt that Cousteau's appointment was a world-class coup for Monaco. Yet the Council wouldn't accept that.

In the end, of course, Rainier got the money to cover the railroad and to bring Cousteau to Monaco. But at times it appeared almost as if the Council—driven by Rey—was engaged in nothing short of a personal vendetta.

By 1959, things had gotten so out of hand that Rainier decided he had no option but to suspend the constitution and take rule by decree. "There was no doubt that changes were needed. We couldn't go on much longer the way we were. It hadn't yet reached the stage where anyone was making serious threats but there was discontent with the old constitution. I decided I wanted to create a genuine constitutional monarchy. Not because I was being pressured into it but because I felt it was better to do it voluntarily than to wait until the National Council or various political figures in the community started making specific demands. So I approached the National Council and we worked it out together. I gave up some power but it wasn't necessarily a difficult thing to do because responsibilities were split too."

Under the new Constitution, dated 1962, executive power would remain in the hands of the Prince, who appoints a Minister of State to run the government. The Minister also represents him in matters of foreign affairs and with the Monegasque parliament.

Because everything is done in the name of the Prince, it is only done with his approval.

But legislative power is split between the Prince and the National Council, made up of 18 native Monegasques elected by universal suffrage to a five-year term.

Rainier explained, "They vote the budget. They debate the laws. They vote the laws. Or they can veto the laws. They're not supposed to interfere with the executive and his duties but in reality we have clashes, especially when they make judgments about how I'm doing my job or say things like, building permission should never have been granted for such and such a project. It's difficult for elected men to look after that kind of stuff because you never really know where their own interests are. The National Council discusses each chapter of the budget and each department of the government must defend its own requirements. If the National Council isn't satisfied, it can reject what it doesn't want. So because it votes the budget it can, if it wants, block the whole system."

Keeping a tight rein on the Council would prove to be a constant challenge for Rainier. But there were others just as difficult. He also had to do battle with a wily Aristotle Onassis, the all-powerful SBM, and the ever formidable President of France, Charles de Gaulle.

Chapter 11

Taking On Onassis

One morning in 1951, while casually strolling through the streets of Monte Carlo, a shabbily dressed Greek multi-millionaire bearing thick black-rimmed glasses, noticed that the old Sporting Club was boarded up.

Aristotle Socrates Onassis was born in Smyrna in 1906, but was forced to flee at the age of 16 when the Turks ravaged the village and murdered his father, a successful tobacco broker. He found a ship bound for South America, jumped on board, and headed for Buenos Aires with just $60 in his pocket. To avoid being sent home when he got there, he lied to the authorities that he was 21. To buy food once he settled there, he worked at night as a telegraph operator.

Even as a young man, Onassis showed the keen eye of a world class opportunist. When he noticed that tobacco was in short supply he became a broker and later parlayed that into a factory. When he saw tobacco ships leaving empty for the return trip, he became an exporter and made a fortune by filling their holds with leather and grain. He soon took over a small fleet of old freighters, negotiated a commercial treaty between Greece and Argentina, and got himself appointed Greek Consul General. He used his title to build up his freight business, which he then diversified into whaling and a fleet of oil tankers. After World War II, when he bought 20 former American Liberty ships at knock-down prices and changed their registry from the US to Panama, the Americans said he was in breach of his purchase agreement and fined him $7 million. But Onassis was such a natural wheeler-dealer that, while paying the fine, he actually convinced the Americans to offer him a $14 million loan to build himself 20 more ships.

If he wasn't yet the wealthiest man in the world in 1946, when he married 17-year-old Tina Livanos and honeymooned in Monaco, he was fast becoming that.

In those days, his Olympic Maritime empire—consisting of 91 ships, of which 70 were oil tankers—had its headquarters in Paris. But French taxes were killing him.

Now, seeing the Sporting Club boarded up, it dawned on him that a building like that would suit him very well, all the better considering Monaco's no-tax politics. So he asked around, discovered that the place had been empty for some time and went to see the company that owned it, SBM, hoping he could rent it.

Their answer was no.

He asked why not.

No one came forward with any explanations.

So he offered to buy the building.

They said no.

Next, he offered to buy the building and the ground under it.

They said no again.

He increased his offer.

And still they said no.

He asked why they were being so stubborn.

They showed him to the door.

This didn't sit well with Onassis, a businessman who was simply trying to do a deal with a company that should have otherwise been anxious to realize the benefits of its assets. It bothered him, not just because SBM was being illogical, but also because when he wanted something, he usually got it.

So he bought SBM.

"As the biggest employer here," Rainier said, "SBM was always trying to exert their influence. But I felt they interfered too much with the running of the principality. A lot needed to be changed, or at least to be redefined. For example, until I looked into it, SBM's payment to the government for the monopoly on gambling was very mysterious. During my grandfather's reign there was always talk about envelopes being passed under tables. It was an unacceptable way of running a business."

Rainier made substantial changes, but one consequence of the war was that wealth and exclusivity were no longer synonymous. A lot of exclusive people were no longer wealthy and a lot of wealthy people were not very exclusive.

"I knew that Onassis was always looking for interesting places to visit," Rainier explained, "so I convinced him to come to Monaco as a sort of a super-tourist. He and Tina started spending a lot of time here. He based his shipping company here. And his yacht, *The Christina*, usually wintered here. After a while he began to think of Monaco as something of a second home."

Encouraged by Rainier, Onassis used 51 front companies, mostly in Panama, to acquire 300,000 SBM shares which he hid in various portfolios before anyone else in Monaco realized what was happening.

It was a costly exercise that put a strain on his cash flow but then, whenever Onassis was short of cash, he turned for help to Stavros Niarchos, the Greek ship-owner who'd married Tina's sister.

Niarchos later swore, "I bought Monte Carlo with Onassis. But when it came to a settlement I was out. Oh well, that's my brother-in-law."

Onassis assured Rainier that he was going to modernize the company, add rooms to the Hotel de Paris, and build a grill restaurant on the top floor. "I will spend millions and make the place a world cultural and tourist center."

Obviously, Rainier liked what he heard. "In the beginning I thought Onassis could be useful to SBM even though he had some slightly odd ideas, like tearing down the opera house. A Greek architect he'd hired told him that the sound was bad and the best thing would be to rip it down and put up a huge shell."

Almost right from the start SBM made money under Onassis, partly because he and Tina were at the heart of the European jet-set—their clique had loads of money to spend—and partly because of a general upturn in French economy. But as the 1950s wore on, Onassis spent less and less on the company.

When Rainier tried to push him into building a new Summer Sporting down the beach, Onassis directed his people to ask the government what their plans were for electricity, roads, sewers, and gas. The bureaucrats took a predictably long time to answer that they'd provide electricity, roads, sewers, and gas based on SBM's plans for the site. But SBM said they couldn't proceed without knowing what the government intended. It went back and forth like this until the bureaucrats finally came up with blueprints. Then SBM questioned technical aspects of those blueprints. The government had to answer those questions. And when they did, SBM posed more questions. Onassis generated a massive, nonsensical dialogue with the government because as long as it was going on, he didn't have to spend any money.

Rainier was both disappointed and troubled by Onassis's attitude. "During the years that he was majority shareholder, none of the big investment programs he'd spoken of were carried out. He patched up whatever needed patching up and left the rest. All right, he built the Grill on the top of the Hotel de Paris. He did it because that interested him. And he painted some of the gaming rooms. But he didn't spend money on things like renewal of the company's activities or the creation of new activities. I didn't find the same enthusiasm in the man once he took over the company as I'd expected."

It's true that Onassis catered to his jet-set friends while the Prince wanted to cut Monte Carlo into an increasingly important middle-class tourist market. Some people over-simplified the problem by saying that Onassis wanted caviar and the Prince wanted sausages. But that's not quite true. Onassis merely saw SBM's assets in a different way. The casino was a kind of big kid's toy. Like his yacht, it was something he enjoyed telling people he owned.

Anything but amused, Rainier threatened not to renew the lease on Olympic Maritime's offices.

In response, Onassis objected to Rainier's interference and in turn threatened to leave Monaco. The Prince didn't want things to go that far so he backed off just a bit.

Then in 1959 Onassis dumped Tina for the opera super-star, Maria Callas. There was no doubt, Rainier understood, that having Onassis and Maria Callas in Monaco was good for business. Except that by this time, Onassis was thinking of SBM as little more than a real estate investment.

That's when Rainier learned what Onassis had in mind.

And it frightened him. "I had certain indications that definitely scared me. I was led to believe that one day he might try to sell off part of the property. He was a very intelligent man and terribly tough to do business with. But when it came to running SBM the way I'd hoped he would, it was almost as if he was too busy with other things."

Eventually, Onassis got to the point where he said he wouldn't put any more money into SBM except for upkeep and redecoration of hotel rooms.

"Even then I didn't like what he was proposing," Rainier continued. "He said he wanted to find some famous decorators and give them each two rooms to do any way they wanted. I couldn't believe it. It would have been a mess. There would have been no harmony. Two people in two different rooms would never have thought they were staying in the same hotel. We had lots of meetings, just the two of us, trying to find a solution. But we got to a point where there was no way out."

Monte Carlo was in trouble.

And Rainier could see that, just by looking at SBM's regular clientele.

A European clan, presided over by Onassis with Stavros Niarchos as his sidekick, they were united in wealth and the pursuit of pleasure, assembling each year at the Hotel de Paris, throwing parties for themselves on each other's boats and gambling together in the *salles privees*.

Italian film producer Dino De Laurentiis was a charter member, at least as long as he was in love with the beautiful Italian actress, Silvana Mangano.

Fiat tycoon, Gianni Agnelli, was also part of the clique.

As was the Italian industrialist known as "the fridge king."

He was an old man who began his career repairing bicycles and expanded that into the largest refrigeration company in Italy. He had absolutely no interests in anything, except Italy's national soccer team and weekends in Monte Carlo. He'd show up in his private plane and toss 5,000 franc chips around the casino as if they were pennies. He managed to average about $1 million in gambling losses a year and went on that way for eight or nine years, until he died.

At this point, thanks entirely to Grace and the publicity she generated, Americans joined the crowd.

Film producer Sam Spiegel mingled with tycoons like Charles Revson of Revlon Cosmetics and real estate magnate Bill Levitt of Levittown fame. Revson docked his boat, *Ultima II*, next to Levitt's boat, the *Belle Simone*, and in those days those two yachts were usually considered the most beautiful in the world.

Still, even with the Americans, the diminishing breed of hard-core gamblers who arrived every summer to stay for a month and divided their time between the Beach Club and the casino, was no longer enough.

By the early 1960s, the Summer Sporting had become a slightly seedy place. It was too small, not air-conditioned, and its tropical ambience was little more than a string of harshly colored lights shining on a couple of palm trees.

A decade later, the Arabs would come with their petrodollars, and super-rich Iranians would be there, as well. They were all high rollers. But even with them, 75 percent of the casino's total takings came in during July and August, Easter week and the week between Christmas and New Year. And 80 percent of the total takings came from fewer than 2,000 known clients.

The rest of the year, Monte Carlo was three or four little old ladies sitting in the Hotel de Paris having tea.

Many hotels, like the Hermitage and the Old Beach, closed for the winter. There was no young, international, year-round community. There were hardly any foreign companies. There was limited industry.

Off-season Monaco was so quiet that when Pan Am sponsored a feasibility study to build an Intercontinental Hotel there, the result was "don't bother."

The state didn't have sufficient funds to back the project and the only other man around who did—Onassis—didn't see any reason to help a company which would be in direct competition with SBM.

Pan Am couldn't come up with a single backer who believed in the future of Monaco.

In November 1962, Onassis tried to force a solution by giving Rainier a 90-day option to pick up his holding in SBM at nearly

$30 per share. But the quoted price was about half that, so the option was left to expire.

Onassis then announced that he was splitting the company into three groups, one for gambling, one for the hotels, restaurants, and the beach facilities, and one for real estate. He said he might even sublease the gambling concession so that he could concentrate on the main holding company and the real estate.

That was the last straw. Around the Palace the drastic step of nationalization was discussed. And for the first time in many years Rainier had the National Council behind him.

"Onassis and I did not quarrel," Rainier insisted. "We just both dug our heels in to maintain our positions."

However, the Prince was quoted at the time as saying, "Mr. Onassis is nothing more than a property peddler with no real interests in the welfare of Monaco."

Finding no equitable way out of the situation, Rainier ordered that the company's capitalization be increased by 800,000 new shares. Those shares were then sold to the state and Onassis was deprived of his majority.

The story told around the principality, romanticizing the shoot-out between the two into a sort of Monegasque OK Corral, is that Rainier offered Onassis $14 a share, when Onassis had paid between $2.80 and $5.60. Onassis refused. So Rainier took Onassis to the government printing plant and showed him SBM's new share certificates rolling off the presses.

Onassis supposedly said, "That will ruin me, that will drive my shares down to under $5."

Rainier supposedly replied, "Either accept $14 gracefully or try to find someone else who'll give you more than that for your reduced holding."

Onassis screamed nationalization and went to court to try to stop it.

Unfortunately for him, this was an away game as the only court with jurisdiction was in Monaco.

Except it didn't quite happen that way.

"That's not my style," Rainier said, although he admitted the new share certificates were printed and that Onassis did see them. "There's no doubt that the law permitting me to print those shares was a huge economic sword to hold over his head. But we didn't nationalize SBM. We bought those shares and paid Onassis a fair price for his. Now, it's interesting that once Onassis lost his majority holding, once he no longer had this personal interest in SBM, he became more reasonable and much more involved. He held onto a nominal shareholding, had a representative on the board, and took a real interest in what the company was doing."

The SBM that Rainier wrestled away from Onassis was antiquated. Stoves in the Hotel de Paris kitchen dated back to 1899. The kitchen staff included men to carry coal to those stoves, and one fellow in the basement whose job it was to receive huge blocks of ice, cut them up by hand, and send them in plastic bags to various bars around Monte Carlo.

Worse still, SBM's personnel lived off the fat of the land.

Until 1967, if you worked in a kitchen, SBM's food was your food. If you worked in a restaurant, SBM's silverware was your silverware. Whatever you needed at home—rugs, furniture, mirrors, linens, plates, and glasses—you simply helped yourself.

And no one batted an eyelid.

Within only a few months of the state finally assuming majority control, strikes and a student revolt crippled France. In solidarity with their French brothers, the unions in Monaco also went on strike. Even the croupiers walked out of the casino, although theirs might have been the only picket line in history where the protesters arrived in Cadillacs and Mercedes.

Rainier orchestrated sweeping changes to SBM as fast as he could, but it took 15 years before the company would invest $100 million in a five-year refurbishment program to modernize the hotels and build a new Café de Paris, in the style of the original 19th century café.

American games which had crept into the casino over the years—craps, slot machines and Las Vegas-style 38 number roulette, as opposed to European-style 37 number roulette—were moved out of the casino and into the rear of the Café. Rainier wanted the clock turned back in the casino, making it into the same sort of elegant private club it was when Edward VII and the Russian Grand Dukes played there.

He understood how the lights might be brighter in Atlantic City, and how the games might be faster in Las Vegas, but he also understood the image SBM should be selling—if you haven't won or lost at Monte Carlo, you're playing in the minor leagues.

And with that change of image, the punters began to return to Monaco, the way the faithful go to Lourdes.

"You can't really compare Las Vegas or Atlantic City with Monte Carlo," he said. "There isn't a lot of elegance in Las Vegas or Atlantic City. Nor is there a lot of charm there either. I would never want to see in Monaco some of the things I've seen in Las Vegas. It was very depressing to see people in wheelchairs stuck for hours in front of the slot machines. The casino at Monte Carlo isn't merely a place for gambling, it's an historic monument."

Even with his backing, nothing happened overnight. Change at SBM has always come at a snail's pace. Consider the fact that it took a 90-minute lecture from the company's managing director just to get the various hotel chefs thinking about a new dessert menu.

Onassis might have lost SBM, but he didn't exactly walk away penniless. He came out with a profit of more than $7 million—somewhere around $45 million in today's money—more than five times his original stake.

Still, when he heard of his defeat in court, he barked, "We were gipped."

Rainier refused to accept that. "The Onassis affair ended as well for him as it did for Monaco. Today the state permanently holds 1.2 million shares, which is a majority stake in SBM, so that one man can never again own SBM. At the same time he made some money on it. But that wasn't really the important thing. He never would have said so but I think he liberated himself from something he'd gotten into which wasn't really in his waters. I sincerely believe that because as soon as the deal was completed our personal relationship improved. On the contrary, it was even better than before because there was nothing to get in the way."

Their friendship continued until Onassis's death in March 1975.

"I can recall the first time he showed me around *The Christina*," Rainier said. "The ship had 12 cabins and I remarked what great cabins they were. He looked at me and confessed, 'But they're always empty.' I asked why. And he said, 'Because I don't know 12 people I'd like to have with me.'"

Rainier said that he and Grace liked Onassis a lot, and got along especially well with Maria Callas. "He was a very human man. Of course the tragedy in his life was the death of his son in a plane crash in the sea off Nice in 1973. The son was working with him and would have succeeded him. I don't think he ever got over that. Nor do I think he was ever very happy in either of his marriages. I'm convinced the only woman who brought him happiness was Callas."

Sailing on *The Christina* several times with Onassis and Callas gave Grace and Rainier a chance to see those two up close.

Rainier acknowledged, "There was a very good rapport between them. They understood each other. After all, they were both terribly Greek. They both had international reputations. They were both self-made. Grace and I agreed they were really meant for each other. We thought that Callas was fun. She was forever playing jokes on him. She was very easy to get along with, except that every morning she annoyed the hell out of him by vocalizing. He absolutely hated that. She'd run through her scales and he'd run around the ship turning up all the radios to drown out the sound. But I will always remember Aristotle Onassis as an intensely lonely man."

Chapter 12

Battling de Gaulle

As if his battles with Onassis and the National Council weren't enough, in 1962 Rainier also had to take on Charles de Gaulle.

The French President had become obsessed with untaxed French money in Monaco. He'd been complaining for some time that French companies basing themselves in Monaco were doing so specifically to avoid paying taxes, and that was no longer acceptable. French citizens living in Monaco didn't pay French taxes either. De Gaulle believed they must.

In March of that year, de Gaulle demanded that Rainier accept a revision of the 1951 treaty that protected Monaco from doing exactly what Charles de Gaulle wanted to do.

Rainier refused.

Firing the first salvo in what would ultimately be a stressful, one-year battle, de Gaulle went insisting on France's right to take over control of Radio Monte Carlo (RMC).

In those days, throughout Europe, governments controlled all sorts of enterprises that today we take for granted as being independent and outside the scope of national ownership. That included the telephone company, the gas and electric companies, the railroads, the airlines, and radio and television stations.

Because the monopoly on broadcasting was absolute, de Gaulle decided that any broadcasts in French, coming from outside France but aimed at sovereign French territory, had to be stopped.

Two years later, in 1964, the famous battle between the non-commercial British BBC and the commercial pirate station Radio Caroline—named for the then seven-year-old Princess Caroline of Monaco—would make headlines around the world. A ship anchored outside of Britain's three mile territorial limit aimed its antennas into the UK, openly competing with the government-owned BBC. The British government of the day declared that unacceptable.

For de Gaulle it was the same story with the principality's Radio Monte Carlo (RMC). It was also the perfect excuse to teach Rainier who was really in charge. So the French president's allies in Monaco strong-armed their way into RMC and got the man running the station fired, on the grounds that he was "too Americanized."

That meant he was playing too much American music and not enough French music.

Rainier was incensed with this blatant intrusion by a foreign government into the affairs of his independent nation.

By April all negotiations with France had broken down.

Except, of course, Monaco wasn't entirely independent of France.

The Council backed Rainier but the Minister of State—a loutish French bureaucrat named Emile Pelletier—sided with de Gaulle.

Infuriated, the Prince accused him of being disloyal.

Pelletier threatened to disclose to de Gaulle information that, as Minister of State, he'd been party to in confidence. Pelletier also threatened to inform de Gaulle of just how anti-French Rainier really was.

Rainier fired him on the spot.

De Gaulle now had the pretext he needed to get at the untaxed funds. He announced that Pelletier's dismissal was an insult to France, demanded that there be a revision of the Franco-Monegasque accords, and warned that, if the situation wasn't normalized immediately, France would shut Monaco's border, "and asphyxiate the state."

De Gaulle's intention was to rewrite the treaties with Monaco even though they'd been in effect since 1861 and 1918.

Rainier was never sure how de Gaulle thought he could get away with it. "He couldn't have done it legally. We were even prepared to go to the Hague. The treaty we've got with France stems from the Treaty of Versailles. You can't just erase that."

Which is precisely what de Gaulle wanted to do.

He was 72 and at the very height of his political powers. His vision of France as an independent super-power that demanded the respect of the rest of the world, was not universally shared. Still, to many Frenchmen he was sometimes, "Monsieur le President," but always "Le General."

His arrogance, combined with his haughty vision of France—and of himself—was matched only by his imposing size.

Charles de Gaulle stood six feet five. By contrast, Rainier was a shade over five foot seven.

"He was such a strange man," Rainier went on. "Whenever we met, when he came to visit in Monaco or when Grace and I went to Paris on what amounted to a state visit, he was very amiable. When he came here he brought gifts for Caroline. She was just a little girl and when she was introduced to him it was as if he was her grandfather. She kept asking him questions, like if he had any ponies. He must have spoken to her for 10 minutes. Still, he was adamant about his position vis-à-vis Monaco."

Despite their many differences, Rainier said, he couldn't help but be impressed by de Gaulle because he was such a formidable politician. "I always compared him to the Eiffel Tower, not because of his

Grace of Monaco

height but because he was something you could admire but couldn't possibly love. He was very cold."

To that he added, "You must understand that as soon as they set foot in the Élysées, every President of the French Republic becomes a monarch."

When de Gaulle discovered, much to his consternation, that Rainier would not give in without a fight, the dispute got bitter.

For de Gaulle, it was unthinkable that anybody would ever dare to stand up to him.

But Rainier understand what was at stake. "He wanted us to align ourselves on the French fiscal system. After someone somewhere in the Finance Ministry got it into de Gaulle's head that a lot of the North African French money was hidden here and that it had to come to France, he took the approach that there was no need for negotiations. That his word was going to be the law."

To prove his point, de Gaulle issued an ultimatum. If Rainier didn't give in, he—Charles de Gaulle—would order customs barriers set up around Monaco to isolate the principality from the rest of the world.

Again, Rainier stood his ground.

In October, de Gaulle fired the first salvo by stopping all mail going into or coming out of Monaco bearing domestic postage stamps. He insisted that those rates no longer applied and that only letters stamped for international mail would be accepted.

At a time when most business was done by mail, this had a staggering effect.

Next, he ordered two companies of gendarmes stationed in Nice to be put on alert. While rumors flew that French paratroopers were getting ready to seize Monte Carlo, the gendarmes constructed barriers at all the roads leading in and out of Monaco. Then, at midnight, Friday, October 12, 1962, French national police along with French customs officers sealed the border.

On de Gaulle's orders, they stopped every car in both directions and asked endless questions. For example, if you had a radio in your car, they'd ask you where you bought it and demand to see the receipt. If your papers weren't in order you were turned away.

By dawn, traffic was backed up for ten miles.

In Rainier's eyes, de Gaulle's actions were a direct threat to the sovereignty of the principality and there was simply no way he could permit that.

Reacting to an intractable Rainier, the French president next threatened to cut off Monaco's electricity and water.

Rainier didn't know what would have happened to Monaco had he done that but he always believed it could have been fatal for de Gaulle.

"It would have been a really stupid thing to do," he maintained, "because there was never any aggression on our part. I was giving interviews at the time trying to show that we weren't being anti-French by standing up to de Gaulle. I was only making a stand against measures that affected us, that were taken in the name of France when we were not given any chance to discuss them."

At one point there was actually talk around the French Foreign Ministry of dethroning Rainier and sending him into exile.

It wasn't until December, with the press continuing to describe Monaco as a country under siege, that the two parties started talking again. Several months of mediation followed.

"Once we got down to serious negotiations," Rainier said, "with the technicians at the various ministries, we knew everything would be all right. We could see that they were even a little embarrassed about all this because de Gaulle had gone too far."

Rainier agreed that French citizens, resident in Monaco for fewer than five years, would no longer enjoy their tax exempt status, and that they would be subject to French income taxes. Furthermore, any Monegasque company earning more than 25 percent of its turnover outside the principality would also be subject to French taxes.

"After all the hassles," he said, "our main concession was that French people living in Monaco would have to pay French taxes as if they were living in France. We worked out a compromise that from 1963 onwards no Frenchman would be allowed to evade French taxes by living in Monaco. But then that's what de Gaulle had been after all the time."

The customs checks disappeared, the gendarmes were stepped down and life returned to normal.

Rainier and de Gaulle were destined to lock horns again a few years later, when the General decided to close the American bases in France and withdraw French military support from NATO.

Rainier, who was staunchly pro-American, announced that US ships would indeed be permitted to stop in Monaco. "De Gaulle didn't like it when I refused to turn my back on the Americans. But this time there wasn't much he could do about it. I didn't invite them to stop here for economic reasons, even though there's always a lot of money at stake whenever a warship comes to call. The guys come ashore and they spend. I just thought de Gaulle's attitude towards the Americans was wrong. I didn't see any reason why we should have adopted that same stance."

Using the words "hard, bitter, and difficult" to describe that period, Rainier believed that one of the ways he got through those times was by learning to count on Grace. "In the beginning she said maybe I should have toned myself down a bit with Pelletier. But she could see that he hadn't fulfilled his responsibilities to me. This was the first serious diplomatic crisis in her career. It was unknown territory for her. She had to learn about it, had to find out for herself what was going on. Once she realized what was happening she backed me up all the way."

He said that they discussed what was happening at great length, that he confided in her and that he turned to her for support.

"She always offered suggestions," he said, "but she never interfered with my decisions. I wouldn't say she was my closest adviser because she never took the position of an adviser. Instead, she was always cautioning me not to be in a hurry. She took the human side, wanting me to keep a dialogue going with the French, telling me not to push too quickly or too hard."

He paused for just a second, then added with a tinge of sadness, "She and I were a pretty good team."

Above: It was Grace's ice-cold beauty—a new kind of sex appeal in the 1950s—that made her a show-business star at the age of twenty (courtesy Photo Archive, Palais Princier, Monaco). *Below:* At Cannes, the day after she met Rainier (courtesy Popperfoto Ltd.).

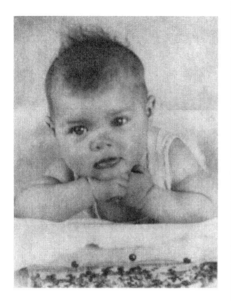

This page, clockwise, from top left: Grace Kelly at nine months, at two years, and at twelve years (courtesy Photo Archive, Palais Princier, Monaco).

Opposite, clockwise, from top left: Rainier at four months; born with a sense of adventure, Rainier always enjoyed motorcycles and fast cars, kept wild animals as pets, and loved the sea (courtesy Photo Archive, Palais Princier, Monaco).

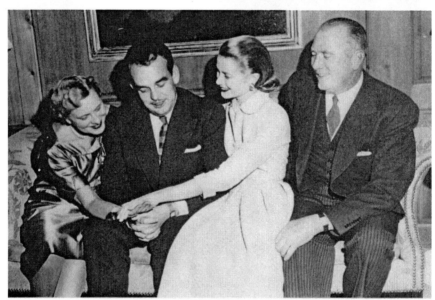

Clockwise, from top left: Grace with the man who made her a movie star, Alfred Hitchcock, on the set of *To Catch a Thief* in 1954 (courtesy Paramount Pictures). Romance blossomed between Rainier and Grace with the help of Rainier's Irish friend Father Tucker (courtesy Popperfoto Ltd.). The engagement ring marked the official start of the endless Rainier-and-Grace-must-now-pose-for-photographs season of 1956 (courtesy Popperfoto Ltd.).

From top left: On the ship to Monaco, photographers followed Grace, here with her poodle, even on lifeboat drills. Grace arrived in Monaco to a standing-room-only harbor crowd in April 1956. Only her hat got in the way of her joyous arrival. *From bottom left:* First, there was a civil wedding at the palace, followed by the religious ceremony in St. Nicholas Cathedral (courtesy Photo Archive, Palais Princier, Monaco).

She was a fairy-tale bride (courtesy F. Picedi).

Clockwise, from top left: Grace and her mother in Monte Carlo (courtesy Photo Archive, Palais Princier, Monaco). Grace and Rainier at home (courtesy Photo Archive, Palais Princier, Monaco, G. Lukomski). Rainier and Grace on official duties with Caroline, Rainier's father, Prince Pierre, Albert, and the nannies (courtesy Popperfoto Ltd.).

Clockwise, from top left: Rainier with young Albert (courtesy G. Lumoski, Photo Archive, Palais Princier, Monaco). Grace at the beach club with Caroline and Albert. Grace with infant Stephanie and Albert and Caroline. Grace walking in Monaco with the children (courtesy Photo Archive, Palais Princier, Monaco).

Chapter 13

Mr. and Mrs. Grimaldi
and Their Family

Within a week of their marriage, Grace was pregnant. She spent much of the summer of 1956 nauseous with morning sickness. That autumn she and Rainier sailed to the United States. It was Grace's first trip home as a Princess. It was also her first trip to the White House.

"We went to Washington and called on President Eisenhower," Rainier said. "He was a glorious figure but a bit dull, the way all military men are when they're out of their element."

They returned to Monaco with two tons of white lacquered nursery furniture, a wicker crib, and toys. The theme for the baby's room would be bushy-tailed rabbits.

Caroline Louise Marguerite was born in the rain on the morning of January 23, 1957. It was a good sign. According to the local superstition, a child born in the rain has health and character and brings prosperity.

She was called Heiress Presumptive, as she would lose her right to succeed to the throne if a boy came later. Still, all of Monaco rejoiced because Rainier had an heir, because the line was secure, because the child born in the rain had assured their continued freedom from the dreaded French tax man.

Towards the end of that year, Grace and Rainier took Caroline to meet her paternal grandmother. Grace was determined to patch up the strained feelings between her husband and his mother.

Charlotte had turned much of the estate at Marchais into a halfway house for ex-convicts. She'd given them shelter in the 100-room castle and hired them to work on its huge grounds with a three-mile moat. Rainier felt it was too dangerous having such types around and he argued with his mother about it. Grace hoped the baby could somehow heal the wounds.

This was not Charlotte's first grandchild, but Caroline would always hold a special place in her grandmother's heart.

Just as "Mamou" would in Caroline's.

Within five months of Caroline's birth, Grace was pregnant again.

Albert Louis Pierre, now the Hereditary Prince of Monaco, was born on March 14, 1958.

Eighteen months later Rainier named Grace regent, issuing a decree that she would rule in the case of his death until Albert was 21. In the meantime, he gave up sports car racing and skin-diving.

The children now occupied much of their free time. They still traveled but Grace flew with Albert in a separate plane from Rainier and Caroline. They began dividing summers between the Kelly family house on the New Jersey shore and their farm in the hills above Monaco, *Roc Agel*, where they moved into all 14 rooms and stocked the stable with two horses and a donkey.

They also did a lot of sailing, although Grace was never much of a sailor.

She convinced Rainier it might be better if he replaced the *Deo Juvante II* with something that didn't rock back and forth quite as much. So Rainier sold the ship in 1958—today it is called M/Y *Grace* and sails tourist charters off the Galapagos Islands—replacing it with a handsome 40-year-old Spanish banana boat.

But that didn't exactly solve the problem because, as Rainier put it, "Without bananas in the bottom it still rolls."

Grace brought teachers into the Palace for Caroline and Albert when they were of kindergarten age, starting them off in school together. But she quickly decided that wasn't very wise even though they're only a year apart.

For much of his youth, Albert suffered from an awkward stutter. And some people think it might have stemmed from that period. Whatever the cause, it was a great concern to his parents.

Like both his parents, Albert was naturally shy. His speech problem only added to his timidity. But as he grew older he realized he could overcome it. Today there is only a very faint trace of stutter. He speaks slowly and at times very deliberately, but the problem that haunted him during his childhood is gone.

Caroline, perhaps because she was that year older, became the outgoing one. She was the one who always organized him and their friends into games. Her favorite game as they grew up was playing school. Albert and the others had to be the students. Caroline, of course, was always the teacher.

On February 1, 1965, Stephanie Marie Elisabeth joined them.

"The thing about them as a family," observed Nadia Lacoste, "is that they were just that, a real family. The Princess would read to her children in the evening. The Prince would balance all three kids on his shoulders or get down on his knees and play with them. They were a team at work and a team when it came to raising their children. They shared the feeling that it was important to be close, to be together. You know, to stick together. The Prince and Princess both wanted to make certain that their children had a happier childhood than they had."

In those days they lived in a terrace, off the main courtyard, Pull-man style, with all of their rooms in a straight line. There was a drawing room, dining room, study, the master bedroom, a dressing room, and the children's room. You walked through one to get to the next one.

All three children were born in the study, which was converted for the purpose into a delivery room. Caroline and Albert shared a room with a sliding partition down the middle that could be closed at night.

When Stephanie came along, Grace put her in Caroline's side of that room. But as the children got older, Grace and Rainier decided the arrangement wasn't very convenient so they built a wing onto the Palace, and together they designed new private apartments.

"In about 1976 or so," Rainier explained, "we found a series of old drawings and plans for the Palace and decided to add a wing on the west side of the main entrance."

Wearing gray slacks and a custom-made pale blue shirt open at the neck with his personal crest on the pocket, he sat on a couch in front of the huge fireplace in the double-storied living room at the heart of his private apartments which take up the entire left wing of the Palace.

A bright, airy room with marble floors, there are enormous French windows overlooking the private gardens and huge leafy green plants climbing towards the ceiling.

"There'd been a wing here up to the end of the 18th century," he continued, "but it was destroyed during the French Revolution when the Palace was occupied and part of it was turned into a hos-pice. Sadly the Palace was emptied of everything it contained. We've since found a few of the original pieces—furniture and paint-ings, that sort of thing—and bought them back. But it would be im-possible to find everything. Anyway, we got our architect to re-create this wing and Grace designed the apartment. This was our home."

Furnished modern, with family photos in silver picture frames on almost every table, there's a small lofted study overlooking the living-room where the Prince sometimes worked in the evening.

Next to it is the small study, which Grace occasionally used.

There's a dining room and a kitchen leading off the living room and down the hall there's a second, less formal living room that doubles as a family room.

The master bedroom is upstairs, with en suite dressing rooms and a large bathroom.

Albert, Caroline and Stephanie each kept a two-room suite there as well, separated by a large communal room where, as children, they had their desks and did their schoolwork.

"Grace was always very concerned with the Palace," Rainier said, "in restoring it to its original beauty. She also paid great attention to *Le Rocher,* which is now an historic monument. The whole quarter around the Palace is protected. In order to build anything here you need a permit based on a very precise plan. You must conform to the traditional style of all the buildings on the Rock. Grace was so concerned with maintaining a sense of historical harmony here that she even changed the color of the Palace. It used to be a kind of pale yellow. She thought that a pale, salmon pink might be better, more harmonious with the rest of the Rock, so that's the color it is today"

Rainier conceded that those early years were especially difficult for her. After all, she was the one who'd made the biggest change. She'd given up her career, right at the top, and in her mind there would always be a distant question mark over what might have been had she stayed in the business. She'd also given up her friends. Apart from Rainier and his father, she didn't really know anyone else in the entire country. She'd moved from comfortable rented houses in California and a well-appointed flat on Fifth Avenue, to a huge empty Palace in the south of France that hadn't been lived in for any length of time in many years.

"The Palace itself was very beautiful," Grace used to say. "It was enormous but it was also a bit sad. It was uninhabited most of the year. But we planned to live in it all year long, to make it our home. So I threw open the windows, opened them all the way, put flowers in the pots, and got a legion of people to sweep away the dust."

Rainier convinced her to design a new Palace projection room and stood by as she re-designed the sky-blue, oval-shaped swimming pool in the Palace gardens.

They brought specialists from Italy to do stone-work and craftsmen from France to put the woodwork into shape. And they spent a fortune restocking the period rooms with the correct furniture and tapestries.

Little by little, the two of them turned the Palace into a home.

They raised their family with some simple rules, Rainier explained, like believing that good manners are a virtue because everything rare is precious.

There's no doubt that, by modern standards, they were strict parents, approving of old-fashioned manners, insisting on basic courtesies like "please" and "thank you" and generally rejecting any arguments in favor of what used to be called the "permissive society."

As Grace once put it, "If one doesn't impose some discipline on one's children at an early age then life will impose it later on perhaps but with a great deal more brutality than any parent could be capable of. There was a time when religious institutions used to take over a child's education if the parents were too weak. Or boys would go off to the army. But the church seems to be falling to pieces and discipline in the army is out of favor."

Believing, "what children need most is the love and attention of their mother," she also tried hard to give her two daughters the confidence they would need to become independent women. "I'm basically a feminist. I think that women can do anything they decide to do."

She used to say that she stressed certain moral principles with her children but agreed that getting any child to believe in such things was a struggle. "You explain certain eternal values, in which you yourself believe implicitly, only to see everything you teach them contested and made fun of by newspapers, films, television, books, and the theatre. I've also tried to treat my children in accordance with their different personalities. I've always respected in them the adults which they will one day become."

She said, "I've never lied to them because I feel that would be tantamount to treating them as inferiors. At home I've insisted that they respect the rules of life which my husband and I have established. And when it comes to those rules, we are inflexible. He and I are both convinced a child senses that the discipline you subject him or her to is nothing more than a reflection of the love you have for that child. A child left to himself is an abandoned child. And abandoning your child is the worst injustice I can think of."

While Grace and Rainier were anxious to raise their children in a normal way, like other children, there was never any doubt that Caroline, Albert and Stephanie were more privileged than most. Even if they couldn't be allowed the same freedom that average children know—they had to grow up with bodyguards nearby—at least Grace and Rainier stressed that privilege should be earned and not simply expected.

"My father had a very simple view of life," Grace would often say. "You don't get anything for nothing. Everything has to be earned, through work, persistence, and honesty."

Caroline was the first to realize they were not like other children. "I was maybe 14. It wasn't a complete shock finding out that we were different from other kids because we'd sort of gotten used to certain things, like people taking our picture all the time. But that's when I started to see there were a lot of things my friends could do that we weren't allowed to do."

Acknowledging that her parents were very strict, she explained, "We weren't allowed to go the beach every day. They wanted us to stay home and read and take our schoolwork seriously. We had to dress properly all the time. My mother didn't want me to wear a two-piece bathing suit when I was a teenager. She thought it would be more proper if I wore a one piece even though other girls my age were wearing bikinis."

There were also issues like walking to school. "We had to have somebody walk us to school and back. We couldn't just hang out with the kids. We didn't understand it then and I'm not sure I understand all of it now. I'm not sure all of it was necessary."

That meant, at least in her mind, it wasn't always easy to have friends. "When I was 12, it was a big deal to go and sleep over at a girlfriend's house. Everybody else did it but Mommy wouldn't let me do it, except for a couple of times when she really knew who the people were. And we couldn't just ask friends over to the house. First we had to ask Mommy. I'd come home from school to ask if so and so could come over and maybe she wouldn't be there or she'd be in her office so we'd have to wait and the day would go by. Then the next day I'd ask if my friend could come over and play and she'd say, maybe another day. When you're eight years old and want to play with your girlfriends and your Barbie dolls, it's not always easy to accept being told, maybe tomorrow. Mommy always used to say, 'Maybe.' She said it so often that I used to imitate her telling me, 'I said maybe, and that's final.' I guess what I'm saying is that we were a little too protected."

Albert had the same reaction. "I couldn't bring just anybody home either. I had to ask Mom and Dad and they always wanted to know who he or she was. It was sometimes hard to handle. But Caroline broke the ice so by the time she convinced our parents that it was sometimes all right to bring friends home, I was able to do it, too."

At least in that area, Stephanie appeared to have had it easiest of all. "I didn't have that much of a problem because I went to school in Paris and lived there with my mother. The rules weren't as tight at the apartment as they were for the Palace of Monaco. I could almost always bring girlfriends home or have a girlfriend stay over. Everything was more relaxed in Paris."

Asking each of them who was stricter, their mother or their father, they laughed and answered in exactly the same way.

They all agreed, "It was pretty even."

But Caroline and Albert both contended that, of the three children, the one who got away with the most was Stephanie.

Being seven years younger than her brother and eight years younger than her sister, they claimed, Stephanie was the one who could do what the other two couldn't. Being freer than they were to bring friends home with her was just one example.

Said Albert, "Stephanie learned very quickly how to wrap my mom around her little finger. And probably my father even more so than my mother. But don't tell him that."

Stephanie, however, didn't see it quite the same way. "I was the smallest one so maybe it seems to them that I got more attention than they did. They were close enough in age that they had many of the same friends. They played a lot together. I was more alone at home. Then they went off to school and Caroline got married and I found myself the only one left at home with my mother and father. That's why they think I could wrap them both around my little finger. But there wasn't much of a contest because I was the only kid in the house."

At the time, she admitted, she thought her parents were particularly strict with her. "I remember when I was 15 or 16 thinking to myself that my father was the only father in the world who was that strict. I kept saying to myself, why are my parents giving me such a hard time? I always thought they were after me. Of course every teenager goes through that. I didn't realize until lately how lucky I really was. Looking back, I see now that it wasn't me being able to wrap them around my little finger as much as it was them being very understanding parents who helped me grow up. Every kid, at one point or another, thinks their parents give them a hard time. But when I look back I can see they did everything possible for me."

Both parents stressed the importance of developing true family values in their children. It was, she recalled, a central theme. "We were raised to respect each other and to be honest with each other and above all to communicate with each other. We were raised to understand that we were a family. When any of us had a problem we'd bring it out, we'd talk about it with each other instead of just keeping it inside. We do it to this day. We've always done that."

Early on both girls were exposed to music, opera and ballet, while Albert was encouraged to pursue his interest in sports. His father even set up a soccer net in the garden so he could play there. Caroline still maintains an interest in the classical arts and Albert still plays soccer and tennis. They've both competed in events like the Paris-Dakar Rally while Albert also became an Olympic class bobsledder.

Stephanie is somewhere between the two. "I did ballet when I was very young but stopped and went into swimming and gymnastics. I liked that. For a while I was even in training to be on the French national gymnastics team. I didn't make it though because I was too tall. I still read a lot but I can't say I read very intellectual books the way Caroline does. She reads philosophy and history. I like a good love story. We both love music but there again our tastes are hardly the same. I can't stand opera. On the other hand, I'm not sure she'd enjoy sitting through a Guns N' Roses rock concert."

Where the three are very similar is that they were each raised to be multi-lingual. They spoke English with their mother and their nanny, but French with their father and the household staff. While they were still very young, Grace and Rainier encouraged them to learn other languages. Caroline, Albert, and Stephanie speak absolutely perfect French and equally perfect English with slightly east coast American accents. They each also speak German, Italian, and some Spanish.

Grace and Rainier mostly spoke English together. Grace however perfected her French, as she used to say, "Because the children demanded that I do. Whenever I made mistakes they'd make fun of me so I had to learn to speak it well."

Chapter 14

Coming Into
Their Own

In 1957, Grace and Rainier had hired a young English woman named Maureen King to be Caroline's nanny. When Albert came along she took charge of him, too.

At about the same time, Grace had hired a young American woman named Phyllis Blum to be her secretary.

The two young women became kindred spirits.

Following one trip to the United States, Rainier returned with some dress shirts that he was very proud of. Maureen was often given the extra chore of ironing the Prince's shirts in a little room next to Phyllis's office.

Being so fond of these shirts, Rainier kept reminding Maureen to be extra careful with them. So Maureen and Phyllis found an old sheet, burned holes it in and waited at the ironing board for him to check on Maureen's progress.

The next time he poked his head through the door, there was Maureen ironing what appeared to be scorched remnants of his shirts.

They thought that was pretty funny.

Only after they convinced him the burnt sheet wasn't really one of his new shirts, so did he.

In 1964 Rainier's father passed away.

Six months later Grace's father died.

In July 1967, while visiting Expo 67 in Montreal, Grace suffered her third miscarriage. She and Rainier wanted another child but it wasn't to be.

The 1960s turned into the 1970s and the decade dawned that might one day go down in Monaco's history as the greatest in modern times.

Grace and Rainier were totally in sync with each other and it showed in the easy way they appeared in public. They were photographed driving in the vintage car rally from London to Brighton. Although it was too chilly for Grace, she cheated a bit, driving most of the way in a comfortable modern car and only getting into Rainier's 1903 de Dion-Bouton in time to reach the finish line. And they were photographed at masquerade balls—Rainier with a bald wig and a huge black moustache and Grace with a fat-cheeked rubber mask and her hair in braids under a straw hat.

They were raising their children to be totally comfortable both as young royals at official ceremonies in Monaco and in touch football games every summer at camp in the Pennsylvania Poconos.

"I don't think there is any formula for handling children," Grace told a women's magazine when pressed to come up with an easy solution to the problem. "All a parent can do is play it by ear and hope for the best. That and raise them with a lot of humor and a lot of love."

No one who's ever seen them up close can doubt the love.

In spite of their earlier experiences in dealing with the press—her days as a Hollywood star and his days as the most eligible bachelor in Europe—it wasn't until Grace and Rainier announced their engagement that they were truly baptized by fire.

Neither of them was prepared for the attention showered upon them. They found themselves sitting through endless press conferences, forever answering the same questions.

Rainier might have been all right in the beginning, during the first few interviews about their pending marriage, but his patience quickly wore thin. Before too long he simply couldn't hide his extreme discomfort. You see that quite clearly in newsreel footage from those days. It's almost as if he's trying to become invisible.

Grace obviously understood and tried her best to protect him.

But at one press conference, just as Rainier thought he was finished, a photographer begged a few more pictures and, after Grace agreed, Rainier was heard to mumble under his breath, "They don't understand that I'm not under contract to MGM."

Then there was the media nightmare that was their wedding.

The principality was bursting at the seams with journalists and photographers. The bar at the Hotel de Paris became the unofficial press headquarters and there was such an overflow of scribes that the management had to fill the lobby with tables and chairs all the way to the entrance.

Mayhem reigned.

Part of the problem lay in the fact that most weddings are basically the same. There is a bride and there is a groom and there are people who cry with joy. Afterwards there are drinks and there is food, so that friends can get together, offer congratulations, and wish the couple luck as they run away on their honeymoon.

But that's really all there is.

Perhaps had Rainier employed a professional press attaché in those days, a few hand-outs could have filled reporters in on who was there, on who wore what, on how many eggs were used for the cake, and how the smiling couple danced till dawn.

Instead, in the absence of any real stories, reporters wrote about Grace's too-big hat.

When a photographer tried to snap Randolph Churchill's picture on the steps of the Hotel de Paris and Churchill punched the photographer, they wrote about that, forgetting to add that the general confusion had worn everyone's nerves to a frazzle.

They also wrote that Rainier's mother, Princess Charlotte, had been driven to Monaco by her chauffeur, formerly one of France's most wanted criminals. She always insisted that she was trying to rehabilitate him. But coinciding with their arrival, there were two burglaries at the Hotel de Paris.

Besides that, there really wasn't much else to write about.

By the time the couple returned from their honeymoon, Grace and Rainier were in perfect agreement that they needed help to manage the media.

Grace asked Rupert Allan if he could recommend someone. Allan told Grace about a young American woman in Paris named Nadia Lacoste who had experience in movie and show business public relations. So Lacoste was asked to come and speak with the Prince.

"I met him in Paris in July," Lacoste recalled. "We talked for about an hour. Then he said he wanted to speak with the Princess and asked me to come to see both of them the next day. We made a verbal deal for a three-month job, to be renewed if they wanted to do that. I said okay and started right in because they were leaving for a visit to the States in September and we realized there would be a great deal of press interest in their first trip to America since the wedding."

In a very real way, Lacoste got to know Grace and Rainier at a time while they were still getting to know each other.

"She was a warm, likeable person. But there was a big difference in those days in the way she behaved when we were alone or with the Prince, and the way she was when she saw the press. It was odd because she had a lot of experience with reporters. I expected her to be relaxed but she wasn't. On the other hand, I expected him to be shy, which he was. But I discovered that he has a wonderful sense of humor. I remember going with them to fashion shows. The Princess would be on his right and I'd be on his left. As the afternoon wore on he'd start to get bored so he'd make remarks out of the corner of his mouth, without moving a muscle. He'd comment on everybody and everything. The dresses. The hats. The people in the room. He was so funny that I'd be in stitches."

Grace and Rainier's first professionally arranged press conference was in September 1956 before sailing to New York on the USS *United States*.

Meeting at the Monaco Legation in Paris, Lacoste put journalists in one room and photographers in another. It was an old trick to give everyone a chance and keep the two groups out of each other's way. And it obviously worked because Grace and Rainier were as comfortable as they'd ever been in front of the press. From there, Lacoste, with selected members from the Legation and a few photographers, took the train with Grace and Rainier to Le Havre.

Because they were relaxed, the photo story that followed was a good one. The group then gathered in their cabin for champagne and caviar before the ship sailed although Grace would not eat the caviar.

"Someone had informed her that pregnant women should not have any kind of seafood," Lacoste went on. "It was what pregnant women believed in those days."

Once Grace and Rainier arrived in America, Rupert Allan took over and handled the press for them there.

"Grace was okay with the press," he said, picking up the story. "But Rainier was still usually pretty ill-at-ease. I'd arranged a few interviews for them and tried to make the ordeal as easy as possible, especially for Rainier. And when he was uncomfortable he tended to scowl. He'd see the photos published the next day, see himself scowling, and that merely served to re-enforce his discomfort when the next photographer appeared. I finally said to him, 'Listen, every time you meet the press, just think of them all standing there in front of you in their shorts. Just react the way you would if they had nothing on but their underwear.' And that old trick worked. The next time Grace and Rainier did a photo session, there was Rainier grinning."

While they were in the States much of their publicity surrounded Grace's new life.

"The biggest difference in my life isn't the title," she announced, "it's changing from being a single career girl to a wife."

There was also plenty of talk of the expected baby. "I've already gained 26 pounds. When I became pregnant I was pretty sick for the first three months. They'd told me about morning sickness but they didn't tell me you could be sick all day, every day. Once I got over that I started eating. The doctor says I shouldn't eat too much but I'm ravenous. I had this terrible craving for noodles and spaghetti all summer. I wake up hungry at night. The Prince is excellent at scrambled eggs but I had to teach him how to make sandwiches. Now he invents ones for me."

With that Rainier chimed in, "I'm the gendarme on her diet. I keep reminding her not to eat but it isn't easy. I really don't mind because she was so thin when we married."

Grace didn't always say she wanted a boy, that "a healthy baby is what's important," but on other occasions she'd concede, "Rainier would like a boy a lot."

She'd also explain that, while her husband had helped choose the layette, he wasn't taking any special lessons on how to handle a baby.

That's when Rainier would chime in with, "When I show the baby to people, I promise I won't drop him. Though I may drop myself."

Knowing that this sort of friendly patter was how they won friends for themselves and for Monaco—the purpose of the exercise—Rupert Allan skillfully manipulated the interviews to highlight Grace and Rainier as real people with real concerns, and all the more attractive for their sense of humor.

He got Grace to say, "I suppose royal babies should be born in a Palace, but I'll feel better, more secure, in a hospital." And, "No matter where the child is born, my husband won't be welcome in the delivery room because that's no place for husbands."

She said she liked the name Henry but the Prince didn't, "So it won't be Henry."

She said she believed in spanking children, "And royal children probably need more spanking than others."

She said she'd eventually like to have three children, "Not more."

Then she pre-empted the next question by volunteering, "So there's your answer as to whether or not I'll be making any more movies. I'll be too busy raising a family."

By the time they returned to Monaco, Nadia Lacoste understood that the key to the couple's public appeal was a combination of their natural charm and the "handsome prince marries beautiful actress" fairy tale.

Her three-month trial as press attaché turned into a lifetime career.

"The difference between him and her," she explained, "at least in the beginning, was that he had nothing to prove. He was born a prince. He knew who he was. But she believed she had to prove that the person being interviewed was not Grace Kelly the actress but Princess Grace of Monaco."

Lacoste acknowledged that Grace was all too well aware that she was being watched carefully and that she desperately wanted to do the right thing. "She didn't want to make any mistakes. She didn't want to do anything that would embarrass her husband or reflect poorly on Monaco. It wasn't a part she could play like an actress. If it was, she could have gotten away with simply playing the role of a princess. That would have been easy for her and she would have played it beautifully. She would have been very comfortable playing a role. The problem was, being Princess of Monaco was real life. Finding her way was not very easy."

Lacoste said that once she got to know the Prince well enough she'd screen newspaper men so that no one ever got in to see him if she didn't feel the two would get along. She'd discovered that because the Prince took an interest in the world and what was happening, he had a tendency to start asking the journalist questions. And on more than one occasion journalists came out of an interview and reported to Lacoste, "I told him more than he told me."

But it took a long time before she could make it work that way with Grace. "I can still see her during her very first in-depth interview with a French journalist in Monaco, literally sitting on the edge of her chair with her hands clenched together. She was grinning too hard and swallowing too hard and her answers were almost too practiced. It must have been excruciating for her. I decided then and there not to ask her to do any other interviews for at least six months, at least until she could find her place in the Palace and get settled into her whole new life."

Even many years later, once Grace had mastered French, she was never totally at ease speaking it for any length of time on radio or television.

Lacoste again. "One afternoon, it might have been as much as 15 years later, I was trying to explain to her that the best way to let the public know about some of the things she was doing in Monaco like the Flower Show and the Princess Grace Foundation, was for her to talk about them. I argued that for me to tell the world about them was of no interest to anyone. She finally agreed to talk about the Ballet Festival."

So Lacoste carefully offered that interview to a radio journalist she liked, one she'd always found to be knowledgeable about the arts. But within 15 minutes Grace was in such a state, so unnerved by the whole thing, that Lacoste had to stop it and ask the journalist to please be kind enough to wait outside.

"Once he left, Grace started to cry. Tears were running down her face. She said she felt totally frustrated being interviewed in French. Of course she'd made comments on French radio before, but when it came to expressing herself in a long, important interview, she said she simply felt too limited by a language which was not her own. She kept telling me, 'This is terrible.' I promised her, 'Okay, never again in French.' And I kept my promise. That was the first and the last in-depth broadcast interview in French she ever did."

Chapter 15

The Press Feeding Frenzy Never Stopped

In sculpting a public image for Grace and Rainier, Nadia Lacoste found, each story created bigger and bigger crowds wherever they went.

At the same time, those crowds generated more stories in the press.

Once, while Grace and Rainier were stopping at London's Connaught, a British paper reported, "Big premiums were being offered last night to house and flat owners near the Connaught Hotel where the couple are staying. These Peeping Toms, for that is what they are, were eager to get a bird's eye view of Grace and Rainier, and blatantly said they wanted to use field glasses and binoculars. 'I was astounded,' said a Mount Street householder. 'An estate agent telephoned me saying he would pay a premium if I let my flat, or one room in it, overlooking the hotel.' Not since high premiums were offered to view the bed in which Mrs. Simpson slept has there been such a rash of peepers."

A few years later, Grace and Rainier visited Dublin.

The crowds along O'Connell Street were estimated by one paper to be 5,000 people and by another to be 20,000. Whatever they were, everyone rushed to get a closer look inside the car bringing them to their hotel.

Panic erupted and 50 people were hurt.

The papers reported, "Princess Grace was escorted into the hotel, weeping and upset, and her appearance at the ball was delayed for more than half an hour. She later made an appearance on the hotel balcony to acknowledge cries of, 'We want Grace.'"

A couple of days after that, thousands of people lined the streets when Grace and Rainier traveled to County Mayo to see the home where her grandfather was born.

One journalist pointed out, "Every bar and restaurant with Kelly in the name—and there are plenty, as I counted eight Kelly's Bars in Dublin alone—are laying on celebrations tonight."

Another wrote, "Among their 800 pounds of luggage was one marked 'fragile.' It contained presents for everyone including, I'm told, all the Kellys in County Mayo." To that he added, "Since Princess Grace has been expected, everyone around here has discovered their name is Kelly."

While a third journalist disclosed, "At a conference among close relations which went on until the early hours today, a compromise was reached. Originally only second cousins of Princess Grace were to be officially received by her. But it was finally decided that one third cousin would also be allowed in."

When Grace and Rainier returned to Ireland on their next trip, this time with Albert and Caroline in tow, they got even bigger headlines.

"A prince and princess were 'at home' yesterday to representatives of the press," commented the Irish Press. "There just is no other way to describe the disarming informality of the press conference given by Prince Rainier and Princess Grace of Monaco. The quote of the day came from Albert who announced in the middle of his parents' conversation with the press, 'I want to milk a cow.'"

Lacoste was, to say the least, overwhelmed with requests for interviews. "We got them every day of the year from all over the world. I think the only country I never spoke to is Russia. Even the Chinese asked for interviews. I'd say that between interviews, appearances, and photographs we got at least 20 requests a week. That's over 1,000 a year. For obvious reasons we accepted very few."

Almost right from the beginning, she never set up more than five or six interviews a year for Grace. And in later years, even fewer, only one or two.

"For the Prince," she said, "there were usually a bit more but they tended to be on specialized subjects. Let's say, the architectural press requested an interview to discuss something about the development of Monte Carlo or a financial journalist wanted to talk about the Monegasque economy. Maybe he did as many as eight or ten interviews a year."

Inevitably, every now and then, something would come up that was beyond Lacoste's control.

Especially embarrassing and all the more infuriating was the photo of Grace at a Monaco carnival shooting gallery.

She'd gone there with her children on a Friday morning to open the carnival, and walked around with them to play at various booths. She stopped at the shooting gallery, took aim with a rifle, and fired at some clay pipes. No one recalls whether or not she won a Kewpie doll because it was Friday, November 22, 1963.

The photo of Grace with the rifle ran in newspapers around the world the following day. The caption under it berated her for being so insensitive as to have played with a rifle when John Kennedy had just been murdered.

But Monaco is seven hours ahead of Dallas and the photo of Grace with the rifle was taken a full nine hours before Kennedy was killed.

However, that pales with what happened the day the paparazzi discovered there was a market in photos of Caroline and Stephanie. That's when all of their lives took a huge turn for the worse.

Noted Rainier, "You can imagine the kinds of photos they're looking for because they all walk around with huge telephoto lenses and hide behind bushes. What no one ever seems to understand is how distressing it is for us to live our lives knowing that they could be anywhere, spying on us. It was especially terrible for the children when they were younger. It wasn't fair to them. They were paralyzed by it, never knowing how to play or what to play because they were always afraid that someone might be photographing them."

The system, he claimed, was based entirely on making someone look ridiculous. The more ridiculous the photo, the higher the price. To get that one big-money shot required snapping tons of pictures. So they paid people at airports to ring them when Caroline arrived. They came to Monaco disguised as tourists with cameras strung around their neck to blend into the background. They sprinkled roads with tacks so that Albert would have to stop his car or risk a flat. They even rented ultralight gliders to sail over the family property at Marchais hoping to get a glimpse of Stephanie.

One photographer, after checking the family flat in Paris to see if anyone was home, discovered there was an empty apartment next door. He somehow got inside and waited there for several nights. The picture he got for all his trouble was of someone—it turned out to be Caroline—closing the curtains. She was dressed and you couldn't see her face but that didn't matter. The photo ran.

"It became unbearable for all of us," Rainier shook his head. "Once, on a skiing holiday in Switzerland, Grace found Stephanie hiding in her room in tears, afraid to go outside because the paparazzi frightened her. I wonder how those photographers would have reacted if their own children had been subjected to those same pressures."

Grace found it just as aggravating to watch the press abuse her children.

One of the things Hollywood had equipped her for was being able now to accept certain comments in the papers about herself. But when they wrote about her children, she looked at it differently.

There were times when she'd be so incensed at the treatment her children were receiving that she'd write to editors to ask them please to leave the family alone, or she'd write to correct them when they published something about her children that struck her as being particularly stupid.

When that failed—which it usually did with the German press in particular—she showed her frustration by going after the entire nation.

"Germany is a horrible country and the Teutonic press is disgusting," she lashed out. "I read some of the things written about my family in German magazines and newspapers and there are times when they say such despicable things that I can't bear it any longer."

The thing that truly panicked Grace and Rainier was when the French or Italian papers publicized the family's address in Paris. They looked on that as a direct threat to their children's security.

"I went after them for that," Rainier said. "Happily, the law in France protects people from that sort of thing. Once they printed pictures that showed where Caroline lived in Paris. You could very clearly see the number of the house and all the nuts in the world starting ringing her doorbell. I wouldn't stand for it. We went to court to stop that."

On several occasions over the years, Grace and Rainier took photographers and magazine editors to court.

In 1978, when an Italian magazine superimposed Caroline's face on the nude photo of another girl, Rainier pressed the case and the magistrates sent the guilty editor to jail.

That was an exception. In all too many other cases, there was little anyone could do. The paparazzi photographed Caroline in low-cut dresses bending over in a nightclub and sunbathing topless on a boat. The pictures were published. Long lenses captured Albert and a girlfriend nude together on a boat. The pictures were published. The paparazzi once even got Rainier in his underwear through a second-floor window. The pictures were published.

Certain big-circulation magazines and downmarket tabloids in the United States, France, Italy, and Germany refused to put a price limit on embarrassing photos of the Grimaldis. It was well known in the trade that anyone with the right photo could name his own price and probably get it.

Certain smaller picture agencies in France, Italy, and Germany considered photos of the Grimaldis to be their bread and butter.

Faced with that kind of market pressure, and not necessarily helped in every country by privacy laws, Rainier conceded, "In the end you can't really do much. You have to let a lot of things go. You just have to write some of it off as part of the apprenticeship of life."

The dual burden of structuring the family's public relations and also defending them against the press fell squarely on Nadia Lacoste.

"Right after the Prince and Princess were married," she said, "whenever they were in Paris, there were always four or five photographers stationed outside their apartment snapping pictures of them coming in or going out. Okay. But as the years went by, the photographers became less and less reserved."

Now they began following Grace and, especially Caroline and Stephanie, on motorcycles through the streets of Paris. Or, during the summer in Monaco, they'd hide in the small stretch of public beach just around the corner from the Old Beach Hotel because from there, with their long lenses, they could photograph Grace in her bathing suit.

In the winter, when the family went skiing, the photographers would follow them to the slopes and hide in the bushes so they could get pictures of them, hopefully falling in the snow. The solution Lacoste proposed was to arrange a family photo call.

Wherever they went, especially if it was on a private holiday, Lacoste negotiated a truce with the photographers. She'd get Grace and Rainier and the children to pose for 15 or 20 minutes and once everyone had their pictures, the photographers were supposed to retreat and leave the family alone.

It was a good idea on paper. And it even worked the first few times. Then one photographer stuck around for a few more days to get the picture that everyone else missed, and before long all the other photographers were doing it, too. Eventually it got so bad that instead of four or five paparazzi on guard in front of the apartment in Paris there were 20.

In 1980, word went around that there was big money in any photos anyone could get of Stephanie at school.

To protect her from daily harassment and allow her to get on with her life, the question became how to keep the press from finding out which school she was attending. It wasn't easy because the family always tried to get together at weekends, either in Monaco or Paris. The paparazzi, therefore, knew that Stephanie would be going back to school on Monday mornings. Their game plan became to find out where they were spending the weekend, then wait them out until Monday.

So Grace and Rainier, with the help of Nadia Lacoste, had to devise new ways every week to get Stephanie back to school without being followed. Life for their youngest daughter quickly deteriorated into one, big, unhappy race between the family's chauffeur and the photographers.

"Dad always told me," Stephanie said, "'If you and your sister weren't beautiful, no one would care, so take it as a compliment.' I guess he's right. If we were ugly dogs and never did anything exciting except sit home desperately seeking a husband, the magazines wouldn't have bothered with us. I guess they're interested in us because we're well brought up and not too bad looking and we do things with our lives. It's hard sometimes, but I always try to find the good side of things."

Stephanie observed that Grace had also been philosophical about the situation, telling her children there was nothing anybody could do but accept the fact that the photographers would be hanging around.

"She urged us not to let it get to us," Stephanie went on, "or to depress us or to make us go completely nuts. She was a great help because she'd gone through this sort of thing when she was in films. She didn't over-dramatize things or allow it to have more importance than it should have. When we were children she tried to get us used to it and warn us that we were going to be hassled and chased around by a lot of photographers. So in a way, when I got older, I was expecting it. I don't think it was so much Caroline's experience that taught me anything because there really isn't anything to learn. Even if I wanted to use the same tricks she did to avoid the photographers, they already knew them. I had to find my own."

Being as strong-willed as she is, Stephanie was the one who always seemed to react in the most candid ways when she was hassled by the press.

There were times when she'd even stick her tongue out at them and tell them to go to hell. "Yeah, I did. When they were rude to me, I never saw why I should have been anything else to them. If they're polite with me, I'm polite with them. If they ask for a picture, I let them take one on the understanding that once they've got what they want they leave me alone. But if they're rude to me, yelling obscene names to me, I'm going to be just as rude back to them. That's the way I am."

Unfortunately, there were times when even her best sword-rattling bravado in the face of Nikons let her down.

Late one winter afternoon, Grace rang Nadia Lacoste to announce that the paparazzi had been massed in front of the house all day and that, because of them, Stephanie was now in tears. Grace said Stephanie was refusing to leave the house and would not go back to school as long as they were there.

"Can you blame me?" Stephanie demanded. "Do you realize how embarrassing it is to be that age and to arrive at school with a horde of photographers behind you? The other kids made fun of me or stayed away from me because of the photographers. It didn't bother me as much when I was with my family, but at school it was horrible. I felt as though it scared them off and I didn't want that. What kid would?"

So it was up to Lacoste to plot Stephanie's escape.

Second guessing the photographers' behavior—obviously they were going to follow Stephanie to school—Nadia phoned Prince Rainier's chauffeur and told him to drive slowly away from the residence. She told him to make absolutely certain the paparazzi saw that Stephanie was not in the car.

She then told him to wait nearby but out of sight.

Lacoste arrived at the apartment a few minutes later. So did the Monagasque ambassador's car, which drove into the garage.

Once it began to get dark. Nadia wrapped a scarf wrapped around her head, got into the back seat of the ambassador's car and crouched down. The chauffeur then pulled out of the garage and raced down the Champs-Élysées.

Convinced Stephanie was in the back seat, the paparazzi raced after them.

It wasn't until they converged at a red light along the Champs-Élysées that Nadia sat up and the photographers realized they'd been duped.

By that time, the Prince's chauffeur had been notified on his car phone that the coast was clear, returned to the apartment, and fetched Stephanie.

"Those were the sorts of silly games we were forced to play," Lacoste recalled. "It became a constant battle of wits between us and the photographers. Maybe a grown-up can understand that sort of thing but it's awfully difficult to make a child understand. It got so bad in the last two years before Princess Grace died that once she stopped her car in the middle of Paris, got out, and berated the photographers to please leave them alone. She said, 'You've been following me around all day. I can take it. But please don't do it to my children. Please stop doing to them what you've been doing to me for years.'"

Her case fell on deaf ears. The photographers merely took pictures of her pleading with the other photographers.

Lacoste continued, "They became so aggressive that they'd follow her into shops and restaurants. And no one would stop them. Although one day when she was in a store and couldn't find anyone to help carry her packages, she turned to a photographer who'd followed her inside and said, 'The least you can do is make yourself useful.' She loaded him up with packages and led him back to her car."

Of the three Grimaldi children, Albert fared best with the press.

He happily admitted, "I was lucky. When the press started getting interested in Caroline and then Stephanie—I'm talking about the European social press—I was at Amherst, in Massachusetts. I wasn't hiding but I was far removed from that whole Paris disco scene. Also, as a guy, I was more capable of defending myself. Yet I think the real reason they pretty much left me alone is because pictures of Caroline or Stephanie or my mother sold more magazines than pictures of me. Sure, we were all bothered at official functions and on holidays, like when the whole family went skiing in Switzerland. I've had to deal with the press from an early age. But, thankfully, I've never been harassed like my sisters were."

It seems that the only times the press bothered him during his four years in the States was the first week of college and at graduation. The rest of the time he was free to roam around and do his thing.

He believed, "I was semi-incognito. It was great. And that's why I have such fond memories of those years. I can still be that way when I go to the States. Not too many people there know me and if I don't tell them they don't necessarily know where I come from. After the 1988 Winter Olympics, I took a road trip with some friends. We drove from Texas to Los Angeles and stopped at some pretty cheap motels in Arizona and New Mexico. It was great fun. No one knew who I was. And no one cared. I enjoyed that."

The nearer Albert got to succeeding his father, the more that changed.

Living in Monaco as heir to the throne, life became a little more difficult for him, vis-à-vis the media.

"I don't like to see my face spread all over the scandal sheets," he admitted, "so I try not to give them a lot of opportunities to do that. I have to be careful where I go and who I go with. But I try not to let it get in the way of my social life. It's hard to do and as time goes on it will be increasingly difficult. Though I'm sure there's always a way to be relatively anonymous."

It's never been very easy for him to be seen in public with a girl, because the photographers are always hoping to get the first pictures of Monaco's next Princess. They've also been known to hound him when he goes somewhere in Paris with one of his sisters. More than once he's had to enlist the aid of a friend to drive a second car behind his just to keep the photographers from catching up.

One night, one of his pals swung his car sideways to block the street, allowing Albert and Stephanie time to get away. Just as he did, the car with the pursuing photographers slammed into him. The friend complained that they'd ruined his car. The photographer who'd been driving replied, "It doesn't matter. With the money we make selling pictures of them we can buy you three cars."

Chapter 16

Grace

A perfect summer's evening party on St. Jean-Cap-Ferrat, what now seems like a very long time ago.

Deep in conversation with someone, Grace slowly wound her way across the huge, well-manicured lawn, down to the squat stone sea wall. Strings were playing somewhere in the shadows. The moon was shining on the water.

As she moved further and further away from the party, men in white evening jackets and women in long, sleeveless gowns, speaking softly, arm in arm, drinking champagne, and eating canapés, drifted that way, too, relaxed, almost unintentionally forming a huge semi-circle around where she stood. Then very gently, as if someone was deliberately lowering the sound track, little by little, everyone else's conversation hushed until the only voice you could hear was hers.

A moment passed.

Suddenly aware that something was happening behind her, she turned to find the entire party simply watching her.

Flustered for only a split second, she clapped her hands, organizing everyone, leading them back towards the beach house where she announced, "Let's go swimming," and from there she lured them all into the water.

The woman could cast a spell.

The Monegasques had welcomed Grace warmly when she arrived, had rejoiced heartily with their Prince when he took her as his bride, had applauded her and had feted her. But deep down they were suspicious of her. They would point at her and say, there's Grace Kelly. They couldn't understand what this foreigner was doing here. It would take her four or five years before the locals began calling her Princess Grace.

"I had so many problems when I first came here," she once explained. "To begin with, there was the language. I still spoke very poor French. What I knew of it I'd learned in school. You know, 'la plume de ma tante.' I was smothered with problems. But I think my biggest single problem was becoming a normal person again, after having been an actress for so long."

During her years in New York and Hollywood, a normal person meant, for her, someone who made movies.

Not any more.

It was, she went on, exactly like learning a new job. "It was a very hard job that I had to take step by step. Luckily I had the Prince, who was very helpful and very patient with me. But even so, there were some difficult moments. I got pregnant right after our marriage. Nobody knew this but it meant taking my first steps as Princess of Monaco while being sick as a dog. I didn't let it stop me though. That's the Irish in me. I can laugh at myself. It's a great help. That's a talent I would never exchange for any other."

Because she knew she had to be seen, had to earn her acceptance, she refused to hide in the Palace. She deliberately set out to create a presence in Monaco. And that wasn't easy.

But, little by little, especially once Caroline and Albert were born, you saw her there. She was visible, not just at official functions when you were supposed to see her, but at normal times when you saw normal people living normal lives. She'd go shopping. She'd have tea with friends. She'd take the kids to school or to the dentist, she'd buy shoes with them or stop at their favorite pastry shop to buy them cakes.

Yet, just as she was winning her way into the hearts of the Monegasques, word spread that she was not very friendly.

Some people went so far as to say she was pretentious, snooty to the point where she would walk down the street and not say hello to anyone. People started asking, "Who does she think she is?"

A better question would have been, "What does she think she is?" Because the answer was, terribly short-sighted.

Without glasses she couldn't see three feet in front of herself. She wasn't snooty at all. She simply couldn't see people across the street to say hello to them.

In fact, one of the things that made her special was that the average person could relate to her. She was accessible in Monaco. People were always coming up to say hello and she was always happy to smile and shake hands.

She was also accessible to people outside Monaco, albeit mostly by mail or through stories in magazines. She spoke to journalists about her fears and her dreams. She might have once been a movie star and she was now a princess but she was also a wife and mother, and she allowed much of the rest of the world to see her as that.

"I think she had fun being a princess," claimed Mary Wells Lawrence, one of America's most successful woman entrepreneurs, founder of the Wells, Rich and Green Advertising Agency and a very old chum of Grace's. "In fact, I know she did. But I also think she was a very motherly mother and a very good wife. She was a woman who enjoyed being pretty. Although I know she felt that she had to make a constant effort not to be an outsider in Monaco. After all, she was an American and it wasn't easy for her to be accepted. It took time."

It also took a special kind of talent, Lawrence added. "Not just anyone could have done it. She had a very specific talent, a gift. She was larger than life. She was not just a human being, she was an idea. She was an idea that Monte Carlo was a fairy tale in an increasingly ugly world. You see, in a world where things were getting more and more difficult, and smaller, and where more and more things were becoming the same, Monte Carlo had a fairy-tale quality. I think there was something about Grace that gave that to Monaco. It was in the way she did things, the way she acted. She was a real star. And in the world today there aren't a lot of real stars. There are loads of people who are famous, but there are very few real stars."

After her secretary Phyllis Blum left for England to get married, Grace hired a young French woman named Louisette Levy-Soussan, who was with her for the next 18 years.

"The Princess was not just pretty," Levy-Soussan maintained, "she was beautiful. But she never flaunted that beauty. It was a perfect kind of beauty and maybe that was one of the things that made her so special. Because she was so perfectly beautiful and yet at the same time so simple in her own way, other women were never jealous of her. Of all her children, I think that Prince Albert is probably the one who is most like her. They have the same temperament. I look at him and I can see her. I'll tell him something and he doesn't seem to be listening and then three or four days later he'll say something about it. That's exactly the way his mother was."

While Grace was very easy to work for, Levy-Soussan noted she was very strict about certain things, especially trust. "Once she trusted someone she would trust them forever. Let's face it, Monaco is a small town and there is always a lot of gossip but once she trusted someone she would defend them and never believe the gossip she'd hear. I remember she once received an anonymous letter from someone obviously involved with the Garden Club because it was about another woman at the Garden Club. It was very nasty. But the princess laughed about it. She said, 'I can just see this woman sitting with a cup of tea writing this letter to poison her friend.' She understood."

Some people have written that Grace was cold, but Levy-Soussan insisted that wasn't the case. "She was poised. She kept her feelings to herself, unless she was with friends and then she'd let them out. People who didn't know her sometimes found her, well, maybe the word is guarded. She didn't show everyone the private side of her that she showed to her friends. But she was certainly not cold. She was genuinely kind and very concerned about other people."

That not only showed in the way people communicated with her, but in the way she reacted to them.

She'd receive letters from people who needed help: a mother asking for money for a sickly child; an old age pensioner wanting a new heater to keep warm for the winter; a battered woman looking for shelter; a young boy trying to get off drugs.

Wanting to help, and seeing that, for whatever reason, the Monaco Red Cross couldn't react quickly enough, she established the Princess Grace Foundation and, at least initially, funded it herself.

"I don't need to have an administrative council decide that someone needs an operation or a roof over their head," she once explained to her press secretary, Nadia Lacoste. "This way I can say what I want to do with the money."

Nor did her concern for other people stop there. When she saw how various artisans in Monaco were struggling to sell their wares, she set up a local boutique as a non-profit venture to help them earn a living. When it proved successful, she opened a second boutique for them.

During the summer months, when she was at *Roc Agel*, she'd often work there, preferring not to come into Monaco, asking instead that Levy-Soussan bring her mail to her in the afternoons.

Letters poured in every day and unsolicited gifts were a regular part of her post. Especially when her children were born. She was inundated with knitted sweaters and booties.

Occasionally, when one of those gifts pleased her, she'd display it on a shelf in her office or bring it back to the private apartments. But most of the time she donated the countless coffee mugs with GRACE written across the face and the ashtrays with her picture on them to charity bazaars. She also gave a lot of her own clothes to the Red Cross for their jumble sales.

One woman in Genoa so admired Grace that she put together scrapbooks of her newspaper and magazine clippings and sent them to her every year for Christmas. Every year, by return post, Grace would send her a handwritten note to say thank you. Every now and then Grace would also invite her to the Palace for tea.

Then there was the man from Moscow who started sending her Russian stamps. Grace responded by sending him Monegasque stamps and their correspondence lasted for years.

When a little girl wrote to ask, "How many hours a day do you spend sitting on your throne and wearing your crown?" Grace wrote back to explain that modern princesses don't do that.

Understandably, she liked to keep in touch with friends and, at least during the holiday season, the mail was the best way to do that. According to Levy-Soussan, Grace had a constantly expanding Christmas card list—"It got bigger and bigger every year"—and she often added a few words in her own hand.

Although shopping was not important to her—"If there is one thing that is foreign to me," Grace would explain, "it is shopping for pleasure"—there's no doubt that she loved clothes and wore them well.

She would say, "I believe that it is right to honor all those who create beautiful things and give satisfaction to those who see me wearing them."

Accordingly, she was a regular on all the various lists of the world's ten best-dressed women.

However, if she was going to spend the day in the office and not see anyone, or when she was at home with her family, she dressed simply. Slacks, flat shoes, and frequently a scarf tied around her head. At *Roc Agel* she often wore jeans and sweatshirt, but it was extremely rare for her to dress that casually in Monaco.

"We live in a palace," she said, "one is thus a little embarrassed to walk about it wearing blue jeans."

When Grace first arrived in Monaco she had a private tutor to help her with French. She worked very hard at learning the language but progress was, decidedly, slower than she would have wanted. Later in life she decided she wanted to speak better Italian so she and a few friends took lessons. As soon as they all felt confident enough, they decided to show off their newfound skills with a private show for a small group at the Palace. Decorating hats and donning masks for costumes, Grace and her Italian class staged a 30-minute all-Italian rendition of *Pinocchio*.

Another thing she got good at, because she enjoyed it so much, was needlepoint. In addition to doing a lot of cushions, she even did a waistcoat for Rainier. In fact, she got so involved with needlepoint that she formed a local needlepoint club. She also painted, did collages, and for many years went to pottery classes.

"I never saw her idle," Nadia Lacoste said. "If we had tea in the afternoon, she'd be sitting there knitting or doing needlepoint. If she had some free time, she'd go walking. She adored that. She used to take the small path that follows the sea and walk along the coast. Or she'd walk up the mountain at *Roc Agel*. She was interested in flowers so she used to carry scissors and a small pouch with her on those walks and stop to cut flowers or pick leaves. When she got home she'd press the leaves and flowers into a book. I don't think you could have pulled a single book off her shelf without flowers and leaves falling out."

As the years passed and her family grew up, Grace found herself at times longing for some of the creature comforts she'd known in America. She never hid the fact that she was American and for a long time she and all three of her children held American passports. Eventually they let them go for tax reasons. Still, she missed certain things about the States and tried her best to re-create them in Monaco.

She brought American furniture with her when she moved to Monaco, used an American interior decorator to help her re-do the family apartments and fitted an American kitchen and American bathrooms. She subscribed to the American Book of the Month Club, and was always receiving a lot of books—especially history books—through the mail. She also subscribed to *Architectural Digest* and the *International Herald Tribune*.

But, most of all, she was especially fond of *New Yorker* cartoons.

Believing there was always a cartoon that was just right for someone she knew, every week, as soon as the magazine arrived, she'd flip through it from cover to cover searching for appropriate cartoons. She'd sit at her desk, grinning from ear to ear, with the magazine and a pair of scissors. Whenever she found one that suited her purpose, she'd cut it out, put it into an envelope and, with great glee, mail it, usually anonymously, to whomever it fit.

The story persisted for years that the Prince had banned her films from being shown in Monaco.

"Not true," Rainier said. "Grace's films were shown here. They've been in the local cinemas and on television. We've also shown them in the Palace. Grace got a hold of some 16mm copies from MGM."

She only managed it, however, after a lot of effort.

Rainier continued, "It wasn't very nice on MGM's part because they were so difficult when she asked for them. They could have been a little more cooperative. They could easily have made a collection of her films available to her but when she asked if she could get copies of her own films all they did was tell us how many problems she was causing by asking. In the end, they said we could have some but we had to sign a paper promising that we'd never show them in public. That discouraged her a bit and I don't think we have all of them."

The moment their engagement was announced, one of the first questions anyone put to Rainier was, will Grace Kelly still make movies? His answer was no. Rainier told reporters months before their wedding, "Grace and I have agreed that she must give up her career. She could not possibly combine her royal duties with those of an acting career."

Right after her marriage, she was approached by Dore Schary to star in *Designing Woman*. She was interested in the film but never contemplated doing it.

"My film career is over," she'd tell anyone who asked, but only occasionally confessed that she was saying it because she wanted to avoid any confrontation about that with her husband.

It was a touchy subject because, at least in the beginning, she really missed everything she'd given up back in the States, including her career. And even years later, she was always glad to spend time talking about Hollywood with anyone from the business who happened to be passing through Monaco.

She also regaled her children with stories from Tinsel Town.

"It was great having an actress mother," her youngest daughter Stephanie felt, "because instead of growing up with stupid bedtime stories, my mom would tell me what was going on in the studios and all the latest Hollywood gossip. She'd sing and tap dance and tell me all about her movies."

Chapter 17

From Princess
to Performer

"There's no way I can win," Grace told friends. *"Whenever I put on a* couple of pounds, everybody thinks I'm having a baby. Whenever I manage to lose a few pounds, everybody thinks I'm finally planning to make another movie. If I go three days in a row to visit a friend in the hospital, right away the newspapers write that I'm suffering from some incurable disease. If I stay in Paris for a few weeks so that I can be with my daughter while she's at school, it gets around that my marriage is collapsing, that we're going to separate. As adults we end up taking all that with a shrug. But the often malicious interest shown in my children is very difficult to accept."

For most of her adult life, Grace ranked high on the list of the most written about, most photographed people in the world. Yet with her hair wrapped in a scarf and sunglasses hiding her eyes, Grace was not always recognized.

Walking with a friend one day across the large, open square in front of the Palace, she was approached by a couple of American tourists carrying a camera.

They said, "Hi."

Grace and the woman with her said, "Hi."

The tourists said, "Where are you from?"

Grace answered, "America."

The tourists said, "Us, too," then thrust their camera towards Grace. "Would you please take our picture?"

She said sure.

The tourists found just the right spot with the Palace was framed in the background and Grace snapped their photo.

The tourists said, "Thanks," reclaimed their camera, waved, "Have a nice day," and walked away.

They never knew.

"When Ava Gardner gets in a taxi," she liked to say, "the driver knows she's Ava Gardner. It's the same for Lana Turner, or Elizabeth Taylor. But not for me. I'm never Grace Kelly. I'm always someone who looks like Grace Kelly."

She swore that happened to her all the time, like in New York when she found the cabbie staring at her through the rear view mirror.

"You know what," he called back to her through the meshed grill that separated his seat from hers. "You look like Grace Kelly."

She said, "I do?"

"Yeah," he said, "you do. Except I think she's a little prettier than you are."

For most of her Hollywood career, Grace managed to avoid the scandal press. Not only, perhaps, because she spent as little time as possible in California, which must have helped, but also because she was very discreet about her private life.

She did not, however, escape completely unscathed.

When she made *The Country Girl*, gossip columnists linked her to her leading man and the photo that proved it showed Grace with Bing Crosby sharing a very romantic dinner. Except, it was tête-à-tête only as far as the picture editor was concerned. He'd cropped the photo tightly enough to eliminate any sight of Grace's sister Peggy, who was sitting on the other side of Crosby.

Not long after that, one of the Hollywood gossip sheets staked out Grace's flat and wrote that William Holden's car was frequently parked outside at night. What they failed to say was that Holden had loaned the car to one of Grace's friends.

The person who gave Grace the roughest time of all during her Hollywood days was columnist Hedda Hopper. For whatever reason, just before Grace started work on *A Country Girl*, the vitriolic Hopper phoned Crosby to warn him that his co-star was "a man-eater."

As soon as Grace and Rainier announced their engagement, Hopper wrote, "Half their friends are betting they never make it to the altar."

Since Grace's death a great deal has been written about her love affairs. All too often the sources quoted are dead and the stories, salaciously embroidered, are accepted as the truth merely because they are now in print and frequently repeated.

That she might have been in love with Ray Milland or Oleg Cassini or Jean Pierre Aumont or anyone else, for that matter, doesn't change the woman she became. When she got engaged to Rainier she told a reporter, "I've been in love before but never in love like this."

That a healthy, grown-up, single, working woman in her mid-20s had normal human feelings and desires hardly seems like much of a revelation today.

When Alfred Hitchcock sent her the screenplay of *Marnie*, saying that he wanted to cast her opposite Sean Connery, she liked the script and wanted to do it. She and Rainier had now been married seven years and, she sensed that he was starting to mellow about her career, becoming less dogmatic about her retirement. Still, there could be no question of making another film unless he approved.

"She and I talked about it," Rainier said. And contrary to many stories that have come out about this since Grace's death, Rainier maintained that he was not against the idea. "We also talked to Hitchcock about it. She was very anxious to get back into the swing of things. By that point I didn't see anything wrong with it. So I suggested we combine her work on the film with a family vacation. They were supposed to shoot somewhere in New England over the summer. I proposed that we rent a house nearby and go with the children. She said, 'If that's your idea of a vacation fine, except working on a film is not what I'd call vacation.'"

So Hitch announced that she was coming back, and before long, rumblings of discontent reached the Prince's ears.

"The appeal of *Marnie* was Hitchcock," Rainier continued. "He was, I think, very fond of both of us and we both trusted him. Grace would never have considered a film with just anybody. But this was Hitchcock. He was totally in charge and I can't imagine that he would have ever done anything or allowed anything to happen that might have in any way belittled the principality or Grace's position as Princess."

Well that might have been, but then the question of her fee hit the papers and rumors spread through Europe that Grace was only returning to films because the family was broke and needed the money.

In response, Grace announced that her entire fee would be put into a trust to help needy children.

That's when MGM added their two-cents worth by claiming that she was still under contract to them.

After that, the French newspapers criticized her for concocting the whole thing just to annoy Charles de Gaulle—remember, this was 1962 and Rainier was locked in a battle with de Gaulle over taxes—and the press was suggesting that Grace was returning to films simply to emphasize to de Gaulle that Monaco would do whatever it pleased.

That was followed by a letter from Pope John XXIII personally asking Grace, as a Catholic Princess, not make the film.

Finally, the Monegasques banded together and petitioned their prince to put an end to this.

Nadia Lacoste quickly found herself knee-deep in press criticism of the plan. "The Prince couldn't see why there was such a public reaction against Grace making film. I told him that to be an actress was a trade, a profession, and that maybe being Princess of Monaco was also a profession, but a completely different kind of profession. I asked him how he'd see the posters for the film. I wondered if he thought they'd bill her as Grace Kelly or Princess Grace or even Grace Grimaldi? I had the feeling that he hadn't thought about that before."

Lacoste felt she needed to make him understand that the answer to how they would bill her was, obviously, as Princess Grace. "The Prince looked at me and said, 'You're so old fashioned.' He pointed out that King Albert of Belgium used to climb mountains. I said, 'But climbing mountains is a sport, making movies is a business.' I just don't think he realized the implications until he thought about what the posters would say."

With the benefit of hindsight, Rainier was convinced that Grace's billing would not have been a problem. "How would they have publicized the film, starring Princess Grace or starring Grace Kelly? It would have been as Grace Kelly because that's the name she worked under."

In the end, the question was moot. Public opinion won out and Grace decided that she would not do the film.

"I must say," Rainier went on, "that she made her decision without any influence from me. I thought it would be great fun for all of us, especially the kids. And I knew she wanted to make more films. It would also mean working again with Hitchcock, whom she adored. Oh well."

He said that she accepted defeat reluctantly. "Yes, she missed performing. Very much so. But mostly she missed the stage, not the movies. That's why she did the poetry readings. She could do it without attracting much criticism. Although people are sometimes such idiots that they even criticized her for reading poetry in public. With some people you can never do anything right."

Sometime after the *Marnie* incident, Grace and Rainier found themselves in Hollywood. The entire family visited a film set, after which she told friends that she'd pretty much given up any ambition of ever making another film.

"It's all changed so much," she said. "I couldn't work like this."

Two years later, however, Rainier encouraged her to appear in a documentary about drug addiction for UNICEF.

Then, in 1970, she stepped in at the last minute for an ailing Noel Coward as host of a major charity gala at London's Royal Festival Hall.

She followed that in 1973 with a British television appearance in a show called *The Glories of Christmas.*

All of this was fun for her and didn't raise too many eyebrows in Monaco. But deep down, she knew it wasn't really show business. That's one of the reasons why, in July 1976, she accepted a seat on the board of Twentieth Century Fox.

By then, Grace was living most of the year in Paris to be near Stephanie who went to school there. Paris had rekindled her need for the cultural bounties of a world-class city, although she did tell certain friends that she was getting anxious for Stephanie to finish school so that she could move back to Monaco. "I'm not as fond of Paris as I used to be. I'm lonesome here. I guess I'm just a small town girl at heart."

Not surprisingly, there were other film offers.

Because a Grace Kelly comeback could have been the biggest box office draw of the decade, she could have commanded an enormous fee. But *Marnie* had shut the door to any lingering hopes she might have had.

It was a time of genuine conflict for her.

"Acting in a film again might have been in the back of her mind," remarked Lacoste, "but she had a lot of other priorities. Don't forget, she came along before the women's movement, before women wanted to prove they could do anything men could do. In her mind she was the Princess of Monaco and the mother of three children and her job was to deal with that. I once asked her if it had been very difficult to give up Hollywood. After all, she quit at the top. But she said no. She answered very clearly, 'To me, marriage has always been more important than my career.' Of course, there were times when she thought about the old days and maybe even missed making movies. She loved to talk about movies, about who could play this part or another part. But to say she was sorry she wasn't still in the movies, no, I never heard that. I never felt that."

Gradually Grace's thinking began to change. Motion pictures were one thing. Performing on stage might be something else. It was less visible. It was also more in keeping with the serious tradition of the legitimate actor.

Rainier was supportive of her and agreed that, if she could find something suitable, she'd be welcome to do it. However, anything she wanted to do would have to be carefully judged and presented in such a way as to be compatible with her image as the Princess of Monaco.

The American Bicentennial of 1976 came to her rescue.

Celebrations commemorating the Declaration of Independence took various forms throughout the world. Even in the United Kingdom. Among them was a special series of American music and drama performances at the highly acclaimed Edinburgh Festival.

In keeping with the theme, John Carroll, who had for years devised special poetry programs for the Festival, scripted a selection of poems under the theme of "An American Heritage" but felt that the best way to present the poems was with American voices. An old friend suggested that Princess Grace might like to do it.

Carroll met her for the first time in Paris. "I went to have lunch with her and we clicked. She loved the idea, although she did say she'd have to discuss it with the Prince. Ten days later she rang to tell me it would be okay."

The poems he chose for her included works by Longfellow, Whitman, Frost, Thoreau, Dickinson, and one by Eleanor Wylie called "Wild Peaches."

Grace arrived in Edinburgh three days before the first performance so that she could rehearse. "I'll probably be a bag of nerves," she told Carroll.

He confided, "I was a bit worried about how she'd take direction. But she was a lamb. When I selected 'Wild Peaches' for her I felt it should be done with Southern accent. I just wasn't sure I could ask Grace to do it that way. Well, after we rehearsed it the first time she turned to me and wondered, 'Shouldn't I do this with a Southern accent?' That's how good she was."

Grace's notices were ecstatic.

Carroll next suggested she should appear in Stratford-upon-Avon as part of the 1977 summer Shakespeare Festival.

She agreed, and he put together a program called, "A Remembrance of Shakespeare."

Carroll staged it at Trinity Church where the Bard is thought to be buried.

"We needed to do a full rehearsal," Carroll said, "so the church was closed on the evening before the performance. Grace arrived that night carrying a beautiful, long-stemmed rose. A typical Grace gesture. She brought it to put on Shakespeare's tomb."

The enormous publicity generated by that appearance was followed by an offer to narrate a film called *The Children of Theatre*, a documentary about the Kirov Ballet School in Leningrad. Grace not only accepted to do the voice-over, she also attended the premieres in aid of ballet charities in New York, Lausanne, and Paris.

Next came Grace's first poetry-reading American tour.

The American International Poetry Forum in Pittsburgh wanted her to do the "An American Heritage" program in the summer of 1978. She asked Carroll's opinion.

He devised a script with poetry and prose around the theme of animals and called it, "Birds, Beasts, and Flowers."

From an opening triumph in Pittsburgh, they flew to Minneapolis, Philadelphia, Washington, DC, Princeton, and Harvard.

By the time she returned to Europe, requests for more appearances were pouring in.

She appeared at the 1978 Aldeburgh Festival in East Suffolk, England and at a charity dinner held at St James's Palace in London with the Queen Mother in attendance.

Believing that these recitals were, as John Carroll put it, "A compromise between her old career and the dignity of her position," she performed in 1979 at Trinity College as part of the Dublin Festival, and in London again at both the Royal Academy of Arts and the Lyric Theatre in Hammersmith, now doing a program called "The Muses Combined," a series of readings on the arts of painting and sculpture.

Those were followed by appearances at Tatton Hall in Cheshire and the English Theatre of Vienna.

"Grace could speak some German," Carroll said. "She learned it from her mother. When she told me that, we added a couple of short verses from Austrian poets referring to the magic of Vienna. Grace recited them in German at the very end of the program and absolutely brought down the house."

Each success brought more offers.

A second US tour was arranged for the end of summer 1980. Grace returned to Pittsburgh to do the Shakespeare program there, then performed something new by John Carroll called *Evocations* in

Detroit, Dallas, Nashville, and Baltimore. It created such excitement that one Dallas paper wrote, there were more millionaires in the audience on Grace's opening night than had ever been seen in one place in the city before.

Between poetry recitals, Grace teamed up with a British writer to do a book on flower arranging. Like all best-selling authors, as soon as *A Garden of Flowers* was published, Grace embarked on a publicity tour, suffered endless interviews for newspapers and magazines, did live radio for the first time in many years and appeared on selected television shows where her hosts were pre-warned not to stray from the subject of the book.

Financially, the book was a huge success and Grace's portion of royalties was soon bolstering the bank accounts of charities such as the Monaco Red Cross.

In connection with that, she put together a homemade film. Titled *Rearranged*, she wrote the script, supervised the direction, and starred in it. Shot entirely on location in Monaco, she included all her friends in it. There is even a cameo, flower-arranging appearance by her husband.

Never meant to be anything more than a fun project strictly for the benefit of the Garden Club of Monaco, it's only had a few select showings. Approaches were made about buying the rights to the film for commercial, public distribution. One offer was as high as $6 million. But Rainier felt that would have entailed re-editing the film and turning it into something it was never intended to be. The print is locked in a Palace vault and Rainier insisted that's where it will stay.

In 1981, Grace was back in England to do a poetry recital for the Royal Opera at Covent Garden. She next performed at Goldsmith's Hall in the City of London and this time she had to share the spotlight with a young girl named Diana Spencer.

Prince Charles had just announced his engagement and this was the first time he and Diana were seen out together.

Diana appeared in a low-cut, black evening dress that made her look very busty. The photographers loved it but that only served to send the naturally timid 19-year-old deeper into her shell. Grace picked up on Diana's discomfort right away and moved in fast to lend moral support.

Carroll remembered, "Grace was very motherly with the future Princess of Wales. Diana was terribly nervous. This was her first public appearance apart from posing for pictures with the press in the garden at Buckingham Palace when her engagement was announced. If you remember she was a bit on the plump side in those days. The black dress was décolleté and it caused quite a stir. Diana was painfully shy but Grace understood what she was going through. She kept whispering things to Diana. She really was exactly like a mother with her."

Grace read at the Chichester Festival in March 1982, then went to Philadelphia to accept the hometown honor of a four-day Grace Kelly Film Festival.

In cooperation with the Roman Catholic Congregation of the Holy Cross in New York, Grace agreed to host a series of three half-hour television programs. "The Last Seven Words," "The Nativity" and "The Greatest Mystery" were filmed on location at the Vatican, St Patrick's Cathedral in New York, and Chichester Cathedral in England. They featured such varied singers as Placido Domingo and Petula Clark doing spiritual music with choral backgrounds plus British Shakespearean actors doing dramatizations from the Bible.

"Grace was totally comfortable with religion," Rainier affirmed. "She was a practicing Catholic and had a very strong, pure faith. She was certainly more rigorous than I was. If we were traveling someplace and it was Sunday, she'd insist that we find a church to attend mass. Maybe I wouldn't have always bothered, but she made it an important issue. I think it was her Irishness."

Convinced that poetry readings were the next best thing to being a working actress again, she scheduled further appearances around her official duties in Monaco.

One night, over dinner in a small restaurant in the south of France at the very beginning of September 1982, Grace told Mary Lawrence, "I'm so looking forward to this year. I'm coming into a whole new period of my life. The children are grown, Monte Carlo is great, everything is terrific. My responsibilities have changed and I can finally do so many of the things I really want to do. I'm excited about the future. Now is my time."

Added Lawrence, "She said she wanted to perform more. She said she wanted to paint more. She said she had all sorts of things set up in different places. They were personal, creative projects that she was going to do, as opposed to being a mother and supporting the children and being an image for Monaco. And I looked at her as she was talking and thought to myself, you have never been as beautiful as you are this minute."

A week later, Grace was dead.

Midday

Every parking meter in Monte Carlo is taken.

In the summer, the public beach along the Avenue Princess Grace is packed with people lying on inflatable mattresses, or on huge monogrammed towels, or on fancy chaise-lounges that they rent by the hour for exorbitant fees, baking in the sun.

Young men with flat stomachs and gold chains around their necks drink *Pastis* and play backgammon.

Young women, the tops of their bikinis casually tossed aside, drink Vichy and rub oil on themselves as small beads of sweat trickle down between their toasted breasts.

Children sit at the water's edge where the gentle ebb and flow of the sea covers the pile of smooth pebbles they've used to build a castle, because there is no sand.

A helicopter flies in from Nice airport.

At the eastern end of the principality, the very private Monte Carlo Beach Club is like something out of Hollywood in the 1930s, with rows of pinkish-colored cabanas covered by green and white striped awnings and an old-fashioned wind sock stuck on the top of a tall pole so the driver of the boat that takes people parasailing knows which way the breeze is blowing.

There's a small wooden pier that juts out from the rock beach to the lake-like sea. And much further out there are two small docks floating on pontoons so that, if you can swim that far, you'll have a place to rest or sunbathe or simply collapse.

A waiter sets tables outside at the Café de Paris.

Facing the port, on the sundeck below the Hotel de Paris, where the indoor pool is heated all year to a constant 82.5 degrees Fahrenheit, old men with paunches, gold Rolex Oysters on their wrists, and spotless white terry cloth robes hanging loosely around their shoulders, walk barefoot to the bar where they order another glass of champagne for themselves plus a Kir Royal with a Nicoise salad for the no-longer-so-young woman in the stylish one-piece bathing suit with the matching gold Rolex Oyster on the next chaise-lounge.

Around the corner from the railway station, a man who runs a small grocery starts taking in his wooden baskets of peaches and green peppers and onions and lettuce so that he can close for a three-hour siesta.

In the winter, the public beach gets only truly hearty types, who take their daily dip no matter what. The Monte Carlo Beach Club is closed. But the Health Club is open all year round and, if you know someone who rents one of the private sauna rooms, you can meet your lover there for what is called here—as it is in much of the world—an early matinee.

Depending on the restaurant, a $4 cantaloupe melon with a small piece of Parma ham on top and served on crested porcelain can cost upwards of $35.

Chinese waiters on one of the larger yachts in the harbor set out a buffet for the owner and his 20 guests, who will board the ship soon for a two-hour cruise to nowhere, consuming $15,000 in fuel, while men in white slacks and blue shirts talk business and women in their summer dresses discuss the price of shoes.

An architect sits hunched over his drawing board desperately trying to finish the final designs on a small block of flats, jammed in between other blocks of flats, where miniscule studios sell for hundreds of thousands of dollars, and even then you have to lean over the balcony, stand on tip-toe and twist your neck to get a glimpse of the sea.

Less than a hundred yards away, an old woman in Beausoleil, just across the Monte Carlo line in France, who always dresses in black and lives in a narrow, two-storey villa with a breathtaking view of the sea, draws her green shutters to keep the afternoon sun out. Then she shuffles towards the rear door, across her polished linoleum kitchen floor, pushing her slippered feet on top of a dish cloth so as not to dull the shine.

Outside, in one corner of her narrow yard, there's a chicken coop. She bends down to fetch an egg and bring it back to her butane stove where she drops it in an old pot and boils it for lunch.

In Monaco, on any given day at noon, between omelets, Nicoise salads, soufflés, quiches, flans, and pastries, more than 2,500 dozen eggs are cracked and cooked.

Chapter 18

Before the Laughter Stopped

One night, when their children were very young, Grace and Rainier went out for the evening, leaving their nanny, Maureen, in charge. Maureen being Maureen decided to have some fun, and stuffed their bed. She took Grace's nightgown and Rainier's pajamas and filled them with pillows.

The night-gowned pillow was reading a magazine. The night-shirted pillow was looking at a picture of Brigitte Bardot. To make the scene complete, she turned the lights way down so that at least, on first glance, it appeared that there really were two people in the bed.

As Grace had just acquired a new puppy which hadn't quite been house-trained, Maureen bought some plastic dog droppings and sprinkled them around the bedroom for good measure. She then went to bed.

When Grace and Rainier returned home, they could be heard shrieking.

Maureen repeated the joke a few years later when Caroline was old enough to be her accomplice. The two of them took an old shirt and some trousers and stuffed them to look like a body. Then they snuck out of the Palace and hid it under some shrubs.

The two of them thought this was a riot. Unfortunately, the security guards who found it weren't nearly as amused.

As Maureen remembered, quite clearly, "It didn't go down terribly well."

Not that Maureen, or her usual partner-in-mischief, Phyllis, always escaped unscathed.

Accompanying the family on a ski trip, they shared a room and left their window open to have some fresh air as they slept. No sooner were they asleep than the attack began.

Grace and Rainier were outside, pelting them in bed with snow balls.

On another trip, a ski lodge piano player smiled at Phyllis while Rainier was watching. He teased her about it, insisting that a romance was obviously on the cards. She protested her innocence. No sooner had they returned to Monaco when flowers arrived for Phyllis from the piano player. The flowers were followed with notes swearing undying love and affection.

Phyllis didn't know how to turn off the piano player, until she found out that Rainier was behind the whole thing.

Another evening, Grace and Rainier had been invited to a small dinner party by some friends, who'd also planned to ask Grace's secretary Phyllis Blum. But at the last minute the hostess realized there were too many ladies at the table.

The hostess rang Phyllis to explain the situation, hoping that she wouldn't mind backing out.

But Phyllis, encouraged by nanny Maureen King had another idea.

She showed up at the dinner party dressed as a man.

Wearing a wig and a borrowed suit, she also sported a beard and dark glasses. The hostess introduced Phyllis to everyone as a famous Polish pianist who'd just arrived in the west for the first time.

When presented to Princess Grace, Phyllis bowed gallantly.

Grace said that she was very pleased to meet him.

When the famous Polish pianist didn't respond, Grace was informed that he didn't speak English.

At one point before dinner, Rainier quietly remarked to someone that the famous Polish pianist seemed to him to be, "a bit on the feminine side."

He was told, "Oh, well, you know how those musical types are."

Over dinner, Grace found herself sitting next to the famous Polish pianist and, being polite, tried to determine what languages he spoke.

The hostess informed her—only Polish and German.

Wrong answer. Because Grace now asked the famous Polish pianist in German if he liked the soup.

When the famous Polish pianist didn't answer, Grace supposedly mumbled, "Perhaps he doesn't like the soup."

Not one to give up, Grace continued trying to make small talk with him in German.

The Polish pianist was unmovable.

Exasperated, Grace finally turned to her hostess and whispered, "Who is this person?"

That's when the hostess confessed everything.

And it was Grace and Rainier who laughed the loudest.

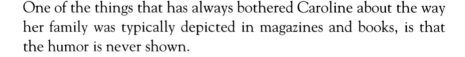

One of the things that has always bothered Caroline about the way her family was typically depicted in magazines and books, is that the humor is never shown.

"They don't show us laughing," she said, "which we did a lot. My mother had a terrific sense of humor and so did my father. No one ever writes about that. Mealtime was a time to tease each other. My parents always made sure that we'd have at least one meal a day together as a family. And when we did we laughed a lot."

Throughout their lives, Grace and Rainier exhibited their humor in different ways.

Rainier could tell jokes, and often did. Sometimes, the dirtier the better. But he also had a natural sense of humor.

While on a visit to Houston, Texas, he was taken to a football game at the Astrodome, the nine-acre, climate-controlled, covered stadium that seats just over 50,000.

As he gazed around at this engineering feat, his host wondered, "How would you like to have this in Monaco?"

Without skipping a beat, Rainier answered, "It would be marvelous. We could be the world's only indoor country."

Grace, in turn, was witty, like the time she realized it was her dog's birthday and decided to throw a party.

"I was maybe about 11," Caroline recalled. "I guess there were 10 or 11 dogs that came. They weren't all ours, of course, we invited some from the neighborhood. You know, our dog's friends. Because this was a birthday party, we wanted to do it right. So we had party hats for the dogs and a paper tablecloth on the lawn. We also had games for them to play and gave the winners prizes. We gave them bones. We had dog biscuits and cookies they could take home and even baked a chocolate birthday cake which we brought out to them with candles. They loved it. But then who doesn't love a birthday party?"

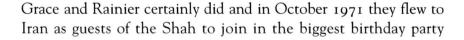

Grace and Rainier certainly did and in October 1971 they flew to Iran as guests of the Shah to join in the biggest birthday party ever—celebrations marking the 2,500th anniversary of the founding of the Persian monarchy.

It was a party that was estimated to have cost anywhere from $100 million to $1 billion.

After gathering in Tehran and going on to Shiraz, the Shah, his Empress Farah, and their 600 closest friends—including 37 heads of state and representatives of 69 nations—moved in armored convoy to Persepolis, the ceremonial capital of the ancient Persian empire. The night's feast was held in the huge state banqueting tent at the center of the spectacular canvas village that had been built in the middle of the desert especially for the occasion.

The food was cooked by 180 chefs from Maxim's in Paris, the Hotel de Paris in Monte Carlo, and the Palace Hotel in St. Moritz. First course was quails' eggs stuffed with golden imperial caviar and served with champagne and Chateau de Saran. Next came a mousse of crayfish tails with an Haut Brion Blanc 1964. Then there was roast saddle of lamb with truffles served with Chateau-Lafite Rothschild 1945, followed by a sorbet of Moet et Chandon 1911. After that, waiters paraded in carrying silver platters with 50 peacocks, their tail feathers put back in place and surrounded by roasted quails. That was served with a salad of nuts and truffles and Musigny Comte de Vogue 1945. Fresh figs with cream, raspberries, and port wine came next, along with Dom Perignon 1959, coffee, and Cognac Prince Eugene.

The only substitution on the menu went to the Shah himself who had artichoke hearts because he didn't like caviar.

With so many dignitaries in one place for the first time ever, it was an opportunity for all of the Shah's guests to mingle with people they might not normally have a chance to see on such an informal basis.

At one point Grace spotted somebody she wanted to meet, walked up to him and said, "Good evening, I'm Grace of Monaco."

Such was the tone of the evening that he simply extended his hand and said, "Good evening, I'm Tito."

Grace and Rainier were two of the 94 guests seated at the Shah's long zigzag head table. Rainier was next to the Duke of Edinburgh while Grace sat next to an Eastern bloc prime minister. She and the gentleman chatted amiably over dinner in French and German, but when he followed dessert with a cigar and inadvertently blew a huge cloud of blue smoke in her direction, Grace sneezed.

Unfortunately, she sneezed so hard that she popped some of the buttons on the back of her Givenchy gown.

And the dress opened.

Horrified, her lady-in-waiting rushed to the Princess's aid.

So did the Prince.

But they were both too late.

Neither of them could do anything more than stand by helplessly while Grace—who figured that her wardrobe malfunction coming as it did after a meal like that, had to be the perfect ending to a perfect evening—instantly doubled up in great convulsions of laughter.

In the summer of 1981, the family took a cruise together on the French ship, *Mermoz*. Stephanie didn't join them because she was at summer camp in the States. But Grace, Rainier, Caroline, and Albert, plus a few old family friends sailed up the coast of Norway to the North Cape for a look at what was left of the late-summer midnight sun.

Typically, the *Mermoz* entertainment program featured a costume night. Grace and Rainier dressed as pirates and stole the show.

A few nights later, the ship's magician performed.

Unbeknownst to their parents, Caroline had already met him and secretly rehearsed with him. So that evening, when he announced that his grand finale would be to saw a woman in half and needed a volunteer, he yanked Caroline out of the audience.

Grace and Rainier gasped.

Caroline lay down in the box as the magician pulled out some very long knives.

Her parents were now in a near state of shock.

After making a point of mentioning how the trick sometimes goes wrong, the magician proceeded to saw her in half.

Much to everyone's relief he also managed to put her back together again.

Rainier said he'd figured out right away that she was in on it. "I was merely hoping that she'd do everything she was supposed to when she was supposed to do it."

Caroline and her parents laughed about that night for years. "It was pretty hilarious."

But when Grace got killed, at least for a while, the laughter stopped.

Chapter 19

Teamwork

Like any good team, with Grace and Rainier, too, there was a distinct separation of responsibilities.

Grace never concerned herself with matters of state, politics, or government. She dealt with anything that had to do with the arts, their social life, the running of the Palace, and what might be called human relations.

Rainier said there were indeed many times when he spoke to Grace about affairs of state, but Grace once told her press attaché, Nadia Lacoste, that when he mentioned such subjects, she considered it as if he was merely thinking out loud.

She acknowledged, "I never give him any advice unless he asks for it."

Not that she necessarily hid her opinions.

When pigeon shooting came to Monte Carlo in the 19th century, they used live birds. When Grace moved to Monaco and saw how birds were still being slaughtered, she begged her husband to abolish it. And he did.

Later, when the new convention center was being built and the question came up of a name for it, she proposed that it be named after him.

The Prince's response was, "That sort of thing isn't important to me."

Grace held her ground and in the end won out.

But, as he was not the type of man who seeks self-promotion, it wasn't easy.

Grace's cousin John Lehman saw the Rainier-Grace partnership up close since his first visit to Monaco in 1965. "Monaco in those days was like something out of Central Casting. Dowager Russian princesses and out-of-work Balkan kings. Monaco was a very stodgy watering spot for European millionaires and down-at-the-heel aristocrats. But you could see changes starting. Rainier was determined to bring Monaco into the 20th century while still maintaining a certain dignity. He didn't view himself as the prince of the millionaires. He wanted to breathe life into the economy, to provide jobs and create a more wholesome environment for the people. Today it's the most remarkable achievement. Grace and Rainier accomplished it together. They were the most totally complete marriage I've ever witnessed. They were very different personalities but you can't separate them. Rainier's vision of Monaco was the guiding force. He clearly wore the pants. But she was no shrinking violet when it came to her own views."

Another person who observed the partnership up close was Rainier's old Lebanese chum, Khalil el Khoury. "In a small group of intimate friends you could see how comfortable Grace and Rainier were together. He was 100 percent Latin and she was 100 percent American and, in spite of their differences of upbringing and culture, they functioned like a team. It was when they were forced to show themselves in public that they were sometimes under strain. Especially the Prince. She made him see more people than he might have tended to. But most couples are this way. They change each other. He became more sociable. She made him realize the virtues of public relations. The world became fascinated with Monaco's image and the family's image. He understood it and did it gracefully. I wouldn't say he loved every minute of it because he's the sort of man who prefers getting to know people on a one-to-one basis. His is the more reserved approach to life and people. But he did it because it was right for Monaco."

It was as a team that Grace and Rainier rejuvenated the Monte Carlo orchestra and brought world-class artists to perform there; encouraged the revitalization of SBM's hotels; built an addition to the hospital; sponsored races, rallies and regattas; oversaw vast improvements in the public utilities and communications; championed construction of the new golf course at Mont Agel and built the public swimming pool at the port.

They traveled together, appearing together at all the right places because being seen helped to bring tourists to Monaco. They worked as a team to create a public image for themselves and the principality. But when it came to stardom, Grace held the ultimate pulling power. She was the magic.

Her talent was understanding how to market Monaco to the outside world without ever once giving the impression that she was selling something.

It was Grace who brought celebrity tennis tournaments to Monaco; convinced American television to tape shows there; attracted bigger and bigger names to the weekly galas; brought major stars to the orchestra, the opera, and the ballet. It was Grace who brought celebrities in every field to Monaco, seeking out writers, artists, scientists, and politicians.

It was Grace who turned Monaco back into a place to be seen. And that, in turn, attracted people who wanted to see.

There were times when you could walk down the street and bump into almost anyone.

Start with Henry Kissinger.

Commented Rainier, "He stayed with us once in the Palace. He was very professorial. You'd ask a simple question and he'd answer with the entire university-level course."

Then add Dr. Albert Schweitzer.

"He gave a lecture here," Rainier said, "and the principality donated an operating room, with all the equipment, for his hospital. I found his attitude to be a very noble one. I don't think enough has been said or written about him. Maybe he's even been a little forgotten. That's too bad. He set a great example, all the more so because what he did had no political resonance at all. He was far above that. His was pure human kindness and concern for people, with no other considerations."

Cary Grant was also a Monaco regular.

As handsome as ever, tall and tanned with snow-white hair, he always stayed in one of the guest rooms at the Palace. Grant returned year after year as a judge at the Circus Festival, giving that event a little extra touch of sophistication.

Of course, Frank Sinatra was there a lot.

Some years he'd only come for a week, others he came to stay for a month. He'd take the big suite on the eighth floor of the Hotel de Paris, play tennis at the Country Club, go to the Beach Club, and hang out at some of the better-known restaurants. But he was most visible every evening when he held court in the hotel bar. And when Sinatra was in residence, business boomed.

Another Monaco regular was Winston Churchill. He came often in the years before the war and returned just after the German surrender. From then, until the end of his life, he made several 10-week visits to the Hotel de Paris.

Rainier said he got to know Churchill fairly well. "But I'm not sure anyone could have gotten to know him very well. He came here a lot when Onassis was here. He was a great character. I found out that he loved to see films so Grace and I used to invite him to spend the evening with us. We'd built a projection room in one of the old stables and once or twice a week we'd show a film and serve a buffet supper. Except that he was such a stickler about food he'd eat dinner first at the Hotel de Paris. He liked coming to us for movies because there weren't too many people and we'd always put a bottle of cognac next to him. I remember one of the films he saw with us was *Lawrence of Arabia*. Afterwards he was very excited and couldn't stop telling us, 'I knew that man.'"

But the stars really came to town for the Grand Prix and the Red Cross Ball.

The Monaco Grand Prix bills itself as the greatest Formula One race in the world. And even if it isn't, it is certainly the best known. Actually it's a pair of events. There's the race, which is a sporting event, and there's the celebration of that race, which is one of Europe's major tourist attractions. The tarmac at the airport at Nice is never covered with as many private jets as it is during Grand Prix weekend. The harbor at Monaco is never filled with as many huge boats as it is during that weekend. The bar at the Hotel de Paris is never as crowded with as many easily recognizable people as it is that weekend.

"What makes Monaco really special," according to racing legend Stirling Moss who raced in Monaco from 1950–1961 and won three times, "is the atmosphere and the demanding nature of the circuit. It's a relatively safe circuit but it's very tricky. It's a beautiful, exciting place with an enormous amount of character, and the public, for whom you are performing, are very close to you. They're virtually on top of the cars. They can see you and you can see them. When I was racing, I'll never forget there was a very cute girl with pale pink lipstick who always stood in front of Oscar's Bar and every time I went past I'd blow her a kiss. Monaco is one of those sort of places."

Jackie Stewart, also a three-time winner there, agreed. "If you think of the history of motor sport, it was created from road racing around cities or from town to town. Racing through the streets of Monte Carlo is really a legacy of the basic origins of Grand Prix racing. It's also the most glamorous because it has as a backdrop the

Riviera, the Mediterranean, the Maritime Alps. It has great hotels, wonderful restaurants and beautiful women. If you think about what Grand Prix racing represents, it's glamorous, it's exciting and it's colorful. Monte Carlo projects all of those elements."

And the sovereign family, he went on, has a lot to do with it. "They're one of the ingredients that make up the perfect pie. They attend the race. They're an integral part of it. Now add in the most glamorous and richest people in the world. Everybody who is anybody arrives. It's just after the Cannes Film Festival so you get a lot of the wash from that."

He noted that the Europeans come, and the Americans come and the South Americans come up after they've been to Carnival in Rio. "They have big yachts or a suite in the Hotel de Paris. They go to the gala in the Sporting. They eat at Rampoldi's. Maybe they're invited to the Palace on the Saturday night. The Riviera is fresh, it's new, not like it is in July or August when it's a mass of people. The grass is still green, nobody's walked on it, the sun hasn't yet parched it. People come down from the mountains. They've had their winter at St Moritz or Gstaad or Vail or Aspen and they've come over for the Grand Prix weekend in Monaco. To have a good suite in the Hotel de Paris for the Grand Prix is a passport to whatever you need."

Traditionally, the sovereign family would watch the start of the race from their private box, then disappear until the end of the race. Grace didn't care for all the noise. But when Rainier handed out the trophies, she was there at his side.

And when the sovereign family made their entrance at the Red Cross Ball every August, he was there at her side.

The Red Cross Ball is without any doubt the largest, most spectacular event of its kind in Europe. It's not just the stars who perform there, it's the designer clothes and, especially, the jewelry. This may be the one night in the European social calendar when people who have serious money, seriously wear it.

Rainier formed the Monaco Red Cross in the late 1940s and for the first six or seven years the galas mainly featured European performers. Only occasionally did anyone come from the United States, like in 1954 when a young singer named Ella Fitzgerald had third billing.

Grace made the difference. She took over as President of the organization and gave the ball a big-money Hollywood stature it could never have attained without her. Yet, she never lost sight of its popular appeal.

Just before Frank Sinatra's first concert there, a friend went to Grace and said, "You ought to up the price for the gala. It's a charity event and nobody can draw a bigger crowd than Sinatra."

Grace's answer was typical. "If we up the price some people I like won't be able to afford it."

She also kept an eye on the show itself, because in the mid-1970s the topless craze had finally hit Monaco.

While women could casually shun half their bikini at the other beaches along the coast, it was frowned upon in Monaco, largely because Grace thought it totally unnecessary. For one ball, when the producer flouted tradition and introduced topless chorus girls in his revue, arguing it's been like this for years at the Moulin Rouge and the Folies Bergere, and Monaco must keep up with the times, Grace remained unconvinced. But she knew that if she protested too loudly she'd merely create headlines in the papers to the embarrassment of everyone involved.

So she handled it with typical savoir-faire. She explained to the producer how she felt it would be more appropriate if his dancers did not show their breasts, at least on this occasion. She won her case when she reminded him, "After all, it's a very dressy evening."

Over the years, just about everybody who was anybody in the nightclub world has performed at the Red Cross Ball. Not surprisingly, the biggest star of all was Sinatra. He was also, probably, the most difficult.

At that first appearance in 1980 he wanted extra tables put on the dance floor so that more people could be there. He wanted the orchestra to fill the stage and then announced he didn't want the dancers to do their number. He said all he wanted to do was walk on, do his bit, and that would be the evening.

Unfortunately, they couldn't put the orchestra where Sinatra wanted it but no one had the nerve to tell him. The chore fell to Grace. She explained to her old pal that people entered the room across the stage. She also had to tell him that it was traditional to have the dance floor available so that she and Rainier could open the ball. He agreed to everything except letting the revue precede him. He said the Red Cross Ball that year was going to be Sinatra and only Sinatra.

The chorus dancers who'd rehearsed an entire revue were furious. They begged the producer to ask Sinatra if he wasn't embarrassed that he was refusing to let entertainers work or had he forgotten what it was like at the beginning of his career?

Again it was Grace who stepped in. She understood how upset the dancers were, so she personally apologized to them on Sinatra's behalf and, to make amends, invited the entire company to the Palace the next day for cocktails around the swimming pool.

Out of friendship to Rainier, Sinatra returned with Sammy Davis, Jr. for the 1983 Red Cross Ball, the most emotional one of all, as it was the first one after Grace's death.

Since Caroline knew she could always count on him, she phoned Sinatra a few years later when Liza Minnelli had to cancel at the last minute because of a sore throat. That year he took to the stage with Elton John.

Another Red Cross Ball that stands out as magical was back in the mid-1970s when Sammy Davis, Jr. didn't show up. That afternoon Davis suddenly decided he didn't like the way things were being organized. He'd heard there'd been a dinner the night before at the Palace and because he wasn't invited he felt insulted. Then he had a run-in with the SBM people. He screamed, to hell with this, climbed onto a friend's boat, and sailed off into the sunshine for St. Tropez. By 9:00 that night, with the guests beginning to arrive at the gala, no one had yet come up with a replacement act.

Looking around the room, one of the SBM directors suggested that as a last resort they simply ask some of the stars attending the ball to do a couple of numbers.

They spotted Bill Cosby. He told the audience that evening, "They asked me to fill in for Sammy because they think I look like him."

He also explained that the first time he'd met Grace someone suggested, "You probably already know each other because you both come from Philadelphia." His response was, "Yes, of course, we know each other. Her family owned my family."

Next they spotted Burt Bacharach and he agreed to play. They hoped Liza Minnelli might sing, but she begged off.

Then they saw the legendary Josephine Baker. An SBM director quietly explained the situation to the 67-year-old French music hall star from St. Louis, Missouri, and asked politely if she'd be kind enough to sing a number or two.

She said, "Normally I'd be happy to but I have no music with me. It might be different if my piano player was here, but he's gone off for dinner somewhere."

The SBM director wondered, "If we send a car to collect your piano player from the restaurant right now, will you do it?"

She said, "Sure."

"Great," the SBM director said, "Where did he go for dinner?"

She told him, "He had reservations at Le Nautic."

The problem was that every village along the south coast of France boasts a restaurant called Le Nautic and there are a lot of villages along that coast. "Which Le Nautic?"

"Ah," she shrugged, "I don't know. Just Le Nautic."

So SBM sent cars to every Le Nautic between Menton and Cannes until they found him and raced him back to Monaco. The show went on and Josephine Baker owned the night.

However, if one night is ever to be called "the most memorable" it might well be the first Red Cross Ball held in the then brand-new *Salle des Etoiles*—Starlight Room—at the Summer Sporting Club.

It was 1974.

Part of Rainier's master plan to modernize Monaco, the room was the centerpiece of a circular complex of discos, restaurants, and a casino built on a small landfill peninsula of colored lights and exotic shrubbery jutting out from Monte Carlo's beach. The room got its name because the roof opens and the sides roll back and on a warm night you're virtually dining under the stars. On a clear summer evening it is spectacular. On the other hand, when it rains it is decidedly less spectacular, especially if the roof is still open. Which is what happened that night.

Jane Powell was on stage, singing and dancing, when a huge cloud moved into position, the roof mechanism jammed and suddenly tons of water came raining down onto the audience.

Everyone in the room ran for shelter.

Except for Jane Powell, who stayed right where she was, singing and dancing on a stage covered with half an inch of rain.

And except for Grace and Rainier. They stayed right where they were—now clutching umbrellas that waiters had found somewhere—fixed in their chairs, because the show must go on.

Chapter 20

Grimaldi Inc.

In the early 1800s the United States was heavily involved in naval commitments along the coast of North Africa.

A pair of costly expeditions against Libyan pirates gave rise to the feeling in Washington that the US Navy could use a refitting and supply station somewhere in the Mediterranean.

Prince Florestan supposedly learned of America's interest, knew that his country's most valuable natural resource was its deep, protected harbor, and considered negotiating the sale of his undercapitalized principality to the United States.

It was not such an outlandish idea.

The Russians later tried to buy nearby Villefranche to use as a base for the Czar's fleet. And Florestan's grandson, Alben I, would one day entertain a similar proposition from the Swiss.

There's no telling how history might have been changed had Florestan gone ahead with the deal.

Perhaps Monaco would today be the 51st state.

Then again, anyone who's ever witnessed bus loads of American tourists taking pictures of themselves on the steps of the casino might be excused for thinking the sale had indeed been concluded.

As Chairman of the Board of Grimaldi Inc., Rainier characterized himself as someone who saw opportunities rather than someone who studied balance sheets and worried about decimal points. Although he refused to accept the description of Monaco as "Grimaldi Inc.," he preferred Chairman of the Board of a business called Monaco.

"In a way, the principality has become a family business," he acknowledged. "I don't think it's really Grimaldi Inc. And I'm not certain it will ever turn into that. But it's much more business-like now than it was years ago. The way the world is today, it had to become that."

When he first married Grace, Monaco was a one product town. There was tourism, which included gambling, and there was nothing else.

Rainier conceded, "It was pretty obvious that no company could survive very long on such a short season and with a regular clientele that was actually smaller than the number of employees in the company."

Until he came along, Monaco's rulers tended to regard the principality as a part-time occupation. Most of them never spent more than three or four months of the year there, and even then they distanced themselves from the day-to-day workings of the country. Projects were only presented at the last stages for final approval. There were no intermediate stages where the prince could ask for revisions, or improve the text of some legislation or just put his own ideas into a project.

"My grandfather did not adequately prepare me for the job," he said. "The fact is, I don't think he was terribly concerned with how

I would get on. He was sickly at the end of his life, recently married and I guess he simply didn't feel he had a lot of time for me."

Rainier noted that although he participated in some meetings chaired by his grandfather and discussed certain things with him, such as the basics of the principality's administration, it was all the more difficult when he succeeded, because he didn't really have anyone he could count on for help.

"The staff who worked for him didn't seem to care much either," he went on. "I was pretty much on my own. Of course, sometimes that's the best way to learn. There were so many things I suddenly had to do that I didn't have a lot of time to worry about how hard it was to learn my job. I sat down and studied all the dossiers and figured out for myself where I was going."

Rainier was the first full-time sovereign, and also the first to approach the running of the country like the running of a business.

Although he couldn't make any decisions under his grandfather's rule, he made himself aware of what was going on. Nor could he criticize his grandfather, which meant he had to keep his opinions to himself. But he was in a position to form his own opinions and once he took over he moved fairly quickly to change things.

Specifically, he changed the economic base of the country.

If it really ever was the "sunny spot for shady people" that Somerset Maugham wrote about in the 1930s, Rainier insisted, it wasn't that any longer.

"The economy is still geared to tourism," he said, "but it's a great deal more well rounded than it was 40 years ago. There's no comparison. We now have a very important convention industry. And we now have a growing sector of light industry that has emerged as a major factor in our economy."

Grace's role was to help establish and to maintain the image of Monaco as the world's premier "jet setting" capital. That went hand in hand with the expansion of tourism that she helped orchestrate by bringing Americans to Monaco. But putting her influence aside, there was never anyone who could rightly claim to have been

Rainier's confidant and adviser in all things. Many of those who were closest to him in those years felt that Rainier's two greatest strengths were his ability to keep things compartmentalized and his uncanny instincts.

Now his instincts told him that he needed to attract new, and very specific types of businesses to Monaco.

"We chose business carefully," he explained, "because we didn't want to ruin the place. The principality was off limits right from the start to any business that would require vast amounts of space, such as an automobile assembly plant. Then, no pollution of any kind could be permitted. No air, sea or noise pollution."

He only wanted industries with a high cost improvement factor, such as pharmaceuticals, perfumes, and some electronics. And with the tax advantages he could offer them—and lifestyle advantages, too—they lined up to come to Monaco.

"We made small electrical components for the Concorde and NASA," he pointed out. "Did you know that the shaving razors for the first astronauts were made in Monaco? They were wind-up razors. There are also certain plastic and rubber parts made here for Renault, Citroen, and Peugeot. There are pharmaceuticals and beauty products either made here or packaged here. The point is that there is no unemployment in Monaco. In fact, we have to import people every day to work here."

To provide for those industries, he had to come up with somewhere to put them. "There were severe space limitations. But by 1974 we'd reclaimed about 53 acres from the sea. It enabled us to create Fontvieille, an entirely new quarter where we could house light industry. It meant that we could actively seek foreign investment and take yet another step away from a dependency on tourism. We expanded our borders peacefully. A rare thing these days, no?"

Along with light industry, Rainier looked to cut Monaco into the European convention business. And with conventions came festivals. He invented the Circus Festival, and welcomed music festivals and television festivals, deliberately scheduled to bring money into the country during the eight months outside the high-tourist season. As someone once wrote about Grace's and Rainier's Monaco, "Find 30 people who play marbles and Monaco will have a festival."

To make that happen, Monaco needed world-class facilities. And when Rainier started this, there was hardly anything suitable. The Hotel de Paris didn't even have a decent room for cocktail parties.

So he built a convention center that could comfortably take groups of 400–1,000 delegates. Next to it, Loews Hotel Corporation constructed a 573-room hotel, the largest on the south coast of France.

There were, however, some minor growing pains. When one of the new convention hotels was being planned, someone noticed that no provision was made to put bidets in the bathrooms. Bidets, the American designers explained, were not used by Americans and this was, after all, "the Americanization of Monaco."

No, the local authorities corrected them, this was not that and, anyway, bidets are a basic necessity in the civilized world. So bidets were duly added to the plans.

Business boomed and for the first time in the principality's history, the younger generation no longer had to look towards SBM for employment, the way their fathers did.

Said Rainier, "Most of them realize that, having gone to university, there are other possibilities open to them. So the old adage that every Monegasque is born with a croupier's rake in his hand simply isn't true any more."

At the same time, Monaco, and in a particular Monte Carlo, was gripped with real estate fever.

It coincided with an outbreak of terrorism in Italy and the real danger that the Communist Party could come to power there. To protect themselves and to protect their assets—many of which had been hidden in Monaco, out of the reach of the Italian taxman—Italians flooded into Monte Carlo.

Apartment prices hit outlandish heights. Building sites sprouted on every corner.

At one point in the late 1970s there were no fewer than nine major construction projects under way, with 85 percent of those new flats pre-sold.

Such was the craziness of the market that some apartments changed hands two, three, and four times while they were still in the blueprint stage.

Everybody suddenly became a real estate speculator. Enormous fortunes were made. It was the '49 Gold Rush, Monaco style. But prosperity was not without its price.

Some people criticized the Prince for not speaking up soon enough or loud enough and for allowing too many unattractive buildings to mar Monte Carlo's skyline. They said it could have been done differently, more tastefully, but because there was so much money involved and because it all happened so fast, controls and checks on the aesthetics of the urban development of Monte Carlo were too lax.

It got to the point that some of the high-rises built along the beach at Monte Carlo were so badly planned that, at three o'clock on summer afternoons, shadows were cast across the beach.

Grace was especially disappointed that the sleepy fishing village she'd moved to in 1956 suddenly looked like Hong Kong on the Mediterranean.

"I didn't necessarily like it either," Rainier admitted. "But what can you do? You can't make regulations that cover everything. As long as the builders are in conformity with the rules you can't say, 'I won't allow this because it doesn't suit my taste.'"

Conceding that it all happened too fast, he didn't want to go as far as to say that Monte Carlo has been spoiled. "The alternatives were to leave the place as it was or to have a spread of low-level building. And that gets back to a question of investment. People won't put their money into a project if it isn't large enough to make it worth their while. As soon as we realized what was happening we did try to change things. We put limits on the height of a building which any individual could build. But then builders started pooling their allocations in order to build very tall apartment houses. They got around the laws. So we tightened the laws."

Another area where Rainier came under some criticism was the often-contentious issue of Monaco's status as "a tax haven."

Here, he was fast to point out, "This is neither Liechtenstein nor the Cayman Islands. They've acquired a certain reputation that we wouldn't want here." And to that he added, "I would never want Monaco to become the kind of banking haven you find in the Caribbean."

Anyway, he shrugged, "Being a so-called tax haven is of no financial interest at all. People live here and buy things here, yes, that's fine. But if someone doesn't pay taxes in England or Sweden, it doesn't matter at all to us."

Grace's influence on her husband notwithstanding, some of the men who worked with Rainier for many years said that no one could rightfully claim to be his confidant and adviser in all things.

They said that one of Rainier's strengths was his ability to keep things compartmentalized. Others suggested that the secret to his success was in his instincts. They portrayed him as an emotional man, true to his Mediterranean heritage, who relied on his feelings and trusted his intuition.

He saw it slightly differently. "I was born here and I've lived here, basically, all my life. When it comes to dealing with the people, understanding them, that's a major advantage I've had over my predecessors."

On the other hand, he said, "I didn't go to school here and I found it was a drawback not knowing my generation very well.

Grace and I decided that Albert should go to the high school here and get his pants dirty with the other guys. When he takes over he'll have grown up with an entire generation here. He'll know them all. That's a benefit I didn't have."

Chapter 21

Caroline

Grace, Rainier, and their three children long had an association with London's Connaught Hotel, which in turn has long had a tradition of catering to European royals. Because some royals are not as stuffy as the Connaught, the two don't always mix.

Very early one Friday morning, with Grace in residence, Caroline and a couple of her friends turned up at the hotel hoping to get breakfast. They'd been to the famous, pre-dawn Bermondsey antique market, making their way through the maze of stalls armed with flashlights to see the bric-a-brac. Then, still clad in jeans and heavy sweaters, they decided to cap the morning with coffee and croissants at the Connaught.

Walking through the front door, Caroline asked the reception manager where they could get something to eat.

Looking down his nose, he suggested that she and her friends were hardly properly attired for the Connaught.

Caroline explained they'd been to Bermondsey.

He shook his head and apologized, "Sorry ma'am."

She said, "All we want is coffee and maybe some toast or something."

He shook his head again and said, "Sorry ma'am, not dressed like that."

"Come on," she protested, "you know who I am. We stay here all the time."

He stood his ground.

She tried, "How about if we take a room?"

He wouldn't give in.

"Okay," Caroline finally said. "My mother's here, we'll have breakfast with her."

She went to the house phone and, despite the early hour, asked for her mother's room.

After a few rings Grace picked up the phone.

Caroline said, "Good morning," and explained the situation. "Just because we've got jeans on they don't want to serve us breakfast."

Grace answered, "Perfectly right, dear," hung up and went straight back to sleep.

———

Caroline was 10 years old when she discovered that her mother was famous.

"I'd seen some movies when I was seven or eight but when I was 10 we went to California and visited some of the studios. They had some of her films in the archives that they showed us. There was so much fuss and commotion made over us that I started to understand who she'd been. But I don't think it affected any of us too much. Albert and I used to tease her a lot, especially about *Mogambo*. There's one scene where she turns to Clark Gable and says, 'I didn't know monkeys climbed trees.' It was the silliest thing I'd ever heard. We'd repeat that to her and then break up. Being children, it was difficult for us to understand that she was acting. I thought it was just Mommy being filmed saying, 'I didn't know monkeys climbed trees.'"

Even though her mother was a film star, Caroline never shared her ambition in that direction.

"Not me. I didn't want to be in films, I wanted to be a dancer. I never wanted to act. I couldn't even make it into school productions. Or the few times I did it was very silent parts. I was once one of the three kings in a nativity play with a big beard. But I used to get such stage fright. When I danced it was better. But when I had to say something on stage, I'd be sick."

Nor did she inherit her mother's general outlook on life. "Mommy was always busy doing something. She got that from her mother who couldn't stand people sitting around doing nothing. So she was always keeping busy. She couldn't just sit back and relax, which of course is miles away from me. I can perfectly well sit back in a chair and not do a thing for two solid hours. But maybe some of my mother has come through to me because when I do sit around like that I feel a little guilty about it. Not that it stops me from doing it, mind you."

After attending primary school in Monaco, Caroline was enrolled at St. Mary's College in Ascot, England, where she was taught by young nuns with a relatively modern approach. Her headmistress was a brilliant woman whom Caroline adored and the two kept in touch for many years.

Initially, Caroline's plan was to then go off to the States to university—there was talk of Princeton—but she wound up in Paris, enrolled at the Sorbonne, and romantically involved with a man 17 years her senior, Philippe Junot.

Junot was well known in Parisian circles as a playboy—and with Caroline being the ultimate playboy's prize—the tabloids kept their romance on the front pages, tracking them from nightclub to nightclub. Their engagement, and every step of their way to the altar was headlined in newspapers and magazines to such an extent that, at least for a short time, they rivaled Burton and Taylor, the Windsors,

Grace and Rainier, and maybe even Romeo and Juliet in history's "most-hyped-love-affair" category.

Throughout it, the media never missed the opportunity to wonder out loud if Caroline would wake up in time to see that this was never going to work. But she was in love with him and her two-day wedding to Junot, on June 28–29, 1978, was the social event of the 1970s. It was a media event to rival Grace and Rainier's own wedding, although this time the press was predicting that the marriage would never last. There was even a betting line started a week before the event that it wouldn't happen at all.

The official guest list topped 600. Because the Palace throne room is far too small for that number, only the immediate family— about 50 people—attended the Wednesday morning civil ceremony.

Thursday morning's religious service had originally been planned for the Palace chapel, but that was also too small. At the last minute, Grace and Rainier moved the service outside so that all their guests could attend.

Desperate to avoid the kind of chaos that overshadowed their own nuptials, they quickly resigned themselves to reality—that there was no chance of making this a simple, family wedding. How could they? More than 200 reporters and photographers were encamped in Monaco, each of them trying to out scoop the other, while none of them had anything more to report on than printed hand-outs.

The first of those handouts noted that the press would be permitted to operate in total freedom, without special permission, in spite of the fact that they would not be admitted into any official ceremony or to any of the several parties planned to fete the bride and groom. The rest of the press kit contained potted histories of the throne room, the chapel, Princess Caroline and what everyone in the wedding party was wearing.

A late entry, complete with a photograph, was everything anyone ever wanted to know about the wedding cake—500 eggs, 145 pounds of sugar, 45 pounds of almond paste, lots of smiling chefs, etc.

Then came the news that Mr. and Mrs. Junot could be photographed while they walked from the Palace to City Hall.

As for photos during the official ceremonies, Grace had asked an old Hollywood chum, Howell Conant, to take pictures. His negatives were rushed off to be developed so that six photos could be chosen as official handouts. In other words, every reporter got the same six photos. It meant that anyone who could manage to get past the Palace walls with a tie-clasp Pentax would have cleaned up.

And a few tried. One of the paparazzi even dressed up like a priest. But they were all caught and no one came up with anything.

So the press did what the press usually does when there's no one to talk to. Reporters bribed taxi drivers, bartenders, croupiers, shopkeepers, barbers, manicurists, hotel concierges, and anyone else who might be able to tell them anything at all about the wedding. But that didn't produce much because the people they were bribing hadn't been invited either. Some media outlets let it be known that they were prepared to pay up to $15,000 for any unofficial pictures taken during the ceremonies, parties, balls, anything at all.

The money went unspent.

The only scoop of the week came when the press mob traipsed off to David Niven's house on Cap Ferrat and learned that Gregory Peck's car had backed into Cary Grant's car. There was no damage, no one was hurt, and everyone involved remained friends. Still, the story made front pages.

The best stories, however, were the ones they didn't get.

Like how, the night before the wedding, Grace was up until 4 A.M. trying to figure out how to seat everybody at the celebration luncheon. There were royals and there were heads of state, and protocol was a nightmare. Tables were set up under the trees on the square in front of the Palace. The whole area had, of course, been roped off from the general public.

It was, as Rupert Allan described it, "The luncheon of the century in that part of the world."

After the luncheon, the Junots flew to Tahiti. And it was there, on her honeymoon, that Caroline began to understand what everyone else had feared, that the marriage would never work.

"It was very paradoxical," she said. "It all had to do with the way were brought up. Mommy said, 'Of course he's the wrong man and you shouldn't marry him but now you've been compromised. You've been dating him for too long, so now either get engaged officially or stop seeing him and go off to the States and finish university there.' She wanted me to go to Princeton. So, of course I said, 'Okay, let's get engaged.' I was 20 or 21 and didn't really want to get married. If I'd lived with him for six months, or even just three months, I'd have found out right away what he was like. But I wasn't allowed to go off on vacations with him or even spend weekends with him, except at his parent's house, which was all very proper. I really didn't know him very well. Getting married was simply the correct way out."

Caroline noted that when she announced to her mother that she wanted to marry Junot, it was with the proviso, "If you're really against it, I won't."

She promised her mother, "I'm not going to run away and get married against your will. Maybe I'll be miserable if I can't see him any more but don't worry, I won't do it."

Her mother answered, "Go ahead and get married. After all, what are people going to think after you've been dating this guy for two years?"

How times have changed, Caroline said with hindsight. "It's amazing. I married Philippe because I was in love with him. That's a good enough reason for marrying anybody. But then one day you wake up and wonder what you've done. I guess I started to wake up and wonder what I'd done while we were still on our honeymoon. He'd arranged with a photographer friend of his to meet us there to have the exclusive rights to our honeymoon pictures. That's when it all started to click. That was terrible. The end started right there. But it took me a year and a half to finish it. A long time."

When she finally gave up on Junot and wanted to come home, her parents were very supportive. "Mommy was very helpful. I didn't dare divorce or even mention divorce because Catholics don't divorce. You're supposed to just make the best of it. But Mommy said, 'You have to get divorced.' I said, 'How can you talk like that? We're a religious family.' I told her I was trying to find a way to work something out. But Mommy said, 'Religion is there to help people, not to make your life miserable.'"

While Caroline continued to go to church every Sunday, she couldn't take communion. But she was never excluded from the church. She filed for and won a civil divorce in 1980. Her annulment inquiry made its way at a snail's pace through the Vatican bureaucracy and by the time it was finally granted—twelve years and two Papal commissions later—life for Caroline had moved on.

Tragically so.

Looking back on that wedding, Caroline shuddered, "Not one of my better days."

She said her mother once told her that she hated the whole fiasco of her wedding, too. "I remember Mommy saying that it was just a circus. Not only didn't they look at their wedding pictures for years after that, on their honeymoon they didn't talk about it. It was madness. She didn't want that for mine."

With the 20/20 vision of hindsight, it's hard to see how Caroline could have avoided it. Her face sold magazines, so much so that she even made it to the cover of *Time* at the age of 16.

"That wasn't my idea at all," she insisted. "They were writing a piece on Monaco and it turned out to be on me. When they said they wanted to ask a few questions, I was frightfully rude. I didn't want to talk to anybody because I was about to go on to university where I'd decided I wanted to be anonymous. I wanted to be forgotten about. But I was told they were going to take a picture. I'd just come back from school, walked into the apartment and the photographer was there. So we went out onto the balcony. As I remember it was a pretty lousy picture."

Not surprisingly, she agreed with her father that it was impossible to get used to all the unwanted publicity. "When I was living in Paris I went everywhere with my German shepherd dog. As long as I was with my dog they tended to keep their distance. Or, at least, they only used their long lenses. Even today when I go out I worry that somebody is following me or hiding behind bushes. You never think you're completely alone or completely free to move around. It's a terrible feeling. The pressure of being spied upon is awful. Lots of people can't understand why I've tried to stop it whenever I can because they think I love it, they think we love the publicity."

She has never collected her own press cuttings and said that when they arrived in her mail—which they do regularly from people who think she might want to have a copy of a story or picture— she hardly, if ever, reads them. "Yet when I do read something, it's like reading about somebody else's life. I look through some of the articles and for the first ten minutes I giggle because it's so absurd. They write such complete nonsense. Then, all of a sudden I say to myself, but they're writing about me and they're lying. That's when I get furious. When they have nothing else to write about they invent things."

She also agreed with her father that being in her position has always made it difficult to make friends. Not because she doesn't want to, but because there is a little voice inside her that asks, what does this person want of me?

Many of her adult friendships, therefore, began in childhood. "The problem is you can't spend too much time worrying about who you're real friends are. You just have to take everybody at face value. After all, if you start worrying, is this one going to be a real friend or behave badly, well it's a shame to have to think that way."

Yet, it was always difficult for her to trust anybody past a certain point. "If you ask them to be faithful and non-demanding and be there to help you, to stick by you and never want anything in return, that's maybe asking a little too much from people. But you can't expect too much or you risk being disappointed. It was lonely at times while we were growing up. I think it's getting easier as I get older. Actually lots of things get easier as you get older. A lot of the nonsense fades away."

At the time of her bust-up with Junot, one of her old chums was Ingrid Bergman's son, Robertino Rossellini. After suffering the stress and embarrassment of a very public divorce, he became a comfort in her life. She was there for him when his mother died. And he was there for her, two weeks later, when her mother died. Friends predicted a wedding, but after a couple of years, the romance lost its glitter. Anyway, by 1983, she'd met someone else.

A tall, blond, quiet Italian from outside Milan, Stefano Casiraghi was three and a half years her junior. She joked at the time that he would make the perfect husband for her because he had a financial interest in an Italian shoe company and there were few things in the world she liked better than shoes.

Hearing that, he had special labels made to put in her shoes saying they'd been created exclusively for her.

The two were virtually living together when she found herself pregnant. A private wedding ceremony was arranged.

The son of a wealthy industrialist, Stefano settled in Monaco where he expanded his own business interests to include real estate and boat building. Their son Andrea was born in 1984, followed by daughter Charlotte in 1986 and their second son, Pierre, in 1987.

The five of them lived mostly in Caroline's house near the Palace, dividing the rest of their time between *Roc Agel*, Paris, and trips to Italy.

Caroline and Stefano spoke Italian at home together although she spoke French to the children.

Seeing her with her children, and with Stefano always near by, it was evident that she'd settled into marriage and motherhood with ease and delight. In quiet moments she and Stefano spoke of someday having six children.

That her life with him had changed her, matured her and given her some substance was unmistakable in one remark she made about how she saw her role as a wife, mother, and Princess. "It wouldn't bother me at all if I weren't Princess Caroline of Monaco. I prefer to be at home with my husband and children than attacked by photographers. I'm just the sister of the future prince, and my children come first. I work my schedule around them."

But it wasn't to last.

On October 3, 1990, Stefano was killed in an offshore powerboat race within sight of the beach at Monte Carlo.

He'd taken up the sport several years before, devoted his energies to mastering it, and in 1989, had won the world championship at a series of races in Atlantic City. This time, in his 200 kph catamaran, *Pinot de Pinot*, he and co-pilot Patrice Innocenti were favorites to retain the title.

About half an hour into the heat, while making a run at 150 kph, the 42-foot boat struck a wave and overturned. Innocenti was thrown clear, but Stefano was trapped inside and drawn under the water. The emergency rescue teams failed to get to him in time.

Caroline was in Paris. It was her father who broke the news to her on the phone.

Within a few hours, a young, black-veiled widow returned to Monaco—accompanied by her best friend and neighbor, model Inès de La Fressange—to face life as a single parent of three very young children.

That Christmas, when someone asked Andrea what he wanted, he answered, "To have my papa back."

As with the accident that had claimed Grace—who hated driving and rarely did—Stefano's death was also filled with ironies. Knowing how Caroline worried about the inherent dangers of power-boat racing, Stefano had announced the week before that this championship would be his last. He was planning to move from racing into the much safer business of boat building.

Then, again, he never should have been racing that Wednesday. Two days before, in an elimination heat, he'd stopped his boat to help a competitor in trouble. That was against the rules and he'd been disqualified.

But Stefano had helped to organize the race—he was the one who brought it to Monaco—and after all, he was the defending champion. So the ruling committee voted to bend the rules and they reinstated him.

Just 30, Stefano was a gentle, soft-spoken man with the confidence to let his wife be the star. He stood by her side whenever he was called on to be with her for official duties, but was not the sort of man who even thought about trying to steal the spotlight from her. He cared for her as much as she cared for him and he adored his children. They were always around him, crawling on him, dangling from his arms, hanging off his back. He laughed with them and he laughed with her and helped her to create the family she had always craved.

Looking for scandal, because that's what they do, Europe's tabloid press discovered that Stefano had managed to escape Italy's obligatory military service. That story, and the inevitable old chestnut that his death was a message from the Mafia, could not soil the dignity with which Caroline and her children, together with Rainier, Albert, and Stephanie handled the tragedy. Anyway, Stefano had been medically excused from his military service and the Mafia link was wholly invented.

Chapter 22

Albert

As sovereign-in-waiting or, more accurately, as Vice Chairman of the Board of Grimaldi Inc., Albert went to the gym every morning early for a swim or a light workout. He stayed in shape, played better-than-average tennis, and held a black belt in judo. After that, he went to his office, where he handled the business of the various associations he patronized.

He attended his father's cabinet meetings and continued to pursue his interests in international sport. When he could, when their schedules matched, he'd have lunch with his father, just the two of them, so that they could talk.

Afterwards, there were always more people to see and more matters to deal with in the afternoon.

As Vice Chairman, he said, he took his job seriously because training for succession was a serious matter. "It's been an ongoing process for years. I guess I was made aware of my future responsibilities from about age five or six. And it's something that's always kind of scared me because I've seen over the years that there's so much responsibility and so many different problems to deal with.

I've come to face some of those problems and to help my dad with the work he does. But it's not easy and I'm not sure if I'm up to it. I mean, I'm fairly confident that I have the right tools to do that kind of work. But I don't know if I can do it as well as he can."

After saying that, he hastened to add that he was not avoiding the issue, just recognizing the fact that he was being called upon to fill some very large shoes.

"I read the papers," he continued. "I know a lot of the press has hinted that I'm just hanging around and not eager to do any work. Well, I think that's unfair. I'm helping my dad and working as hard as I can. I'm giving my best. Whenever the time is right, it will happen. I don't see any reason why I should press the issue because I'm enjoying the present situation and as long as my dad feels comfortable with the present situation, that's fine. Whenever it's going to happen it will happen. There's no timetable. We'll just both know when it's ready."

The closer he came to the day when he would assume the responsibilities of his birthright, the more he saw his father's legacy as being inexorably tied to his mother's prominence.

He maintained it was very much a team effort. "My mom and dad did more for this principality than anyone else in history. They did it together. They gave Monaco a prestige that no one else ever did or probably ever could have. It's hard for me to put into words but just look around. I guess that's a good indication of what's been going on here. It used to be a kind of happy-go-lucky, half-asleep spot on the Mediterranean that only catered to tourism. Now it's a vibrant, busy little city, much more than just a tourist stop. He and Mom have to take the credit for that."

Having mentioned Grace, the conversation naturally turned to her.

Albert confided that one of his fondest memories of childhood was discovering that his mother had been a major movie star. "I was in my early teens and I remember it was a pretty nice revelation. We used to talk about the movies and she used to tell me stories.

I'm still interested in films and filmmaking and I've taken a few courses in it. At times I've thought about what I'd like to have done if I didn't have these other responsibilities and doing something in films has come to mind. But it's such a tough business. Anyway, I was never a great actor. I did a few operettas at summer camp. I never acted at school although I was always tempted. Something always held me back. Maybe I'm too shy. But just trying to understand film is fun. Maybe I would have liked to do something behind the camera."

As a matter of fact, he did have a brief film career which started and ended in 1999.

Billed as Albert Grimaldi, he made his screen debut in *One Man's Hero*, which starred Tom Berenger. Albert played an Irish mercenary fighting for Mexico during the Mexican-American war.

His character's name was Kelly.

"Don't expect an incredible acting performance," he warned.

The reason he did the film was because some friends of his were in it, and because they'd asked him to come along and because, well, "just for the fun of it."

He announced in Monaco that he was going on vacation and, without saying anything more, flew to Durango, Mexico. There, he lived with the cast and crew for several days on a hot, dusty set. The script called for several characters to be executed at the end of the film, including Albert's character.

"Being hanged," commented director Lance Hool, "would have been a great topper to his acting debut."

Instead, Albert was called back to Monaco before the final scene was shot. Rainier was not pleased with his son's moonlighting. And anyway, his entire performance wound up on the cutting room floor.

Not that he ever expected to duplicate his mother's film career. "It wasn't even supposed to be a speaking part," he said.

Still, as a young teenager, it was only when he'd realized who his mother had been and who her Hollywood friends were, that an important revelation began dawning on him.

"It really amazed me who I was meeting and that I could interact with them," he said. "I used to think, hey, I may be the only 14-year-old in the world who could pick up the phone and ring Frank Sinatra or Gregory Peck or Cary Grant and actually get them on the phone."

Understanding the access he had and how access translates to power, he claimed he was always careful not to use it flippantly. "I'm not sure if I always use it the right way. At least I know enough not to ask for favors because the reaction of those kinds of people to someone asking for a favor is the same reaction I have when someone asks me for a favor."

Yet, he insisted, he wasn't shy about picking up the phone when he had to. And in that respect, he said, he's different from his father. "Dad hates the phone and prefers writing letters. He's a tremendous letter writer. But I'm not a great writer so I call people. He's always after me because he thinks I use the phone too much. As soon as I start dialing he says, 'Who are you talking to? Why do you have to call them?' You know what I like best about the telephone? Sometimes I call people I may not know and I tell the secretary, 'Hi, it's Prince Albert,' and they say, 'Yeah, sure.' It's very funny. I've learned to let my secretary dial calls. Except I really love it when someone tells me, 'Yeah, sure you are, come on, who is it?'"

Unlike some middle children, who believe that is the most difficult place to be, Albert maintained that he never felt stuck between his sisters. "We've always been very close, although Caroline as a kid was pretty bossy and pretty independent. I went along with it for a while. Sure she annoyed me a few times when we were kids. Sure we used to fight. All brothers and sisters do. But when I was about 11 or 12, I was taking judo lessons. Once when she was harassing me, I did a hip movement and threw her to the floor. Ever since then we've had a good rapport."

When asked if she recalled that particular incident, Caroline winced. "I certainly do. We've always been a very close family, and I was especially close to Albert because we're only a year apart. The thing was that he and I used to fight like cats and dogs while we were growing up. I mean we'd fight with the determined intention of causing vast amounts of pain. Well that day, just because he'd been taking judo lessons, he threw me on the floor so hard I knew that was the end of that. There could be no more picking on baby brother."

Stephanie escaped that, being so much younger.

As Caroline pointed out, "There's eight years difference between us so I guess I always felt responsible for her. I guess I was always playing the older sister with her. I babysat for her and watched out for her."

Albert felt just as protective. "I played with Stephanie a lot when we were kids. Probably because I love younger kids and even at that age I was kind of fascinated by this little baby in the family. So we always got along great. We've always had a good relationship. I know she went through a lot because of the accident. It affected her more than most people can imagine, maybe even more than we think. She had a very difficult time adjusting afterwards, simply in terms of relating to other people. Hence her chaotic lifestyle."

Because Stephanie has always had such a high exposure, because the press followed her and bothered her for years, he understood how everything about her life got blown way out of proportion.

He continued, "Because of her age and some of the things she's wanted to do, I think there's been additional pressure on her and worry that she'd get hurt somewhere along the line. I really feel for her. She never asked for any of that. She just wanted to do her own thing for a while, and she got caught. My dad and I have had long conversations about it and he's been very worried about her. But that's only normal. I think she's learning who to trust. She's a very sweet girl who puts up a cold, hard front because she's shy and she doesn't always know how to deal with certain people. That's strange in a way because as a family we've been in different situations where we've had to deal with people. But she's always kind of resisted that and now it's working against her. When she does open up to some-

Breakfast with Caroline and with Frank Sinatra in the gardens of the palace apartments (courtesy Photo Archive, Palais Princier, Monaco, G. Lukomski).

Toddler Stephanie with Grace in the garden (courtesy Photo Archive, Palais Princier, Monaco).

Caroline, Albert, and Stephanie in 1973 (courtesy Photo Archive, Palais Princier, Monaco).

Clockwise from top: Grace and
Rainier with Caroline and
Stephanie in 1975 (courtesy Photo
Archive, Palais Princier, Monaco).
Albert and his mother (courtesy G.
Lukomski, Photo Archive, Palais
Princier, Monaco). Caroline as a
teenager with her father (courtesy
Frank Spooner Pictures Ltd.).

At the finish line of the London to Brighton Vintage Car Rally in Rainier's 1903 De Dion-Bouton. The Grimaldis watched the start and the finish together, but for most of the race, Grace, Stephanie, and Caroline sacrificed glory for the warmth of a modern car (courtesy Popperfoto Ltd.).

Above: Rainier sometimes fancied himself a drummer. A playful Grace did not (courtesy Photo Archive, Palais Princier, Monaco, G. Lukomski). *Left*: Stephanie with Grace at a Red Cross Ball (courtesy Popperfoto Ltd.).

Opposite, top row:
One of Grace's
favorite portraits
(courtesy Sam
Levin). Rainier
and Grace out
on the town
(courtesy SBM).

This photo of Grace shooting
a gun at a local fair ran the day
after President Kennedy was
shot in November 1963 and
was interpreted as tasteless,
although it was taken hours
before the assassination
(courtesy Photo Archive,
Palais Princier, Monaco,
G. Lukomski).

Above: Maria Callas and Aristotle
Onassis at the Hotel de Paris,
Monte Carlo (courtesy SBM).
Left: At the Red Cross Ball with
Frank Sinatra (courtesy SBM).

Grace loved needlepoint and
wrote a book about flower-
arranging (photos courtesy
Photo Archive, Palais Princier,
Monaco, G. Lukomski).

Right: Reading poetry—here with actor John Westbrook—was the closest Grace could get to a show-business comeback (courtesy Photo Archive, Palais Princier, Monaco). *Below:* Diana's first public appearance after the announcement of her engagement to Prince Charles was at a Princess Grace's poetry reading. Grace was especially sympathetic to Diana's discomfort at the public attention she was suddenly exposed to (courtesy Reg Wilson, Royal Opera Press Office).

Clockwise from top: Grace's final Red Cross Ball in July 1982 (courtesy Popperfoto Ltd.). A family in mourning (courtesy Photo Archive, Palais Princier, Monaco). Gracia Patricia, November 1929–September 1982 (courtesy Photo Archive, Palais Princier, Monaco).

Opposite: Grace's last Circus Festival in December 1981, with Cary Grant, Caroline, and Rainier (courtesy Frank Spooner Pictures Ltd.).

Caroline with her late husband
Stefano Casiraghi, their sons, Pierre
and Andrea, and daughter, Charlotte
(courtesy Photo Archive, Palais
Princier, Monaco).

Stephanie with her father, walking
their dog in Paris (courtesy Gilles
Merme, Frank Spooner Pictures Ltd.).

Albert with Rainer (courtesy Photo
Archive, Palais Princier, Monaco).

one maybe she opens up too much. Maybe she's been too easily influenced by the wrong people."

That was a problem, Albert admitted, not at all unique to his little sister. "I'm discovering that the more I get involved with my job the lonelier it is. Sure you have people around you to help, advisers, but it's really up to you to take the final decisions and I guess the more I move towards a position of power and leadership, the more people I find around me claiming to be my friend. That's hard to deal with. I tend to trust most people, but I've been disappointed a lot."

Chapter 23

Stephanie

She was the tomboy of the family.

Just like her older sister, Stephanie started school in Monaco, took piano lessons, and attended dance classes. Just like her older brother, she was encouraged to pursue her interests in sports. And because her mother and her sister both attended a convent school for proper young ladies, it was only natural that Stephanie would also attend such a school.

She didn't want to go to Caroline's alma mater in England, so she was enrolled in a convent school outside Paris, and she absolutely detested it. The sisters were old and grumpy, and the place was decidedly stale. The setting was also pretty grim, totally isolated in the middle of some woods. But neither Rainier nor Grace realized just how awful it was until they saw it. Once they did, it caused a minor row between her parents. Rainier wanted to find Stephanie another school. Stephanie also wanted to find another school. Grace insisted she stay at this one.

Rainier recalled, "We took her there by car for the first term, but as soon as we got there I knew I didn't like it. They'd announced a swimming pool but that didn't exist. They'd announced tennis courts, but there was nothing more than a mud plot with a net strung across it. It was a real disappointment. By the time we drove away and left her standing there, waving goodbye, she was in tears. I said to Grace, 'We've really made a mistake. Let's turn around and go back.' But she said no. She was stronger than I was about that. I was absolutely prepared to bring Stephanie home to Paris with us."

The very mention of the place made Stephanie wince. "I thoroughly hated it. I only spent one term there, September to December, but it was more than enough. I'd broken my foot so I was in my room a lot. Can you believe they had bars on the windows and two German shepherd dogs that they'd let loose at night to keep the girls from running away? We weren't allowed to put anything up on the walls or even to have a radio. It was an experience! Frankly, I still don't understand why I was sent to that place. I wasn't that bad, to be stuck there like that. Of course, looking back, I guess it was at the time of my sister's divorce and my parents probably wanted to keep me away from that whole situation. But I left as soon as I could. A week before Christmas break I escaped. I just took my things and got out of there."

Rainier sympathized. "The school did have some pretty silly rules. To begin with, the girls had to wear dark blue skirts down to their ankles, with big pleats in them and white shirts with long sleeves. Then, the girls had nothing at all to say in the running of the school, the way Caroline and her friends could voice their opinions at St. Mary's. In other words, at this place, the girls did what they were told to or were punished for disobedience. Worst still, there was a limit on the number of showers they could take each week."

"Two," Stephanie blurted out, disdainfully. But she quickly discovered that her distaste for desserts could save her from that. "Mom didn't raise us to eat a lot of sweets. None of us in the family like desserts. Albert might have some sweets sometimes, but when we were growing up, my mom would put fruit or yogurt on the table for dessert. We didn't get to see a lot of cakes and cream pies. Well, it didn't take me long to find out that some of the other girls were more interested in my desserts than they were in their own showers. So I negotiated away my desserts and wound up with a shower every day. I'd rather be clean and starving than fat and dirty."

At the end of that single term she transferred to the more congenial atmosphere of a well-known boarding school in Paris, not far from the family apartment. "That was so much better because I could go home on Wednesday nights and on weekends. I liked that school. I had my own room and there were no convent rules. I took a shower every day without being hassled and still didn't eat my desserts."

She passed her French *baccalaureat* exams in 1982 and had planned on further studies, but the car accident that nearly killed her—and did kill her mother—changed the course of her life.

Everyone grieves their own way. Stephanie's was, promptly, to drop out of everything.

Her boyfriend at the time was Paul Belmondo, son of French actor Jean Paul Belmondo. He'd visited her in the hospital, comforted her there and, in time, brought her back to Paris with him. They watched videos together all day long. She stayed there with him, hiding in her shell. Rainier, Caroline, and Albert were justifiably concerned. When she announced that she didn't want to go on to university, they urged her to change her mind. After a while, she said she was interested enough in fashion that she might do something with that. It took a year before she could bring herself to do anything, but in the autumn of 1983, she enrolled in a fashion course in Paris. At the end of it, an old family friend, Marc Bohan, hired her as one of his design assistants at Christian Dior.

Before long, the old Stephanie was starting to re-emerge. One day she showed up with her hair dyed punk orange. The powers at Dior sent her home with orders to wash it out immediately. They warned her about returning with orange hair. So she did what she was told, went home, and washed it out, and the next day showed up with her hair dyed punk green.

"My time at Dior was a great learning experience. I went to work every morning at 9:30, stayed there until I was supposed to leave and had a pay check at the end of every month. It was a real job. I had a little apartment in Paris and lived on my own. I was flattered that my father would trust me to do that. After all, I was barely 18. But I learned so much. I learned everything I know about fashion from Marc Bohan. He was great and I'll never be able to thank him enough for taking me in."

She traded Paul Belmondo for Anthony Delon, son of French actor Alain Delon, left Bohan and made a deliberate move to cash in on her good looks by becoming a model. "Actually, what I wanted to do was create my own bathing suit company. I planned it with a girl I'd met at Dior, but we needed to raise some money. I didn't want to ask my father for it. I have my own pride. I wanted to do it myself. Well, I knew a girl who worked as a model and she convinced me that I could earn enough modeling to start my company. So I became a model."

Five foot eight, thin, boyishly exotic, and with absolutely stunning blue eyes, she had no trouble at all getting work. There's no doubt she could have made it on looks alone, but being Princess Stephanie didn't hurt, and she quickly commanded fees of $5,000–$10,000 a day.

"I made the rounds with my portfolio under my arm," she recalls, "just like all models have to. And believe me, it's not a lot of fun. Most models are exploited. I know I was. I worked very hard at it, but most of the time photographers were more interested in their camera than they were in me. They didn't care how hot it was under the lights or how long the session lasted. If I complained they simply picked up the phone and asked for another brunette."

Talk was, at the time, that Rainier was not pleased with Stephanie's modeling. But she insisted that wasn't quite the case.

"If he was really unhappy about it he would have made me stop right away. The truth is that he let me go through with it."

A New York agency decided she was hot, and set up a US tour to launch her as a major new face in the States. They put a lot of money into promoting her, knowing how high the stakes could go if she hit it big. But, at the very last minute, the tour was cancelled. She'd called it off. Talk was, at the time, that Rainier was so upset with Stephanie that he'd simply pulled the plug on her career and forbidden her to go.

But she said, "That's not what happened."

She gave it up because she'd been working too hard in the months leading up to the tour and very suddenly took ill. "The day before I was to leave for the States, I'd been on a job. It was supposed to be done by six that evening but we didn't finish until two the next morning. I was so exhausted from working 60-hour weeks and such crazy schedules that when I got home I passed out. A friend found me unconscious on the floor and rushed me to the hospital."

Modeling had by this time put enough cash in her bank account to enable her to go into the bathing suit business. She and her partner brought out a line of swimsuits under the name Pool Positions, which they described as "sexy without being vulgar." They showed their first collection in Monaco, packed the audience with famous faces and immediately sold their wares to major outlets like Bloomingdales, Macy's, and Harrods.

It surprised her as much as anyone else that, in her very first year she'd invaded the market the way she did. "I'd like to think that most of our success was based on the bathing suits themselves and not merely on the fact that my name was involved. Sure we did the fashion show in Monaco because that helped. Why not? But in the end you have to please the buyers. If they can't sell the bathing suits in their stores it doesn't matter a damn to them who the designer is. If the bathing suits weren't good they would have said, 'This is all very nice but thank you anyway, we'll wait till next year.' Instead we had books and books of orders from around the world."

However, the partnership wasn't to be.

Personalities clashed, and only two years into the venture, the friend she'd started the company with walked out. "I felt betrayed and hurt when she left because I always considered her to be my friend. Friendship for me is so important and so hard to find. I guess maybe it's that way for everybody. I have one true, true friend in Paris whom I've known for 12 years. He's the kind of person I know I can call any time of the day or the night and if I need him, he'll be there. I just think it hurts more to be betrayed in friendship than it does in business or even in love."

Stephanie might have stuck with it, and made a go of it on her own, but Pool Positions soon took a back seat to music and acting when someone offered her the chance to cut a single. Her song, "Irresistible," shot to number one in the French charts. Although her voice was thin and there could never be any comparisons made to say, Barbra Streisand or Celine Dion, the record sold an impressive 1.3 million copies in Europe in the first 90 days and went on to pass five million. Her critics were fast to claim that the song didn't matter, that she'd merely cashed in on her name and big sales were to be expected.

"I wasn't expecting it to happen like that," she said. "I never thought the record would sell the way it did. But given the chance to sing I discovered that's what I really want to do. Singing and acting."

Parlaying a French pop song into a French acting career might have seemed logical for anyone else, but the downside of her chart success was the increasing awareness that if she was ever going to be known for what she did and not who her parents had been, she couldn't stay in France.

It began with the terror of having nearly been kidnapped. In November 1984, a couple tried to force their way into her car and drive off with her. "That was very strange. And there was a police station just across the street. I was pulling into the garage at my father's apartment when a guy put a gun to my head. I froze. My body was like jelly but my mind was functioning. I kept trying to squirm around in the car. I kept thinking, if he's going to shoot it's better to get it in the arm or the leg and not in the head. So I kept trying to push the guy away."

Stephanie went on, "Suddenly the girl accomplice appeared at the other side of the car and began yelling, 'Shoot her, shoot her.' Out of the blue I said to the guy, 'Look, my father is upstairs. If you want to speak to him, let's all go up there and talk it out.' I said, 'That's the best thing. Let's go upstairs and talk because nobody is going to pay for a dead body.' That's when the guy freaked out and left. He and the girl turned and ran away. That's when I freaked out, too. I crawled into the concierge's apartment and I was a mess. It was all very weird."

Next she had to confront the jealousy that seems to be one of the inevitable results of success. "It was driving me crazy. People kept asking me why was I working. They kept telling me that I was taking something away from someone who deserved success more than I did. They hurt me a lot. There was so much crap in the papers about me. They were saying that it was only because I was a princess that my record worked. My answer was, 'Selling five million records can't be because it's me, it's because people like the music.' Maybe I could sell 100,000 records because I'm me. But come on, never five million!"

No matter how she tried, she couldn't accept the way she was treated. "It gets down to sheer nastiness. You can be number two and everyone will always love you. However, if you're number one they have to try to destroy you. Did you know that when my record was number one on the French charts, a girl who had a song further down the list purposely tripped me one night while I was going on stage to sing and I broke my ankle? Can you believe that? I would never ever think of doing that to someone. But it doesn't happen like that in America. When I was looking for back-up singers in Los Angeles for my album, George Michael was there and he arranged for me to use his back-up group. He wanted to help me. I decided I couldn't handle things in Europe any more so I moved to America."

Underneath it all, she admitted, another factor played a part in her decision to leave France: the accident. "There was a lot of pressure on me because everyone was saying that I had been driving the car, that it was all my fault, that I'd killed my mother. It's not easy when you're 17 to live with that. There was so much magic that surrounded Mom, so much of the dream, that in some ways she almost stopped being human. It was difficult for people to accept that she could do something so human as to have a car accident. People figured I must have caused it because she was too perfect to do something like that. After a while you can't help feeling guilty. Everybody looks at you and you know they're thinking, how come she's still around and Grace is dead? No one ever said it to me like that but I knew that's what they were thinking. I needed my mother a lot when I lost her. And my dad was so lost without her. I felt so alone. I just went off to do my own thing."

In October 1986, Stephanie moved to California to pursue her singing and acting ambitions. She got herself an agent and started reading for parts. At one point she was getting 30 calls a week but turned everything down because it wasn't absolutely perfect. In the meantime, she began spending two hours a day with her vocal coach and meeting three times a week with Nina Foch, her acting coach. And while she was still one of the most recognizable women in Europe, no one seemed to care about that in Los Angeles.

Which was just what she'd been hoping for. "In Paris I get recognized all the time. Although once a woman came up to me in a bakery and said, 'It's incredible how much you look like Princess Stephanie.' So I answered, 'Don't talk to me about her. Every day somebody tells me that. Every day. What do I have to do, cut my hair not to look like her? I have enough of her. I'm really fed up with Princess Stephanie.' The poor lady kept apologizing and saying how awful it must be to look like her."

In California, she said, it was mainly French people who asked if she was Princess Stephanie. And then, of course, they always asked in French. "I found that if I stared at them and said in English, 'What? What did you say? What language is that?' they'd go away mumbling, 'No, no, it's not her.' Funny, but for Americans I'm not Princess Stephanie, I'm Grace Kelly's daughter. When Americans recognize me that's what they ask, are you her daughter? But what I really like about Los Angeles is that people don't bother with too much stuff like that. I'm just one well-known face among thousands of well-known faces. The average soap star is much more famous in LA than I am."

Unfortunately, in California she embarked on a series of romantic interludes that made the papers. There was a much publicized on-again, off-again fling with brat-pack actor Rob Lowe. There was even talk of marriage and supposedly, they gave each other friendship and/or engagement rings. The *New York Daily News* covered the affair much the way newspapers cover boxing matches, giving punch-by-punch descriptions for each round. A wedding was planned, then it was off, then they were dating again, then it was over for good.

Then she was linked with a twice-married, former waiter from Marseilles who had a criminal record for sexual assault in the United States. That romance lasted nearly two years.

"My dad wasn't exactly thrilled about him." She paused a moment before admitting, "but then nobody was. And I can understand why. But I look at it this way. I did what I had to do and eventually realized it wasn't what I wanted, so I got out of it. Life goes on. I don't regret anything. Dad must have understood what I was going through because I don't think he would have let me go through it for so long if he didn't know I was going to eventually realize it wasn't for me and come out of it all right. Otherwise he would have had me on the first plane back."

She felt he proved that he believed in her by letting her learn her own lessons. "He knows me pretty well. Sometimes he says that I'm the one who is most like him. I think it's true. We have very much of the same character although I don't get as carried away when I get angry as he does. I shake when he gets angry. It passes quickly. He doesn't stay angry long. But his voice changes and it gets pretty scary for a few minutes. Then he calms down and he's a sweet little pussy cat. Still, when he starts growling, it's best to get out of the way. He makes his point and you say to yourself, I don't think I want to get him angry ever again."

The episode strained Stephanie's relationship with Rainier.

Yet the door was never closed.

She said they both purposely made every effort, no matter what, to keep it open. "Sometimes growing up I forgot the door was open and my parents freaked out. It's the same with all parents and their children. I sometimes thought they were the ones closing the door when I was trying to keep it open, but I know now that wasn't quite the way it was. I realize how lucky I was because my parents always kept the door open."

Because her father kept the door open, she said it put their relationship on a different level. They began to communicate differently. He stopped thinking of her as his little baby. He still tried to protect her when he could but, she felt, it was on a more adult level. She hoped she'd proven to him that she could do her own thing in life, that she was responsible, and that their relationship was based on advice and support.

It was while living in California that she discovered, "He doesn't lecture me. I ask for advice and he gives it to me without insisting that I follow it. He'll say, 'This is what I think, now you go ahead and make whatever you want of it.' He and I are much closer than we've ever been."

Chapter 24

Rainier on Stamps, Russians, Prison, Banishment, and the Money in His Pocket

There are only two things you can do with a postage stamp.

You can stick it onto a letter and send it to someone.

Or you can put it into an album with a whole lot of other stamps and look at it from time to time.

But any stamp paid for and then pasted into an album is a service paid for and never returned in kind. Which is why post offices throughout the world—and Monaco among them—encourage stamp collecting.

It was Prince Charles III who, in 1885, created the principality's own stamps bearing the sovereign's effigy. Today they not only trace the principality's history but have also commemorated trains, planes, fish, fauna, flowers, racing cars, boats, local churches, saints, great works of art, animals, radio, television, sport, and the circus.

In short, anything and everything that might be considered a category for collecting.

Rainier took a personal an interest in the stamps, approving every new issue, not necessarily because he collected them—although the Palace museum exhibits every issue of the principality's stamps—but because for Grimaldi Inc., this is a very big business.

"We deliberately aim at the collectors' market," he explained. "While most other countries use modem offset printing methods, we engrave our stamps because we want them to appreciate in value as an encouragement to more collectors. However, it's a very delicate business. If you bring out too many stamps no one wants them and they lose their value in the market. If you bring out too few stamps you can't make enough money because you don't have the products to sell."

Grace's likeness had been appearing on Monaco's postage stamps since her marriage, and they sold to collectors in large numbers. "Grace" stamps were big business. But the image was always of "Princess" Grace.

Meantime, in 1993, the United States Postal Service decided to honor Grace with a stamp. But because federal law prohibits depicting foreign heads of state, the image they chose was from *Country Girl*, the 1954 film that had earned her an Academy Award.

Rainier agreed to use the same image.

So on March 24, 1993, two stamps were issued simultaneously—in Monaco, a five franc "Princess Grace" and in Hollywood, a 29-cent "Grace Kelly."

It marked the first time that Monaco officially acknowledged her film career with a stamp for collectors, and the first time that the US ever so honored a screen actress.

"Did you know," Rainier asked, "that the Russians used to come here during the Cold War? That's right. Soviet hydrographic ships came here because there is an International Hydrographic Bureau here. It was interesting because they always let people visit the ship. School children or anyone else who might be interested. We also got Russian trawlers stopping here. But they never let anyone visit those ships. I often wondered what they could fish because they had so many antennas sticking out of them. I was always amused when they pulled in here because the Russian sailors were allowed to walk around and see this capitalistic inferno. Funny, but I think most of them rather liked it."

Q: What's not to like?

A: There are some things I don't like.

Q: For instance?

A: For instance, gossip. I've already told you, gossip was invented in Monaco. Except that I couldn't care less about it. If somebody is going to bed with somebody else and they enjoy it, good for them.

Q: What about gambling?

A: It doesn't interest me. No member of the sovereign family is supposed to go into the casino here anyway. No nationals are supposed to play. It was clever of Prince Charles to do that. He didn't want Monegasques to lose their money and become a burden to the state.

Q: Horse racing?

A: That's fun. You go down to see if the horse has blue eyes or if the jockey is dressed in the right colors and bet on him. My father-in-law, Jack Kelly, used to invite friends and business associates, all men, to go to the Kentucky Derby every year. I went two or three times. He'd rent an entire train to take us from Philadelphia to Kentucky. It was really one gigantic booze-up. We'd arrive on Friday and stay on the train for the races on Saturday. The mint juleps never stopped. It was great.

Q: Do you know anything about horses?

A: I don't know anything about horses except the front from the back. But one Friday, I think it was the last race, there was a horse called Caine Run and the odds were so high they couldn't even post it. I decided to bet $25 on it. Jack Kelly and a few other guys tried to talk me out of it. They thought it was out of the question that the horse could win. Well, I felt this was such a poor horse that someone ought to put something on it. I finally talked them into forming a little syndicate and we each put $5 down. Guess what? The horse came in. I was worshipped from there on out.

Q: Do you still go to the races?

A: In Paris, every now and then. Because you can see what's happening. I could never get fascinated with a little ball spinning around a wheel. Although I will say that blackjack can be fun. For a while. I used to play a little gin rummy but I get bored with card games if they last too long. Poker is too slow. And as for board games, like Monopoly, I've never had much fun doing that. It goes on forever.

Q: My grandfather never played any card games and while my mother adored bridge, all I ever heard were arguments. "Why didn't you bid spades?" Or, "Why did you play a heart instead of a club?" It would go on for days like that. People would get so annoyed with each other that I've made it my business to stay away from it.

A: Any other games, like bridge?

While there are real differences between the influence a big country can exert and a small country can exert, being a small country like Monaco still has its advantages.

"To begin with," he noted, "we're not interested in possessing what our neighbors have. Then, because of our size, we're vulnerable. But that very vulnerability makes small nations the best champions of peace. Our survival depends on peace. The problem is that the voices of the world's small nations are usually so feebly heard."

It was under Rainier that Monaco was granted full-nation status at the United Nations. He also made Monaco's voice heard on matters such as pollution of the seas.

He'd been "infuriated that the seas have become a dumping ground for garbage and sewage in the midst of mankind's general indifference. Life depends on the water cycle, so what's endangered here is life itself. And we're not talking about something that can't be avoided because no unavoidable pollution exists. It's all caused by man. Pollution can be prevented. It only takes the will and the means to fight it."

And that's the hard part. "You can always get scientists to work, you can motivate them because they understand. The problem is in motivating the bureaucrats. They won't budge because it's against their nature. They're suspicious from the start. Our biggest hurdle was the French. Instead of worrying about pollution, they were more concerned with who'd have the day-to-day authority."

That's what big governments do, he said. "They get bogged down in their own bureaucracies. On the other hand, small governments can make things happen quickly. Big governments become encumbered. They become overburdened."

Monaco is one of the very few nations in the world that doesn't have a prison.

But there are 37 modern holding cells for people awaiting trial which stretch along the outer wall of *Le Rocher* facing the Mediterranean.

However, the rumor that this is "a slammer with a view of the sea" is not true. The best view any prisoner gets is of the sky. The only thing that makes the place special, Rainier mentioned, is that the warden's wife personally does the cooking. So Monaco's is almost certainly the best fed cellblock in the world.

Justice in the principality is rendered in the name of the prince, who can pardon or diminish sentences. But as the National Council long ago abolished capital punishment, the prince cannot decree, "off with his head."

And, even if he could, Rainier grimaced, he didn't intend that he ever would. "That's a pretty messy business."

Yet he can expel someone from the principality and, if he wants, by agreement with France, he can order the expulsion to include the three neighboring French *departements* which are the Maritime Alps, the Var, and the Lower Alps.

Not that it happens very often. That's usually restricted to people who are condemned in Monaco for criminal activity, such as cheating in the casino.

According to Rainier, "France has the same interest as we do in keeping certain people out of the region. The only exceptions to this are Monegasques. I cannot deprive them of their right to live in Monaco. Otherwise, they'd have no place else to go."

Another great benefit of a small country like Monaco, he said, "is that the contact is direct. You can get to people. Now, as the chief executive of my government, I'm not going to ask for something that's impossible because the National Council won't let me have it. But if there's something I feel should be a priority, then I can make it a priority even if the administration is holding it back. You can only do that in a small country."

His favorite example was his campaign for new-style national identity cards. When he first proposed them, he ran head first into a National Council which simply couldn't imagine why anyone would want to replace the old large, clumsy, over-sized piece of cardboard that folded three times, with something the size of a credit card.

"Look at this." He reached into his pocket and pulled a new Monaco ID card out of a small leather aide-memoire. It bore his photo, his name, and his registration number, which in this case happened to be 0001.

"Great, no?" He was very proud of how compact it was. "It doesn't take up any space. But you'll never believe how they fought me on this. The bureaucrats kept saying no, it will never do."

He waved it about triumphantly. "Of course, now everyone is lining up to take the credit for having thought of it."

That's when an odd question suddenly came to mind—What else do you keep in your pockets?

One of those rare questions he'd never been asked before, he shrugged and searched through his pockets to produce a packet of cigarettes, a lighter, the keys to his office safe, and the keys to his desk.

Then, out of the aide-memoire, he produced his driving license and a $100 bill. "I keep this for luck."

Q: No house keys?
A: No.
Q: No other money?
A: Yes, but I won't tell you how much.
Q: Oh, come on.
A: Enough, so that if I'm driving to work and run out of petrol I can fill up the car.
Q: Do you work every day?
A: There's always something to do. Even when I'm not in Monaco, there's always so much to read and there are always people to see.
Q: Don't you ever think of retiring?
A: Constantly.

Grace of Monaco

Q: Really?

A: Of course. I'll retire someday, except I can't tell you precisely when it will happen because I don't know when. It will be when Albert and I both feel that he's ready to take over. When he feels settled and confident. It will also have to do with when Albert gets married.

Q: Do you see yourself ever retiring here as a gentleman farmer?

A: No. I'm not that knowledgeable about farming.

Q: What grows here?

A: Mostly rocks. Farming is very difficult in this region. It used to be a beet-growing area, you know, sugar beet, until the economics of the region changed and now everybody grows corn and a bit of wheat. But I'm not terribly interested in that.

Q: So what will you do?

A: I have a lot of interests to keep me busy. I used to play tennis and ride horses but as I've gotten older I find I play more golf. I still ski and swim and scuba-dive every now and then. When I can find the time I also enjoy fishing. It's good for the nerves but I'm not very knowledgeable about that either. All I know is that when there's a storm they bite better.

Q: Do you have any good fishing stories? You know, about the one that got away?

A: With me they all got away.

Q: There must be more than fishing and golf.

A: There are plenty of things I'd like to do if I had the time. A mixture of traveling and seeing people I want to see, not only the ones I'm obliged to see. I'd like to spend more time in my workshop and arranging my property. I'd like to spend time at *Roc Agel* and Marchais and maybe even on my boat. I'd love to have the time to read all the diaries my great-grandfather left. They're handwritten accounts of his scientific expeditions.

Q: That's not bad. But is that all?

A: Maybe not.

Q: What else?

A: Ah, you know. Get into a lot of mischief. Take my revenge on society. Be rude to people. (He grinned widely and nodded several times.) Just do all the things I can't do now.

Chapter 25

Caroline—
Life Goes On

With Stefano's death, her life and family were thrown into turmoil, so Caroline withdrew to a farmhouse in the Luberon village of St. Remy, some three hours away from Monaco, to be alone with her family and to mourn.

She enrolled the children in the local school, and with great courage, helped them to get over the loss of their father. Unknowingly, they, in turn, helped her to get through that time. They were, she said, the reason she got out of bed every morning.

There is no doubt that she handled her husband's death with the same dignity that marked the way she handled her mother's. Still, the strain was evident. She lost a lot of weight, cut her hair very short, and dressed soberly. On those rare occasions when she was seen in public during the first year after Stefano's death, it was to visit his grave.

Rainier, trying to protect her from the media while allowing her time to grieve, excused her from all of her official duties, saying that she could resume them when she felt she was ready. Albert and Stephanie stepped in for her, not because Rainier wanted them to, but because they, too, shared Caroline's pain.

As Nadia Lacoste said at the time, "The calendar of the palace and the calendar of the heart are two separate things."

It took a full year before she felt confident enough to make her first few tentative steps back to public life. It took somewhat longer before she started to laugh again.

Caroline has always been a joyous woman but joy was slow in returning, hardly helped by tabloid gossip that placed her in dire financial straits. It wasn't true.

By leaving Monaco for the Luberon, she believed, it was easier for her to protect her children. They had all the obvious advantages there of small village life—like animals in the back yard—none of which they would have had as part of the sovereign family back in the Principality. She also hoped her children would be less accessible to the press. She was convinced that she and her brother and sister had been way too overexposed to the media in their own formative years, and that, in turn, the press had mistakenly come to believe that the three Grimaldis belonged to them, that the media had every right to follow them for the rest of their lives.

It was precisely the situation she wanted to avoid with her own children. All the more so, she said, because times had changed and these days that kind of exposure brings with it all sorts of ramifications.

In her mind, the security of her own children was paramount. But the media didn't care about that. The paparazzi staked out her home and followed her children to school. It took some time before the locals stopped giving tourists directions to her house, and once they did, only once they began showing their displeasure when photographers arrived to stalk Caroline and her children, did life take on some semblance of normalcy.

Throughout that first year after Stefano's death, and for the ensuing years, too, she stayed in touch with Stefano's family, understanding their loss, and also so that her own children would never feel estranged from their grandparents, aunts, uncles and cousins.

Sometime around 1990, or so, the tabloids linked her name romantically with a young French actor named Vincent Lindon.

For a while, Caroline and Vincent seemed more than just comfortable together, in spite of the fact that they had plenty of quasi-friends happy to relate the progress of their affair.

After tracing his paternal forebears to the Citroen automobile family and discovering that, on his mother's side, there was once a Third Republic government minister, the press took their gloves off and reported—on several occasions—that Caroline and Lindon had married.

Each time, the Palace had to deny the reports.

Eventually Rainier himself stepped in, promising journalists that if and when Caroline married, the Palace would announce it the same day.

But marriage with Lindon wasn't to be.

And with that Kelly-green Irish courage that so plainly marks all three of Grace's children, Caroline continued to get on with her life.

She had, since childhood, been a competent pianist and an avid reader with a wide range of interests—from the classics to 19th century opera critiques to contemporary fiction. At one point, just after her first marriage ended, she'd even flirted with the idea of writing.

In 1981 Caroline was approached by the *International Herald Tribune* in Paris to pen an article for them about her life in Monaco. She titled her professional debut as an author, "A Compulsive Need for Blue."

"The temptation is to glamorize one's childhood," she wrote. "It probably is in all small towns with beautiful surroundings. The weather is lovely throughout the four seasons. You spend a lot of time outdoors. But as children we were never quite aware of the total beauty. We never thought we lived in a place others considered unique."

She wrote that it wasn't until she was older and had traveled more that she came to understand how much she longed for the Mediterranean and its cloudless sky.

Then she gave an insider's view of the relationship shared by the locals and the invading armies of visitors.

"The rules are simple," she went on. "If you're part of the jet-set you don't just go somewhere, you make an entrance. Your conversation centers on other people's private affairs. You have your dinner on the terrace of the Hotel de Paris and fiddle with the caviar on your plate. The buses drive by endlessly. The people in them stare and point at the women, the champagne, at you. So on the one hand there are groups who stagger out of hot, smelly buses. On the other there are people trying to be beautiful and desperately cool, swelling with pride at the mere thought of showing off. Where and how do the Monegasques fit into this social jigsaw puzzle? Quite frankly, I don't think we do. We've had to learn to keep the visitor content, although it's not been without some grunting and groaning. Now we superbly ignore the anonymous masses as well as the insolent elite. Over the centuries, starting long before people traveled for pleasure, our unique concern has been to preserve a sense of national identity and to cling to it rather fiercely."

Unfortunately, the newspaper printed no more than excerpts of the piece, putting it next to an insipid photo of her aged eight or nine. It was a personal disappointment to Caroline, who'd worked hard to make the article right, and also to her mother who'd read it and felt Caroline might one day take her writing further.

Undaunted by having her work so badly mishandled like that, she wrote for French magazines and among her journalism credits was a very competent interview with the Italian opera star Ruggero Raimondi.

Although motherhood remained her first priority, she occasionally put pen to paper and along with a few friends in Paris helped out an annual satirical magazine.

She also had official duties in Monaco to cope with, especially when Grace died, because the burden of being Monaco's first lady fell on Caroline. She took over the Monaco branch of the Princess Grace Foundation and the Princess Grace Dance Academy, which had been designed by her mother to help young dancers. In addition, Caroline also assumed the president's chair at the Monaco Arts Festival.

"When Mommy was president of the festival," she noted, "it was a sort of curious formula, spread out throughout the year, where various performances came under the auspices of the festival. I know she was thinking of grouping everything into a two or three week period but never had a chance to do that. One of the things I did was make it a proper festival, taking up three weeks in Easter."

Putting her own stamp on the festival, Caroline helped to revive forgotten 17th and 18th century operas, catering to a more knowledgeable public. There was also a Baroque Music Festival, films on opera and music, sculpture exhibits, painting exhibits, photography exhibits, and some experimental theatre. And, in keeping with Monaco's tradition for ballet, Caroline completed her mother's work of creating a professional ballet company for the Monte Carlo opera.

It was, she said, a lot of work. "Setting it up, getting bookings and organizing tours, setting up the repertoire and getting the right choreographers. We try to keep a careful balance between Diaghilev and Ballet Russe repertoire and the big classics like *Swan Lake* and *The Nutcracker*. We also do some modern, experimental stuff."

At the same time she established a project of her own, called *Jeune J'ecoute*—a phone line to help young people in trouble with drugs, or the police, or their parents, or who are just unemployed and need some guidance.

Accepting the fact that much of the void left by Grace had to be filled by her, for all intents and purposes, it was a part-time job. Her children would always come first and Rainier appreciated that. He understood Caroline's desire to live in harmony with nature and out of the constant glare of publicity that dogged her life in Monaco. But then, he knew, perhaps better than anyone, why she wanted to raise her children in a way that her parents could never raise theirs.

"Sometimes," she said, "there's so much going on I don't even have time to think about it. The hardest thing is when you get these desperate letters from people who need help, whose lives are in a real mess. The hardest thing is to find a way to help them. Every day we get requests for help. I feel most of the time I'm really just a social worker trying to help people."

But again, that's not the way the press painted the picture. They saw her as a conniving sister intent on mounting a Palace coup.

So, she was asked, how about all those stories about wanting to take over the throne?

Her eyes lit up. "You mean the ones that say that I'm maneuvering in dark corridors in the Palace? All that intrigue and counterintrigue. Richelieu and Mazarin look like kids compared to what I'm apparently doing. The truth is that whenever I have any free time, instead of plotting, I spend it with the children. Frankly I can't wait for Albert to get married because then I can pass along a lot of my duties to his wife. Of course he keeps telling me he has to find the right girl. Well, at this stage I have so little time for myself and my children that sometimes, albeit only in my weaker moments, mind you, I think even I'd settle for Joan Collins."

While Caroline was still a teenager, Grace had arranged for her to meet one of Europe's most eligible young men. The rendezvous, well chaperoned, took place while Grace and Caroline were on a visit to Germany.

In Caroline's mind, this was never going to be anything more than tea and polite talk. On the other hand, Grace, the eternal matchmaker, was hoping that something might someday develop.

What it turned into was a ride in an uncomfortable car.

The young German fellow had just bought some sort of fancy sports car and, to show it off, he invited Caroline for a spin.

She couldn't say no, although when she saw how tiny the car was, she wished she had. It was so small she felt like a contortionist getting into it and then, once in it, she couldn't get out of it.

Back home, the episode turned into one of her funniest routines as she recounted—and even demonstrated—with great hysterics just how awkward the whole thing had been.

As for the German chap, she told her friends, it was an otherwise boring afternoon.

Twenty years later, she would find him considerably more fascinating.

As her romance with Vincent Lindon drew to a close, she and the German fellow rediscovered each other. It was during a ski trip in Switzerland.

He was Prince Ernst August of Hanover, head of the clan, and long married to a Swiss heiress, with two young sons.

Caroline and Ernst began meeting secretly.

Around the same time, autumn 1996, she started losing her hair.

Generally considered one of the most beautiful women in Europe, Caroline handled the problem with her usual elan, refusing to hide. Instead, she took an "in your face" attitude, donned turbans, scarves and hats, and even then allowed herself to be photographed without the turban—head shaved—in characteristic defiance to the press.

When the media reported that she was suffering from *alopecia areata*, a nervous condition which causes hair loss and is usually temporary, she refused to confirm or deny anything.

Next, the press decided, it must be something worse and guessed that she was having chemotherapy treatments for some undisclosed cancer.

Albert announced in an interview that Caroline's hair loss was due to a skin condition. But she wouldn't discuss it because, in her mind, it was absolutely nobody else's business.

She went about her life, which meant raising her children. And also spending time with the man who was fast becoming a part of it, Ernst.

Two years her senior, and tall enough so that she could wear heels, the customarily good natured Ernst was the oldest of six children to Prince Ernst August of Hanover and Princess Ortrud of Schleswig-Holstein-Glucksburg. His youth was divided between Marienburg Castle and a family estate outside Hanover.

Leaving school at the age of 15—because his hair was too long and he'd been caught smoking—he went to work on a farm, but returned to his education to study at the University of Guelph in Canada and at the Royal Agricultural College in England. Now a wealthy businessman and landowner—with property in Germany, Austria, London, and Kenya—he is the titular head of the House of Hanover, Germany's oldest royal family. He is also, a British royal. His great-great-grandfather, Ernest Augustus, was King of Hanover, Duke of Cumberland, and the uncle of Queen Victoria.

Being a woman meant that Victoria was ineligible to take the German throne, so the line passed down through her cousin and, eventually, to the young Ernst August. That makes him a cousin to Queen Elizabeth II. Which means he holds a British passport, in addition, of course, to his German passport.

Over the winter of 1996–1997, Caroline and Ernst took a holiday together in Thailand. Soon after they returned to her home in the Luberon, Ernst's wife of 16 years, Chantal, filed for divorce. It was granted in September 1997, awarding her around $10 million, but stipulating that the couple should have joint custody of their two boys, then 14 and 12.

Described in the press as Caroline's "bespectacled suitor, with his amiable, slightly chubby face and frizz of hair falling on to his forehead," he'd never been much of a headliner maker in Germany. Or, for that matter, in London where he and Chantal had been raising their children.

However, if there is such a thing as "the curse of the Grimaldis," it is that they shall not be free from tabloid prying, and Ernst soon discovered how the paparazzi's constant presence made it easy to make all the wrong kinds of headlines.

His temper flared once too often when cameras were shoved into the couple's faces and a German photographer wound up on the wrong end of Ernst's umbrella. The episode ended up in court and cost Ernst over $50,000, the bulk of it supposedly to keep the photographer from filing criminal charges.

The press was also, certainly, the reason why their wedding on January 23, 1999—which happened to be Caroline's 42nd birthday—was not announced until the day before.

At 11:30 that morning, the couple was married in a private ceremony held in the Mirror Room at the Palace. It was attended only by close friends and family, including Rainier and Albert, Caroline's aunt Antoinette, Caroline's three children, and Ernst's two.

For her own reasons, Stephanie was not there.

Once their vows were taken, Caroline became Her Royal Highness Caroline Princess of Hanover, Duchess of Brunswick and Luneburg.

Not surprisingly, there'd been speculation about the wedding for months. The media decided that it would happen momentarily, not just because they'd photographed Caroline and Ernst in the royal box at the Circus Festival, but because they'd cottoned onto the rumor that she was expecting her fourth child. The Palace refused to confirm or deny that rumor, even though it was true.

Before any wedding could be planned, however, the couple had to secure certain permissions. They needed Rainier's consent. And because of Ernst's status as a member—albeit distant—of the British royal family, they also needed authorization to marry from the Queen of England.

Presumably, they bothered to ask.

Technically, there was no way she could have refused.

Chapter 26

Albert— Friends and Lovers

The greatest problem, Albert found growing up—echoing his father's and sisters' sentiments—was recognizing true friendship. "I don't think there's any clear-cut recipe. You just have to feel the person out. You watch them in certain situations. I was going to say you test them, but that's not really what I do. I find it's interesting to see a person's reaction to a given situation. Of course, it's not always fair to define the terms of friendship because a lot of friendships are based on help-ing each other. But when it starts becoming a one-way street, when that person is asking you for a lot of favors, I suppose that's when you have to start taking a longer look at that friendship."

Which is not something that, as an adult, got any easier to deal with. "I know Dad had a lot of wonderful friends but many of them have since died so I guess it's especially tough for him. It's difficult for him to make new friends. Even if he has a lot of acquaintances, it's not the same as an old friend he knows and can trust."

He noted that while his father managed to cope with being alone and working alone and not seeing other people for a certain period of time, it was different for him. "I can't. I need to have people around."

Another troublesome area was his constant need to be aware of his own visibility. "Someone told me once that my mom was working a lot more than my dad because she was seen giving prizes and going to charity meetings. They saw her more often than they saw him so they assumed she was working more than he was. Some of the functions that we do, in fact most of the functions we attend, I consider work because I wouldn't necessarily choose to be there if I didn't have to be there. But there's a big difference between representation kind of work and sitting behind a desk. I'm understanding that not everyone makes that distinction for us."

Once Grace was gone, Albert moved back into the private apartments at the Palace. "Otherwise my father would be living alone."

He didn't mind. It's a very comfortable place to live and, anyway, he enjoyed spending time with his dad. "We talk a lot."

Albert knew that his father appreciated having the company.

Rainier was also very understanding when, on certain nights, Albert announced that he wouldn't be home.

He kept an apartment in town—when Rainier was a young man, they were called "love nests"—because Albert and Rainier both believed it would be inappropriate for him to bring women back to the private apartments to spend the night.

Like his father, when Albert reached a certain age, he, too, got labeled, "most eligible young man in the world."

But the title confounded Albert. "It's funny, but I've never seen myself as the most eligible bachelor in the world. It still surprises me when I read that. People are always trying to fix me up. I have a whole file of mothers trying to marry off their daughters, complete with pictures. It's hysterical. I also get pictures of girls practically offering their services. But the worst is when an old friend of the family says, why don't you come for dinner because I'd love you to meet so and so. I can't stand that."

His name was romantically tied—real or otherwise—to Cathy Lee Crosby, Brooke Shields, Daryl Hannah, Sharon Stone, Brigitte Nielsen, Fiona Fullerton, Kim Alexis, Lisa Marie Presley, Claudia Schiffer, Naomi Campbell, Italian television presenter Gabiria Brandimarte, and actress Catherine Alric, who allegedly returned his apologetic flowers, along with his luggage, with a note which read, "Love without faithfulness is like a flower without sun."

Granted, meeting women was never very difficult. "At discos or restaurants or at parties or on the beach or even on the street, I say hello to girls. Why not? I like that sort of thing."

But forming a serious relationship that he could take seriously was quite another. "I always have to ask myself, is she with me because of me or because of who I am. When I meet women it's, okay, she seems nice, but what is she really here for? What is her hidden agenda? Also, I know very well, that when the time comes the woman I marry will have to withstand not only pressure from the media, but also from local people. She's going to be under intense scrutiny and will have to withstand inevitable comparisons to my mother. That's not an easy burden for anyone to live up to."

Nor was easy for him to deal with the media's obsession with one very specific question—when will Albert get married?

"It's been very annoying," he said. "It is very unpleasant, and I don't know what to say now to calm everybody down. I'm sure everyone will know in time when the real one will be here. It's a question of timing. You don't feel ready or you don't feel confident or you haven't met the right person. Maybe it's my desire to be independent that has also prevented me from having a steady relationship. But I won't get married just to please people."

Rainier said often, "I would like him to take things in hand and at the same time to set up a family. This is important."

But all parents say that about their unmarried offspring and Albert insisted, "I will make the right decision when the time for that decision is right. I will marry when I find the right person."

For the record, there was no requirement that Albert marry a Catholic, but his children have to be raised in the faith because they will be next in line. Should he never produce an heir, the line would pass through Caroline to her son Andrea.

Rainier long ago resigned himself to Albert's timetable, although there were moments when he displayed mild impatience. Like when *Time* magazine asked him, "Are you worried that Albert is still single?"

He responded, "No. He is very choosy. And the example of his sisters' divorces affected him. But he will have to found a family, that's important."

Unfortunately for Albert, hand-in-hand with being such an eligible bachelor, came the dangers of being a target for women with their own agenda. A passionate encounter in 1986 with a German model led Albert into the embarrassment of a paternity suit. A court ordered blood test proved he wasn't the father.

Also, as is the case with many men who reach a certain age and are not yet married, rumors circulated that he was gay. And those rumors proved hard to shake off because many people wanted to believe he was.

Credit to Albert, however, he didn't lose a lot of sleep over those rumors. "I was hurt by the allegations. Those kinds of things are never very pleasant. But I learned to shrug them off. The people I care about know the real me. I stopped paying attention to that stuff a long time ago. When I first heard those rumors, I protested whenever I could. Seeing how that merely gave more attention to the rumors, I finally gave up because there is very little we can do."

After graduating from Amherst with a degree in Political Science, Albert served six months in the French Navy, as junior officer on the helicopter carrier *Jeanne d'Arc*. He spent the next five months in the management trainee program at Morgan Guaranty Trust in New York. He followed that with a short management apprenticeship at Wells, Rich and Green Advertising in New York and a training program in Paris in the marketing department at Moet Chandon.

"The stay at Moet was my father's idea. He wanted me to get a feel for the way a major French conglomerate operated. But the look into banking and advertising was my idea. I then returned to New York in the spring of 1986 to spend some time in a law firm, doing all sorts of paralegal stuff."

Albert was not only the first prince to attend high school in Monaco, he was also the first to have been trained in the ways of the corporate world. "I think banking and marketing are part of what my job is all about, although it's hard for me to give a clear-cut program or to express my ideas and tell you what I'll do when I take over."

Reluctant to be too specific, he believed Monaco should continue developing tourism, light industry, real estate, and banking. He was equally interested in exploring new areas of expansion. "I'd like to see Monaco become a major European financial center but we have to be careful how we go about that and with whom we're going to do it."

While none of his plans were in any way conflicting with the options his dad had chosen in recent years, he cautioned, "If I express them too strongly, people will think that I want to push him aside."

With no firm indication coming from Rainier when it would happen, except to say, "It will happen when we both feel ready for it to happen," rumors of Albert's immediate ascension to the throne regularly cropped up.

On the eve of the 700th anniversary of Grimaldi rule, Rainier told *Time* magazine, "I don't want to hang on, but I want to find the appropriate moment, when Prince Albert and I feel that he is ready to take over. Now we are in a period where he is acquiring the experience to run what is in effect a big business."

People claiming to be close to Rainier took that to mean it would happen on Rainier's 50th anniversary in 1999. It didn't. But then, that's what they'd predicted when Rainier turned 70; had promised it would happen in 1997 as part of the 700th anniversary celebrations; and guaranteed it was in the works for 1998 when Rainier turned 75.

Throughout those years, whenever he was asked about it, Albert found himself in a no-win dilemma. "If I say, I'm ready now, then it will be interpreted that Albert wants to kick his father out of here, and that's the last thing I want to do. If I say I don't know, then they say that Albert is so weak and so shy, he's not interested. I'm no ogre for power, trying to kick him out. When it's time, I'll be there."

Anyway, he'd grown comfortable with the status quo. Learning his trade at his father's side was a working relationship that both of them enjoyed. And for many of those years, both of them had come to terms with the inevitable, that succession would happen when it happened. Neither Rainier nor Albert ever hid their hope that succession would happen while Rainier was still alive, so that father could sit in his easy chair in *Roc Agel* and look down from the mountain to be there when son needed advice. But just as marriage had to be Albert's call, succession would always be Rainier's, and deep down both of them understood that it might only happen with Rainier's death.

In that lengthy 1997 *Time* interview, Rainier expressed his full confidence in Albert, certain that the Grimaldis would endure. "We've handled ourselves very well up to now even though a certain press likes to exploit all kinds of things. Members of royal families are human beings like other people, with their faults and their good qualities. I get very annoyed at the tendency to mix up information and indiscretion. But I think the Grimaldis have worked a lot for the principality. Our great strength is the union between our family and our people."

He later said, in a speech to his people, "It is a proud principality, altruistic, and confident in its future, that I would like to leave for Albert," and called on his people, "To assure me and to assure him of your support, your faith and determination."

That prompted all sorts of speculation that Rainier was really saying, Albert wasn't ready, that Albert still had a lot to learn. But some insiders felt that wasn't at all the case. They argued that Albert was more than ready by the time of the 700th anniversary. Rainier's stepping aside then was a viable option, as it was the following year on the 50th anniversary of his reign. That he didn't abdicate said more about Rainier than it did about Albert. No one knew the workings of the principality better than Rainier and no one knew better than him that those waters were filled with sharks.

That he didn't step aside when all the indications were right to do so was because he so feared what those sharks might do to his son.

So while he waited for the ultimate promotion to ruling prince, Albert presided over several charities, including the Red Cross, was head of the tourism board, and chairman of the 700-year Celebrations Committee.

In 1985 he became a member of the International Olympic Committee and in 1994 was named president of the Olympic Committee of Monaco. He attended more than 300 official engagements a year, both at home and overseas, doing everything from handing out prizes to school children to cutting ribbons at fairs, from representing Monaco at the enthronement of Emperor Akihito of Japan and at the funeral of Norway's King Olav, to accompanying Monegasque trade delegations around the world, drumming up business for the principality.

He said he never minded most of the work he did as prince-in-waiting—admitting that he even enjoyed a lot of it—but that he was never totally comfortable in the limelight. "I bear it."

At times he bore it very well. At a Princess Grace Foundation dinner in New York, he was introduced to Tyne Daly, who insisted he sing a duet with her. They did "True Love," the song Grace did with Bing Crosby in *High Society*. It proved he can sing. And if he was uncomfortable on the inside, he seemed to be enjoying himself on the outside.

Where he was always totally at one with himself was when he was involved with sports in general and bobsledding in particular.

He'd seen bobsledding firsthand at the 1980 Olympics, first tried a two-man sled while on a skiing holiday in St. Moritz in 1985 and, the following year, formed the Monaco Bobsled and Skeleton Federation. He intended to put a team together to represent the country at the 1988 Winter Olympics in Calgary, Canada.

It meant starting from scratch, hardly an easy thing to accomplish in a country with no mountains, no snow, and hardly anyone who'd ever been in a bobsled. He nevertheless managed it, and he captained Monaco's first two-man bobsled at the Calgary games. They finished way down towards the bottom, but this wasn't about winning races. He was never under any illusions about that. "It's difficult to put a bobsled team together from a country that only has 6,200 nationals." This was about Albert saying he could get a team there to compete, and doing it. In that sense, he won big.

"There were some people in Monaco who weren't thrilled at the idea of me going down an ice track in a sled going 90 miles an hour," he said. "I heard all the rumors, like how this was just my toy, that I was just doing it to show off. But I didn't start this for myself. I loved the sport and I wanted to bring it to Monaco."

Immediately following Stefano Casiraghi's death, Albert announced his retirement from a sport that was, decidedly, very risky for an heir to a throne. But by 1992, he and Team Monaco were back competing at the Albertville, France games and returned two years later to the games at Lillehammer, Norway. His final appearance as an Olympiad was in a four-man in 1998 at Nagano, Japan. Never having finished higher than 25th in a two-man event, that year he only came in 26th.

But at every one of his four Olympic appearances, he reinforced the point that Monaco could compete, and win friends for the country. It was not as much an exercise in international diplomacy as it was a statement about international sportsmanship.

To everyone's surprise—albeit typical of a man whose image is that of "the people's prince"—the sporting press discovered what the tabloid press had never known. That Prince Albert was good at being just plain Al Grimaldi, a guy who shunned fancy hotel suites to live in the decidedly less-than-luxurious conditions of the Olympic village.

"I don't consider you get the fullest experience out of the Games if you don't live in the village," he explained, as if they should have guessed by now that's the sort of person he is: an athlete who could be just one of the guys. A man born with a silver spoon in his mouth who was equally comfortable with plastic trays, paper plates, and cramped rooms. Someone who was rarely allowed to be that kid at summer camp in the States or that young man in a dorm at Amherst.

"It is a relief from everyday duties," he said. "A great way to clear your mind. I don't ask for extra privileges. It's rare to get such privacy."

But four Olympics weren't just about clearing his head or a search for privacy. Competing in sports, he said, had also given him one very important thing that neither money nor position could buy. And that was, confidence.

"I had a big confidence problem when I was growing up. I went through a period when I was very shy and had problems expressing myself. I had some therapy, but sport has helped me an awful lot. It is not only the physical change that goes along with being competitive in sport but also the character and the dedication you need. It makes you grow as a person."

He announced at Nagano that those games would have to be his last because the demands on his time were getting in the way of the rigorous training schedule that this level of competition required. "I never thought I was going to last 12 years."

Age was catching up to him, too. "There have been times when I have come back from a function and gone to the gym at one in the morning." And while he admitted that there have been times when, at official functions, his mind has wandered back to bobsledding—"It happened to me once at a concert. I tried to visualize a track and had my eyes closed. People must have thought I had fallen asleep"—with some obvious remorse he told the press at Nagano, "I think we're looking at pretty much the waning moments of my 12-year career."

What he didn't say was that Rainier was increasingly concerned—"not outwardly anxious," as one friend put it, "just increasingly concerned"—that the heir to his throne was still engaged in such a dangerous sport. In turn, Albert was increasingly concerned with his father's health. Although Albert didn't help matters when he joked that his retirement from the sport might only be temporary. "I seem to have come out of retirement a few times already."

That sort of candor was one of the things that marked his style. Like his mother, he always demonstrated just how approachable he could be. And how disarming, too, especially when it came to humor. At that same press conference, a cellphone rang. He noticed it belonged to a female reporter. Before it could ring a second time, Albert quipped, "Would you like me to answer that?"

Chapter 27

Stephanie— Following Her Heart

As Stephanie slipped through her mid-20s, she seemed more settled and more together than at any time in the previous 10 years, thanks in large part to an American record producer she'd fallen in love with, named Ron Bloom.

"My father likes him," she said at the time. "He's in his mid-30s, writes music and lyrics, plays 20 instruments, and produces my records. He and I have a lot in common. We have a great relationship. He's a very intelligent man, with strong family values and roots. He's someone who's been raised with family values and that's important to both of us. After my breakup with my previous boyfriend, when I might not have been on the best of terms with my father, Ron was the one who helped me realize how important it was to get back on good terms with my dad. He helped me a lot with that. He told me, 'The most important thing you have is your family. They love you and will always love you so don't close yourself off from them. Show them that you love them, too.' That was very important to me."

Bloom was the catalyst in patching up her relationship with her father.

Stephanie and Rainier spoke two or three times a week by phone talking about all sorts of things and telling each other the latest jokes. "We're very close," she said, "all four of us. At one point or another I guess one of us might have drifted off for a while to do his or her own thing but we always come back home. A family is a family and that's the best thing in the world."

Before she and Bloom were romantically involved, while she was trying to get her life straightened out, he kept saying to her that he wanted them to have a real relationship but that he also wanted them to take their time. "He said he didn't want me falling into his arms because I was under some sort of emotional stress. He kept saying, 'I'll be your friend until you're ready for something more.' That was the best form of respect anyone's shown me in many years."

When they both felt the time was right, they decided to look for a house together. "We lived together for four months in a hotel while we tried to find a place. That's the toughest test I can think of for a relationship. Four months in a hotel room. If you can survive that, you can survive anything."

They eventually found a house in the Valley, with a domestic who came in twice a week to help with the housework and a gardener who stopped by a couple of times a week to work on the shrubs. But otherwise they had no staff. Stephanie did the shopping and most of the cooking—just for the record she is probably the best cook in the Grimaldi clan.

When Rainier visited Stephanie in Los Angeles, he was happy enough with what he saw of her life there to stay an extra five days.

Although he stayed in a hotel, he arrived at her house every morning at 10:30 and, just like so many dads everywhere, showered his little girl with gifts. The very first day he got there he walked around the house, took note of what she needed and promptly went with some of his friends to a local shopping mall to buy her, among other things, a microwave oven.

Her first album was released in the United States in spring 1989. The songs on it were written by her and Bloom. "It was tough work but it was good work. I love performing. It's weird, I can't stand up and make a speech to people because I get so nervous but when I get up on a stage and sing I'm not nervous at all. And then there's the applause. It sends shivers up my spine. It's really a high. It's the most beautiful thing to have a contact with your audience, especially when you're singing a ballad and everybody in the audience holds up their lighters. It's like a huge birthday cake."

Singing was now more important than just about anything else, but she deliberately made a point of showing her father that it was not at the expense of her responsibilities back home in Monaco. "I have always done whatever I'm asked to do and, among other things, I'm on the organizing committee for the Circus Festival. The thing is that people tend to forget how young I am. People tend to say, Stephanie doesn't do anything and refuses responsibilities. But it's only been a couple of years that anybody's asked me to do anything and when they've asked I've accepted."

The romance with Bloom came to an end in early 1990. The two broke up quite suddenly, and the next anyone knew, Stephanie was being escorted all over Paris by a young French real estate developer, Jean-Yves Le Fur.

She was also being reliably quoted as saying, this is the real thing.

Le Fur apparently won her father's approval and in April of that year, the Palace officially announced Stephanie's engagement. She never hid the fact that what she wanted most in life was to find the right man, to settle down, and to have a family of her own.

For a while, it seemed as if she'd finally found it. But by mid-summer, the wedding date was still not fixed and some of her friends were beginning to say it wouldn't happen.

Stephanie returned to California to finish recording her album. Her father accompanied her. Talk of marriage was abandoned.

To get her singing career off the ground, she embarked on what she hoped would turn out to be a world tour. Because Prince Rainier understood the security implications involved in a prolonged series of public appearances, part of her entourage included a young Monegasque policeman named Daniel Ducruet. By the time she returned from that tour, she and Ducruet were an item.

A local fellow, born in 1964 just across the Monaco border, on the French side, in Beausoleil, Ducruet came to their relationship with a bit more baggage than Rainier appreciated. Described by one reporter as, "Gold chains, tattoos, and a coppery tan," Ducruet was divorced when he met Stephanie, but living with another woman with whom he'd only just had a son. But none of that mattered to Stephanie who, typically headstrong, moved into a small apartment in Monte Carlo with him.

Their first child, Louis, was born in November 1992. Their second, Pauline Grace, followed in May 1994. That they still hadn't bothered to marry shocked a lot of people.

But Stephanie couldn't have cared less. "If I shock people," she said, "tough luck."

With motherhood, a radiant new Stephanie emerged.

She and Ducruet set about making a life for themselves. He left the police and started some small businesses, among them a private protection agency. He also took up rally car racing.

Rainier's health was not good and doctors ordered a double bypass. When he came out of the hospital, still smoking cigarettes against the strict orders of his physicians, Stephanie went to her father and secured his permission to marry Ducruet.

It was probably not by coincidence that it happened when it did.

Rainier's heart problems presented his three children with his immortality.

Perhaps the illness had mellowed him a bit, too. Although, at his insistence, the prenuptial agreement stripped Ducruet of any claims on Stephanie and also of custody rights to their children.

Stephanie and Daniel Ducruet were married in a private ceremony at the Palace in July 1995. Both their children were there, as was Ducruet's son.

So, too, Albert, Caroline, her children and, of course, Rainier.

A mere one year and eight weeks later, Ducruet proved Rainier right in having demanded a prenuptial agreement. On a trip to Belgium, Ducruet met a stripper whose claim to fame was that she'd been Miss Nude Belgium. Several weeks later, the two ended up cavorting nude on the edge of a swimming pool at a private villa just down the beach from Monaco in Villefranche.

No fewer than 40 pages of photos suddenly appeared in Italian magazines.

Such massive publicity didn't do any harm to Stephanie's career, but it was enough to ruin her marriage.

Ducruet's excuse was that he'd been set up.

Stephanie's reaction was to ring for her lawyers and within a few months, the Palace announced that she'd finalized her divorce.

Privately she began telling friends, "I see men in a very different way now."

Publicly she admitted, "The best way I've found to deal with it was just to look at it straight on, facing people's looks and their remarks. I don't know if you gain wisdom by suffering, but at one point you just say, now, enough is enough."

To raise some money and, at the same time, in a vain attempt to get back into his ex-wife's good graces—he would tell anybody who asked that he was still the perfect match for her—Ducruet published a book in France called, *Letter to Stephanie*. It was marketed by the publisher as, "An apology."

But, in lieu of serious contrition, he filled the book with gossip, explaining for example, how the first time he and Stephanie met, they took one look at each other and knew they were meant to be. A few days later, he said, she summoned him to a 2 A.M. hotel suite rendezvous. He justified the pillow talk nature of the book by noting that it was in the best of taste because he did not go into any graphic detail about their lovemaking.

This, from the same man who justified his having been caught with a stripper by saying, "I was trapped." He was now claiming that there was some sort of drug in the glass of champagne the stripper had given him. Although he eventually admitted that he had no proof of drugs being present.

His rationalization was, "If I had had all my mental capacities, I would never have done what I did."

Seizing on the story, one French newspaper claimed that Ducruet had been set up by the Italian Mafia. Another insisted that the divorce settlement included $3,000 a month alimony which Stephanie would pay to Ducruet. A third reported that not only had the photographs been widely sold, there was also a video of Ducruet and the stripper on sale just across the Italian border in the market town of Ventimiglia.

A columnist for the prestigious French newspaper *Le Monde* actually blamed the whole mess on the Grimaldis themselves. He wrote that they had been, "caught in a trap of its own making, having systematically auctioned off photo albums on any and every occasion."

As far as Ducruet was concerned—at least, according to what he told Britain's *Telegraph* newspaper—he'd made just one mistake with the stripper. "My only fault was to go to that villa out of stupidity. But I was sorry for her. She sounded sad when she phoned me. And you know, I had no female friends because I couldn't risk being pictured even taking coffee with a girl, so for me it was nice to have female company for once."

He said he'd offered up to $2 million to get the photos back, and could have raised the money from friends, but whoever had them refused, reinforcing his theory that, because money was not the issue, character assassination was. "Everything would have been different. I would have paid and it would have saved my marriage from divorce. But they didn't want my money. It's really too bad."

Commented the *Telegraph*, "His words betray him as much as any photographs. Where a better actor would stick to the script of re-pentant humbug, he veers off into a description of his ideal world, where the eleventh commandment—Thou Shalt Not Get Caught—is worth all the others rolled together."

Following her divorce, Stephanie remained low key, dividing her time between her main priority—two children—and the business she'd set up some years before, the Replay Cafe and Store. It was a bistro and boutique where she tended to work every day, sometimes in the restaurant, sometimes selling in the boutique, taking the venture seriously. She stubbornly molded out a normal life for herself and her two children.

As she told Diane Sawyer in an American television interview just after her divorce, "I think the main thing is I learned a lot about myself. And the best way I found to deal with it was just to look at it straight on, look at the problem straight on. And so I did it that way by being in my store and my restaurant right after everything happened and facing the people's look and their remarks. And that's what helped me. I don't know if you really gain wisdom by suffering, but you know, at one point, you just say, enough. You know, stop pointing at me. It's just, enough is enough."

To that she added, "I'd like people to try and put themselves in my skin."

Rumors that she was pregnant for the third time began circulat-ing in February 1998, when the ever-present paparazzi decided she'd started taking on weight.

At Monaco's Rose Ball, a month later, they watched her every move, and confirmed her pregnancy when they decided she was carrying a bouquet of flowers in such a way as to hide her bulging tummy. That Caroline was also carrying a bouquet of flowers did not change their opinion.

Questions from the media went unanswered. Neither Stephanie, nor the Palace—at Stephanie's express request—would confirm her pregnancy. Nor would anyone reveal the name of the baby's father. The press was left to conclude that the baby's father was her latest boyfriend, a 30-year-old French ski instructor named Jean-Raymond Gottlieb.

When they next spotted Stephanie and her two children at a local ski resort without Gottlieb, they claimed the pregnancy had been the cause of the couple's breakup.

Camille Marie Kelly Grimaldi was born on July 15, 1998.

Although Stephanie had raised her first two without in-house help, Camille's arrival left her with very little time and she finally gave in to her father's, brother's, and sister's advice and hired a live-in nanny.

Stephanie continued to appear at various music awards' shows taped in Monaco, and also co-produced and co-hosted the annual Champions of Magic show on America's ABC Television Network. Her only demand in the taping schedule was that she wouldn't work Wednesday afternoons. "My kids have sports activities. That's a non-shooting day for me."

She cut her hair short, donned large glasses, stayed pencil thin and chain-smoked.

Into her mid-30s, with nothing to prove to anyone, she was still constantly confronted like a rebellious youth and, much to her own annoyance, forever trying to convince the media, "I am not a rebel princess. I have simply lived the life of a girl my age. I've always respected my family and protocol."

She showed up at all the events where her presence was required and at most of the events where her presence had been requested. She maintained her dignity. But still the media trailed after her, looking for other stories to tell.

But when they got it, which they did at the Circus Festival in 2000, it wasn't the wild child, rebel princess story they'd been hoping for.

Rainier was in hospital.

Stephanie was there when the announcer asked the crowd to acknowledge the work Rainier had done for the festival and the principality.

The entire audience rose to their feet and tumultuously applauded her father.

And his baby daughter broke down in tears.

Chapter 28

The Accident

One afternoon in Monaco, late in the 1970s.

Grace was driving alone in her converted London taxi. It was an amusing car, easy to handle in the narrow streets. And with its big back seat there was always plenty of room for her kids, for other people, and piles of packages.

She was a slow, deliberate driver. So slow in fact that whenever her children came along they'd tease her, "We could walk there faster."

Now she pulled the old cab out of the Rue Grimaldi and into the Place d'Armes. She had her glasses on—she always wore them when she drove—but she must have come into the intersection without looking because an Italian, with the obvious right of way, shot across the square directly in front of her.

She rammed him broadside.

Startled but unhurt, she got out of her car to apologize. She was clearly in the wrong and she was willing to admit it.

But the Italian was too furious for polite conversation.

He jumped out of his car, pointed to the damage, and screamed at her.

She tried to calm him down, saying, you're absolutely right and please don't worry because my insurance will cover all the damage.

The Italian didn't want to know. He yelled at her and insulted her.

Within seconds, the policeman guarding the road that goes up to *Le Rocher* rushed over, saluted her, and asked the irate Italian to calm down.

The officer told the man, "Madame says she's sorry and will take care of all your expenses."

But the Italian was too far gone. "This bitch ran into me."

The policeman strongly advised the man to keep quiet.

With arms flying about, the Italian shouted at her again, his vocabulary descending into the gutter.

Now the officer took control, warning the Italian in no uncertain terms, "If you open your mouth one more time you're going to jail. If you insult the Princess of Monaco one more time, I'll arrest you."

That stopped the Italian. He spun around to take a close look at the woman who'd smashed into his car and finally realized who she was.

She continued to reassure him, "It was my fault and everything will be taken care of."

A car soon arrived from the Palace to fetch her.

The damages to the Italian's car were made good by her insurance company.

And Grace began telling friends, "I'll never drive again."

It was a promise she failed to keep.

September 1982

On Friday morning the 10th, Stephanie returned to Monaco from Antigua where she'd been spending the last few weeks of her summer holidays. While she was in the West Indies, she'd suffered

Grace of Monaco

a water skiing accident and split open her head so badly she needed stitches. A chauffeur brought her from Nice airport to *Roc Agel* where she spent the next few jet-lagged days trying to reassure her parents that she was all right.

On Saturday morning the 11th, Nadia Lacoste rang Grace at *Roc Agel.*

Stephanie and Grace were booked to catch the train from Monaco to Paris on Monday night, arriving early Tuesday morning so that Stephanie could start school on Wednesday.

Lacoste was concerned with how Grace planned to keep the paparazzi away from Stephanie on her first day back. She suggested Grace and Stephanie should not spend Tuesday night at the family apartment in Paris.

She told Grace, "The photographers will undoubtedly be hanging around the apartment on Wednesday morning, so why not spend Tuesday night at someplace like the Hotel Maurice? It's close to the school and no one will find you there."

Grace thought it was a reasonable idea. Although she did have to concede, "No matter what we do, they're bound to find out."

On Sunday the 12th, Grace's former secretary, Phyllis Blum, now Phyllis Earl, rang from London to talk about Grace's trip to England in 10 days' time, and the poetry readings that were planned for the third tour of America. At one point in their conversation, driving was mentioned and Earl told Grace, "Don't forget to wear your seat belts."

That same afternoon, Caroline flew to London to spend the week at Forest Mere, a health farm in the Hampshire countryside.

On Monday the 13th, at around 9 A.M., Grace woke Stephanie, then went into Albert's room to say good morning. He'd been to Italy over the weekend to see a soccer match with friends and had got back to *Roc Agel* late the night before.

"Mom came to wake me up," he recalled, "and we talked a bit. Then she said, 'See you later.' I had to come down to the Palace for something that morning, so I said, 'Sure, see you later.'"

While Grace was getting ready to leave for the Palace, her chauffeur brought the ll-year-old, metallic green Rover 3500 out of the garage and parked it in front of the house.

Normally Stephanie would have done that.

All three Grimaldi children had been allowed to drive the car from the garage to the house at *Roc Agel* before they had a license. All three had scooted around in Rainier's golf cart or played with his jeep there. All three practiced driving at *Roc Agel*.

But Grace and Rainier had also laid down very strict rules that, as long as they were under age, they could only drive on the family's private property. Until they had their license, none of their children could take a car beyond *Roc Agel*'s gates.

When Grace came out of the house, her arms were full of dresses that she spread flat across the rear seat of the car. A maid followed with other dresses and large hat boxes and together they filled the rear seat. Then Grace called for Stephanie who was still trying to wake up.

Grace's chauffeur was standing by the car ready to drive the two of them down to the Palace.

She liked the Rover. There wasn't a lot of mileage on it because she didn't use it much, but she still insisted it be well maintained. It hardly, if ever, went any further away from the Palace garage than *Roc Agel*. And even then it was usually driven by a chauffeur.

Now, however, with the back seat covered, there wasn't room enough for Grace and Stephanie and a chauffeur. Grace told her chauffeur that it would be easier if she drove.

He knew she didn't much like driving and didn't do a lot of it any more, so he tried to convince her, "There's no need to do that. If you leave the dresses here I'll drive you down now and then come back for them."

She said, "No. Please don't bother, I'll drive."

He argued, "It's better if I drive. Why don't I call the Palace and ask someone to come up for the dresses straight away?"

She said, "No, believe me, it's all right like this."

Grace of Monaco

He kept trying to change her mind. "I really don't mind coming back for them."

But she kept saying, "It's just easier if I drive."

So Grace got behind the wheel and Stephanie climbed into the passenger seat. And at about 10 A.M. they pulled away from *Roc Agel*. The chauffeur watched them leave.

The road from the farm winds down the hill and eventually into La Turbie. There you must skirt the large Roman monument in the center of town to arrive at a narrow point in the two-lane road where you turn left, across oncoming traffic, and past an old woman who sells wicker baskets from a stall at the edge of the village car park.

The road from La Turbie down to the Moyenne Corniche, which takes you into Monaco, is called the D-37. It's two lanes, but in most places the road is so narrow and winding that you can hardly ever overtake another car.

It goes straight for a while, running between old, yellow stucco two-story houses with green shutters and geraniums in window boxes, and sometimes you see laundry hanging out of a top-floor window to dry.

Then comes a slight bend to the right where you find yourself going fairly steeply downhill. A few hundred yards more and there's a bend where you pick up speed again as the road down gets steeper still.

To your right, an angular valley cuts through the mountains, leading to the sea with houses teetering on the edge of cliffs, just waiting to tip over and tumble down.

For a moment, the road straightens out, but it is never straight for very long—bending right, bending left, then snaking back again—always getting steeper as it brings you down the hill.

A sign says, "Beware of falling rocks."

Far below, the stubby thumb of St. Jean-Cap-Ferrat juts out from where the water comes to meet the valley and forms a small beach. And now the whole expanse of sea is there in front of you, a huge greenish-blue semi-circle. And now there are several very sharp turns.

Approximately two miles from the monument at La Turbie, there is an especially steep bend where you have to brake very hard and fight with your steering wheel to follow the road 150 degrees to the right.

Grace missed that turn.

The Rover slammed into the small retaining wall, then went through it, somersaulting as it crashed 120 feet through branches of trees, careening off the side of the slope, tossing Grace and Stephanie around inside.

Rainier was called at *Roc Agel*. He rushed into his car and immediately drove to the hospital in Monaco. His uncle, Prince Louis de Polignac was already there. Albert came down from *Roc Agel* in his own car and met them at the hospital. Members of the government started to arrive.

Everyone stood around waiting for the doctors' reports.

It took a long time before the news came that Stephanie was badly hurt but that she was going to be all right. Grace was hurt, too. And at this point the doctors felt she would be all right as well.

As late as three hours after the accident, all Caroline had been told was that Grace had broken her collar bone, fractured her hip, and had lacerations. She was assured that Grace's injuries were not serious enough to warrant her return home that night. So she made reservations on the first flight from London to Nice on Tuesday morning.

Over the next few hours, with the entire hospital staff mobilized and specialists called in, three medical bulletins were released by the hospital. None of them suggested the true extent of Grace's injuries.

Stephanie, only semi-conscious and in terrible pain, was diagnosed as having cracked her vertebra. No other serious injuries and no internal bleeding were found. Doctors secured her neck in a brace and eventually announced that with proper care she could be home in about two weeks.

But Grace, now in a coma, was not responding to treatment.

Doctors suspected a brain hemorrhage. They needed to do a CAT scan but the hospital, ironically named for Princess Grace, didn't yet have one.

They debated their options. A helicopter to a Swiss clinic was ruled out because they feared she'd never make it. Even taking her to nearby Nice was considered too dangerous. In the end, Grace was secretly moved about 400 yards in an ambulance to the office of a private physician where the CAT scan was performed.

The scan showed that Grace had suffered two severe strokes. The first, before the accident, caused her to black out. The second, brought about by the accident, was so massive that the French neurosurgeon, Dr. Jean Duplay who'd been rushed from Nice to Monaco, determined that no surgical intervention was possible.

Duplay told his colleagues that Grace would have needed treatment within 15 minutes to have had any chance of survival. And even then, as Professor Charles Chatelin, the doctor in charge, told Rainier later, had she somehow managed to survive, at least half her body would have been paralyzed. She was brought back to the hospital and placed on a life support system.

On Tuesday night, September 14, Rainier, Caroline and Albert assembled outside Grace's room to speak with Chatelin. He wanted them to know the truth. Rainier and Caroline and Albert listened as he gently explained that Grace's condition had deteriorated and that she was now far beyond anyone's help.

"We had a long talk with him," Rainier explained. "He was an extremely nice man and very understanding with us. He explained the uselessness of continuing with the life support machine. He showed us the pictures and helped us to understand in a very clear way that the machine should be turned off."

Rainier and Caroline and Albert made the decision together.

The Prince's voice got very soft. "It was a difficult decision sentimentally." He paused. "But from a rational, human standpoint it was an obvious decision. There was no reason to keep her on the machine."

Rainier and Caroline and Albert went into Grace's room to say goodbye for the final time. When that was done, the life support system was turned off.

First came the rumor. There's been an accident. Next came disbelief. It's not true. The Princess is in *Roc Agel* and Stephanie is with her and so is the Prince and so is Albert. Then word spread throughout the principality that the rumor was true.

Disbelief turned to shock.

Next came confusion.

People believed only what they wanted to believe. The Princess is all right. Stephanie is all right. The car was badly damaged but they've both escaped. People wandered through the streets of Monaco reassuring each other, they're all right, there's nothing to worry about, they're going to be fine.

The press swarmed in on Monaco like locusts, and now the rumors exploded. She's dead. They're both alive. She's in a coma. Stephanie has escaped unhurt but Grace is critical.

Shops closed. Offices closed. People went to church to pray. Photos of Grace began appearing in windows, draped in black. People went to stand in front of the Palace, waiting for news.

The announcement came late on Tuesday night. "Her Serene Highness, Princess Grace of Monaco, died this evening at 10:15 pm."

Total silence blanketed Monaco.

Like a thick, eerie fog hanging heavily, it made its way through the streets and into the corners of every home.

At the Palace there was shock and disbelief and confusion.

A state funeral had to be arranged. But no one seemed to want to take the initiative. It was almost as if everyone knew that once they began making arrangements, that would mean it had really happened. For the longest time no one could summon up the strength to begin. Ironically, the one person who might have been able to organize such an event was Grace.

The burden fell on Rainier, Albert, and Caroline.

And although the government and the cabinet carried some of the weight, it was Rainier who, despite his enormous grief, somehow found the courage to carry on.

Albert and Caroline did their part.

But it was Rainier who took charge.

"Daddy was wonderful," Caroline recalled. "He was so brave and strong. He was amazing. It was such a lesson to watch him handle that. I can see now, all these years later, that my mother's death brought the family closer together. Not that we were far apart before she died. But after she died we learned to work more together, to be more careful about each other, to pay more attention to each other's lives."

Over the next several weeks, thousands of telegrams and tens of thousands of letters poured into the Palace from all over the world. Someone counted 450 baskets of flowers, many of them from complete strangers.

Grace lay in state for three days in the tiny private chapel at the Palace, constantly surrounded by a guard of honor and flowers—white roses, white and purple orchids, white lilies. Her hands held the green stones of her rosary beads. Her wedding ring was clearly visible on the fourth finger of her left hand. And thousands of people filed past her.

At precisely 10:30 am on Saturday, September 18, she was taken from the chapel and brought to the Cathedral in a procession marked by the mournful beat of a single drum, led by her husband, her son and her eldest daughter.

Stephanie, in traction, lay on her back in her hospital room looking up at a television mounted high on pillows so she could watch the funeral. Paul Belmondo was with her. But as soon as it began she broke down and after a few minutes, she was so distressed that she passed out. Belmondo turned the TV off. For the rest of the morning he just held her hand and they wept together.

Once the high mass was said, Grace lay in state for the remainder of the day. A private burial had been planned for later that afternoon. But at the very last minute Rainier decided Grace would not be buried in the crypt that night. He gave instructions that he wanted it made larger.

So she was buried the next day, after workmen had prepared a place next to her where he, too, would rest.

Chapter 29

After Grace

The Monegasques had lost their Princess.

The dignity that characterized their mourning was only surpassed by the elegance of the woman herself. There were, however, a few incidents that posed a minor risk to the solemnity of the event.

When First Lady Nancy Reagan's limousine came within sight of the Cathedral—she was not only there representing her husband, the president of the United States, but as a personal friend—the Secret Service spotted someone on the roof. They whisked her round to the rear door while agents cornered the man who turned out to be a specially assigned film photographer with authorization to be there.

Even most of the paparazzi showed their respect.

Although a few of the principality's foreign residents had an oddly warped view of the future. Some of them had grown smug in their belief that, as long as Grace and Rainier were on the throne, all would be well with their non-taxable world. Now, with Grace gone, the things that concerned them were: Will all of this change? Will Rainier abdicate? Will Monaco collapse?

For them, the death of an ideal was sad, the death of one's financial security and one's quality of life was something serious.

Stephanie had been tabloid fodder all her life, but never more than after the accident. Within hours, the then 17-year-old Stephanie was accused of driving the car.

She wasn't.

Caroline, who'd moved into Stephanie's hospital room to live there with her until she was fit enough to go home, was the only member of the family to have spoken to Stephanie about what happened in the car that morning.

As Caroline explained, "Stephanie told me, 'Mommy kept saying, I can't stop. The brakes don't work. I can't stop.' She said that Mommy was in a complete panic. Stephanie grabbed the handbrake. She told me right after the accident, 'I pulled on the handbrake but it wouldn't stop. I tried but I just couldn't stop the car.'"

It was many year later when Stephanie spoke about the accident, for the first time, on the record, for publication.

And it was for the original edition of this book.

"I remember every minute of it," she said, trying to control her emotions. "It's only in the last few years that I've been starting to cope with it. I had some professional help and especially in the last eight months I've been learning to deal with it. I still can't go down that road, even if someone else is driving. I always ask them to take the other road. But at least I can talk about it without crying. Although it's hard for me to get it out in front of my dad. As far as I'm concerned, I can live with it. But I still can't talk to my dad about it because I know it hurts him and I don't want to do that because I love him."

To set the record straight, once and for all, this is what happened:

Grace had gone through a very busy summer. She was always exhausted at the end of the season, but this one had been even more hectic than usual. The cruise on the *Mermoz* had helped. But she was still tired, irritable, suffering from high blood pressure, and going through a very difficult menopause.

Caroline confirmed, "She wasn't feeling too well. She was incredibly tired. The summer had been very busy. She hadn't stopped going places and doing things all summer long. She'd done too much. She never mentioned it or complained about it though. But she wasn't in great form."

On that fateful morning, Grace and Stephanie drove past the French policeman directing traffic near the monument at La Turbie. He later reported that he'd recognized Princess Grace at the steering wheel and had saluted. A truck with French license plates followed the Rover down the D-37. The driver later testified that Grace was driving.

Somewhere along the road Grace complained of a headache. It continued to bother her as they headed down the hill. Then suddenly a pain shot up through her skull. For a fraction of a second she blacked out. The car started to swerve. When she opened her eyes she was disoriented. In a panic, she jammed her foot on the brake. At least she thought it was the brake. It appears now, she hit the accelerator.

The French truck driver reported that he was 50 yards behind the Rover, nearing that very steep, sharp curve, when he saw the Rover swerve violently from side to side, zigzagging across both lanes. Then the car straightened out and shot ahead very fast. He knew the road and knew that the bend was coming up and, in those two or three seconds when he didn't see any brake lights on, he realized what was going to happen.

At that instant, Grace screamed to Stephanie, "I can't stop. The brakes don't work."

Stephanie lunged across her seat to grab the handbrake. She also somehow managed to put the car into park. But the car kept going. Stephanie said she'll never know for sure if her mother got the accelerator and the brake pedal mixed up or just didn't have the use of her legs. But when the police investigated the accident and checked the road, there were no skid marks.

Neither Grace nor Stephanie were wearing their seat belts. A gardener was working on the property below the road. He heard a loud noise and immediately recognized the sound. He later reported that in 30 years it had happened at least 15 times. He also later claimed to have pulled Stephanie out of the driver's window, giving the impression that she'd been driving. Seeing the interest he created with those remarks, he continued embellishing his own role in the tragedy through so-called "exclusive interviews" which he sold for a fee to any magazine or newspaper that paid him.

The fact is, he wasn't the first person on the scene.

And he did not pull Stephanie out of the car.

She got out herself from the passenger side. "I found myself huddled under the space below the glove compartment. I lost consciousness as we fell down. I remember hitting the tree and the next thing I remember is waking up and seeing smoke coming out of the car. I thought the car was going to blow up. I knew I had to get out of there and get my mom out of there and so I bashed down the door with my legs. It wasn't hard because the door was half gone anyway."

She said she ran out, saw a lady standing there and started yelling, "Please get help, call the Palace, I'm Princess Stephanie, call my father and get help."

The woman, who lived at the house, sat her down.

Stephanie was in shock.

The stitches in her scalp from her water skiing accident had opened and she was bleeding badly. She'd also cut her tongue and lost a tooth. And now pain began shooting up through her back.

She kept screaming, "My mother's in the car, call my father."

The woman and her husband kept asking who her father was. She told them, "He's the Prince. I'm Princess Stephanie and he's the Prince of Monaco."

It was several minutes before anyone understood her and several minutes more before they believed her.

She said, "I kept pleading with the woman, 'Call my father at the Palace. Please get help. My mother is in there.' Everything else is blurred in my mind until the police came."

Grace had been shoved into the back seat and pinned there by the steering column, which opened a severe gash in her head. She appeared to be conscious but was covered in blood. Stephanie said, "The firemen got Mom out of the car and put her in an ambulance. I waited there for another ambulance."

The car was severely damaged and someone who examined it closely later that afternoon asserted that the only area not twisted beyond recognition was the space under the glove compartment in front of the passenger seat. Only someone hunched down in front of that seat, where Stephanie was, could have survived.

When something like this occurs, there are always lingering, unanswerable questions.

For instance, why didn't Grace let the chauffeur drive?

For example, why was she fated to black out at exactly the wrong spot on that road? If it had happened 100 yards further up the road, Stephanie might have been able to swing the car into the hill and stop it. If it had happened 100 yards further down the hill, they would have passed that dangerous hairpin turn.

Ironically, a few years later, Grace's brother Kell would die while jogging of an identical cerebral hemorrhage.

As the accident had occurred in France, Rainier was approached by the French Government who'd immediately ordered an official investigation and asked if, under the circumstances, he'd like that investigation accelerated.

He said no, that everything should be done step by step, by the book. "I wanted them to do whatever they had to do without any interference. All right, the car was taken away from the spot right away. We were criticized for that in the press. But we had to do that otherwise we would have had tourists chipping off bits of it as souvenirs. It was the French gendarmerie who told us to take it to a police garage in Monaco. The local French judge who was in charge of the investigation told his colleagues in Monaco to seal off the garage so that no one could tamper with the car. They did that right away. No one in Monaco had anything to do with the final report or could influence it in any way."

Rover engineers, expressly flown in from Britain, went over the car to check for mechanical failure. They also investigated the possibility of sabotage. But no mechanical failure was found. The brakes, they wrote in their final report, had been in perfect working order. The French investigation concluded that the accident occurred when Grace blacked out and lost control of the car. In spite of a mountain of evidence that corroborated the findings of the French investigation, the tabloid press and a few hack journalists writing books, continued to fuel the fires of doubt.

But Rainier never had any doubt. "When I got the phone call at *Roc Agel* that morning, I drove down to the hospital immediately. The doctors didn't want to say anything in the beginning because they wanted to do a thorough examination. But the press was diagnosing faster than the doctors. Based on the information supplied by that wretched gardener who says he found the car, and supplemented by the gendarmes, rumors spread very quickly. But it took a long time before the doctors knew what the situation was. They'd come out and tell me they'd found a fracture here and a fracture there, then go back inside and look for more. As they went on finding things they'd tell me. I waited a long time before I knew how serious her condition was and I knew before the press did. It's the press who wouldn't let the story alone."

One down-market American supermarket tabloid sent no fewer than 17 reporters. Armed with cash, they paid anyone who'd speak to them. The result was a continual stream of speculation about how the accident happened, who was driving and how the medical teams at the hospital were too slow in their treatment of Grace.

"They did their best to keep the story running," Rainier said, "and didn't show much human compassion for the pain that we were suffering. It was dreadful. There was all sorts of speculation about what we should have done to save Grace. I just can't understand why. Practically everybody at the hospital was mobilized for her. And I don't know how many times we've had to say that Grace would never have allowed Stephanie to drive her down to Monaco, especially on that road as dangerous as it is. Yes, Stephanie did drive the car from the house to the garage at *Roc Agel* but she never drove that car off the property."

He stopped to shake his head, then confessed, "When the press makes up a story about the Mafia wanting to kill Grace, though I can't for a moment see why the Mafia would want to kill her, if there was some interpretation that seemed even only minutely possible, I'd say, all right. But when they keep rehashing the story that Stephanie was driving and they know it's not true, when they know it's been proven that she wasn't driving, it hurts all of us. It's done a lot of damage and that isn't fair. Maybe if there had been some sort of mechanical error, I don't know, but if there had been, Stephanie might have been able to master it better than her mother. But that's not the point. The point is people don't know to what extent Stephanie has suffered."

Psychiatrists have noted that there is a fairly common reaction when someone survives an accident in which someone else is killed. It's known as the "Why Me?" syndrome. The survivor keeps replaying the accident over and over again, asking, why did I survive and the other person die? In Stephanie's case the unanswered question was made even more perplexing by those well-meaning people who reminded her what a wonderful woman her mother was and then added, "Too bad she had to die." It was a subtle way of suggesting, "Those of us who admired your mother would have found it easier to accept your death instead of hers."

Two other things made the problem especially complex for her. The press, by constantly playing up the possibility that Stephanie was driving, subjected her to enormous stress. She tried to fight back by saying, "How can they think I killed my mother?" But because her voice wasn't as loud as theirs, no matter how much she continued to protest, they merely rehashed the story, and her stress refused to subside.

Even then, the tabloid press might not have mattered so much if there wasn't also the guilt that lingered every time she thought about grabbing the handbrake, every time she told herself that she'd tried to save her mother, and every time she remembered that she could not stop the car.

It's clear that, had this been anyone else besides a Grimaldi, a Windsor, or maybe a Kennedy, what happened that day in September 1982 might be accepted as an understandable explanation for the way Stephanie behaved in the years following. But lurid stories linked to Stephanie Grimaldi—true or false—sell newspapers and magazines. In the end, from her point of view and from her father's, the treatment Stephanie received in the media since the accident was, in some ways, almost as tragic as the accident itself.

Nearly 100 million people around the world watched Grace's funeral on television. But at the time, neither Rainier nor Caroline nor Albert in the church, nor Stephanie in the hospital, knew just how widely the world was sharing their loss. Any solace that might have come from the outside escaped them that day.

And like that famous scene so long ago when a three-year-old boy watched as the caisson rolled by bearing the casket of his President father, and he saluted—the scene so indelibly etched in the memory of that morning in Monaco is of Rainier, in his uniform, shattered with grief and of his oldest daughter, ashen and veiled in black, reaching out to touch him.

Chapter 30

Moving On

Burdened, and greatly troubled by the false rumor that she'd been driving the car, and haunted by that accident, Stephanie's otherwise chaotic love life might be easily understood and otherwise accepted.

That is, if she was anyone besides herself.

Instead, because her face sold magazines, virulent stories of romances with unsuitable men—including one who had a criminal record—were followed by tales of her father disowning and disinheriting her.

But even if Rainier had, at times, been displeased with his daughter's antics, she was still his daughter and he was still her father.

And even if there were times when he was angry at her, he said without any hesitation, "No matter what, the most important thing is to keep the door open."

Rainier's worries were naturally shared by Albert and Caroline. And both of them were willing to admit that, to some extent, Stephanie herself had created a lot of the forage that has fed the tabloids.

Albert never hid the fact that, "She is not always very careful, maybe, and leaves herself a little open to that sort of attention."

After the birth of her third child, she fell in love with Franco Knie, an animal trainer and owner of the circus that bears his family name. Family and friends were dubious, but they accepted that Stephanie has always been impulsive. Anyway, most of them had long ago decided that liking Stephanie means accepting her the way she is.

She lived in Switzerland with Knie for 18 months, left him and promptly fell in love with, and married, circus acrobat Adans Lopez Peres. She was 38, he was 28. That marriage lasted eight months.

Although her reputation as a wild child followed her into her 40s, Stephanie never considered herself anything but a normal, healthy young woman with an unreserved outlook on life. But then, she willingly conceded, "It all depends on what you consider normal."

Fast approaching 50, she is a remarkable, beautiful, and confident mother of three who continues to live her life her way. But, she insists, she has never forgotten that there are people who cannot.

In 2003, Stephanie created a charity called Fight Aids Monaco. Three years after that, she was appointed a joint ambassador to the United Nations Program on HIV/AIDS. Next, she made a brief return to music, assembling a group of singers for a charitable single called "L'Or de Nos Vies" ("The Gold of Our Lives"). And in 2010, she opened La Maison de Vie (The House of Life) in Carpentras, France, which offers material aid to people with HIV/AIDS.

When Albert and his father felt enough time had passed—when they decided that it would not be trespassing on Grace's memory—Albert moved into his mother's office, two floors above Rainier's in the Palace tower.

He shifted Grace's desk around to the far wall, facing the windows and changed the colors from greens and yellows to Japanese bamboo.

Grace's favorite painting—that New York scene—was rehung in his secretary's office. In its place, he put up his own favorites, including a huge color photograph of himself with his bobsled before a race at the Winter Olympics in Calgary.

Caroline, in the meantime, immediately stepped into the role of Monaco's First Lady.

She'd always been very daughterly, Rainier said, and now spent a considerable amount of time caring for him.

But she still had her own life to lead, and that wasn't always easy.

It was fifteen months after her mother's death when she married Stefano Casiraghi. Then he got killed, leaving her a single mom with three children. Retreating to Saint-Remy, she still had her father in Monaco, and responsibilities there, and although it took some time, she eventually found a balance between her life as a Princess and her life as a single mum.

Then came the long affair with actor Vincent Lindon, the new one with Ernst of Hanover and her marriage to him.

Caroline's daughter with Ernst, Alexandra, was born in July 1999 in a hospital in Voecklabruck, Austria, some 40 miles east of Salzburg, where Ernst has a large property.

Walking into the hospital that day, Ernst was surrounded by photographers. He asked that they not take his picture and when one of them refused to comply, Ernst tried to take his camera away. The police arrived to send the photographer packing. And security around Caroline's room was stepped up, so that no one could get close enough for a photo.

Caroline, Ernst, and their collective family now divided their time between the Luberon, Monaco, and London. It seemed, at least for a while, that she and her husband could settle down to a normal family existence.

But battles with the media were never far away.

In 1998, they'd secured an apology from the French magazine *Paris Match* for doctoring a photograph of Caroline and Ernst. The magazine had digitally brought them closer together and removed people standing between them. In May 1999 they'd sued the German magazine *Bunte* and won $51,000 on the grounds that the magazine had practiced "irresponsible journalism."

Then, in January 2000, Ernst's temper put them back in the news.

Caroline and Ernst, along with six-month-old Alexandra, had been vacationing at Ernst's villa on the Indian Ocean resort island of Lamu, off the coast of Kenya. The German owner of a disco just across the water on a neighboring island, had been playing music too loud and too late and Ernst didn't like it. He'd asked several times that something be done.

"Every night there was music until five in the morning," Ernst complained. "And every night between Christmas and New Year he trained a laser beam on my house."

Ernst was not alone on the island in asking that something be done. Several neighbors had also filed complaints with local officials. But the club owner simply chose to ignore the problem. So, one night when Ernst spotted the club owner in Lamu, he confronted the man.

By all accounts, what followed was a boisterous argument that ended in punches being thrown. According to the disco owner, Ernst showed up armed, and with 15 thugs who held the man down while Ernst throttled him. As a result, the club owner claimed, he had six broken ribs.

According to Ernst, any injuries the man suffered did not happen that night. He swore that he did not arrive with a gang and that he was absolutely not armed.

One German news agency quoted Ernst as saying, "I had the great pleasure of giving the man a left and a right."

But by the time the story hit the international media, especially the British, French, and Italian tabloids, the club owner was hospitalized.

Ernst then took out full-page ads in several papers to refute the man's claims.

His ad in the *Daily Nation* and *East African Standard* labeled press reporting of the incident as, "one-sided." It went on, "If the prince was indeed involved in an altercation with one of his compatriots on the island of Lamu, it is inaccurate that he was accompanied by gangsters and even less that he was armed."

Flushed with his 15 minutes of fame, the German club owner quickly told every reporter who bothered to inquire, "I'm happy to still be alive."

None of this amused Rainier.

He accepted Ernst's presence at his daughter's side—after all, compared to Stephanie's choice of men, Ernst was bordering on sainthood.

But, according to an old friend, Rainier was "less than thrilled" with this story and worried that his son-in-law's temper might now be provoked by the media, on purpose, to produce more headlines.

"He hates these kinds of scandals," the old friend said of Rainier. "He's had more than enough of them to last a lifetime and is sick and tired of the way his family seems to be a magnet for this kind of negative publicity."

Compared to the rest of the family, Rainier was probably the least approachable in public and the least photographed. However, his face is just as well known and when he was outside Monaco there were often occasions when someone would come up to him, point a finger and ask, "Don't I know you?"

If it was a very pretty woman, he might suggest she did know him. But most of the time he kept to himself and avoided public confrontation by denying that he was Prince Rainier.

He would tell people, "Funny you should say that because I'm often mistaken for him. In fact, you're the third person today who's asked me if I'm him."

That's when they'd take another long look and decide, "Well, no, I guess you're not him. But you sure do look like him."

After that, they would leave him alone.

But people on the street were very different from the paparazzi.

"Even if you've lived with it all your life," Rainier noted, "you never get used to the pressures of living in a fishbowl. There's no denying that we've had our difficulties with the press but you have to understand that as soon as something gets printed it's too late. No matter what you do afterwards it's still always there in black and white. People believe what they read the first time. Retractions, when you can get one, are usually too little and much too late."

Typical of the way the press dealt with him, especially in the years after Grace's death, was to link him romantically to every woman he was ever seen with. That's what they did, for instance, to his friendship with Ira von Furstenberg.

A princess in her own right, her title came from the first of three well-publicized marriages, this one in 1955 at the age of 15, to an Austrian nobleman.

"Her father was friendly with my grandfather," Rainier explained, "so they used to come to Monaco when she was growing up. We've known each other a long time. She's good company and she's amusing, but that's all. There's never been any question of marriage. But I guess each time I go to say hello to a woman the press immediately invents a romance because it makes for a better story than the truth."

The way the story got started was innocent enough. Von Furstenberg came to the principality on business in 1985. She'd taken a stand to exhibit antiques at Monaco's biannual show. She and Rainier were not only distantly related, he'd been to school with her first husband. Anyway, as old friends it was to be expected that when Rainier toured the exhibit he would stop at her stand to say hello.

That's when they were photographed together.

A few days later Gianni Agnelli arrived in Monaco on his yacht for the annual Red Cross Ball. He hosted a luncheon on the boat and quite naturally invited Rainier. He also invited Ira von Furstenberg, who happened to be his niece.

As it turned out, strictly by coincidence, Rainier and Ira arrived at the same time.

That night, at the ball, she sat next to Rainier.

The photographers now had pictures of them together all over Monaco, which quickly led them to the obvious conclusion that their engagement would be announced at any moment.

With great authority, one scandal sheet noted, "His 28-year-old daughter, Princess Caroline's second marriage to wealthy former Italian playboy Stefano Casiraghi is shaky. And his other daughter Stephanie, 20, is constantly in man trouble. Rainier hoped that strong-willed Ira, a close friend of the Grimaldis for many years, could help him overcome these problems."

It was total fiction and both Rainier and Ira denied that anything was going on.

But then her son might not have wanted to believe that the rumors were just rumors, and announced it was a sure bet that his mother would marry Rainier.

The story stayed on the front pages for over a year.

The very same photo of Rainier and Ira von Furstenberg walking onto Agnelli's boat was later run by newspapers and magazines around the world with a caption describing Rainier and his fiancée in the Caribbean; Rainier and the future Princess of Monaco in the South Pacific; and Rainier and the new Princess of Monaco on their secret honeymoon.

The episode only ended when she did, in fact, get married—to somebody else.

Wearily, Rainier conceded, "What can I say? It sells magazines."

Chapter 31

In a Talkative Mood

Rainier had spent the entire day at his desk.

His office, in the Palace tower, was a large room, filled with half a century's worth of stuff. There was a table to the right of the door, covered in folders and silver picture frames—his children and his grandchildren—and near that there was a large, very old safe that was locked shut, protecting, one imagines, large, very old valuables.

His desk was set back in the far corner of the room, facing the door, with a couch and a chair and a coffee table in front of that. On the tables next to his desk there were more silver picture frames.

Of course, there were several pictures of Grace.

In the corner of the room there was a private lift, a sort of decorated triangular cage that took him up one flight to a second office he used mainly as a conference room. That was the room just below Albert's office.

The same size as Rainier's main office, there was a round, green felt table off to one side and a small desk against the opposite wall. There were more family photos on the tables but here there were also several glass cabinets filled with mementos, such as a collection of life-sized sterling silver crustaceans and fish.

There was a large bronze telescope aimed out of the east window and a huge architect's mock-up of the museum Rainier was building to house his automobile collection. There were several paintings on the walls, including a particularly striking one called *Storm*, which depicts a small boat being hurled about by waves far out to sea. The sky in that painting exactly matched the steel-gray blue of those office walls.

Back in his main office, dressed in a blue blazer with gray slacks and a white shirt with a blue wool tie, he reached for a cigarette, then sat down in the chair next to the couch. There were no lights on in the room, and as the sun faded, as the room grew dark, he spoke quietly and reflectively about his reign.

"Mistakes?" He thought for a moment, then nodded, "Yes. Who doesn't make mistakes? One would be terribly boring if one didn't. But I'd like to think there have not been any major mistakes which have handicapped the principality in its development. I suppose, though, there have been minor ones. In fact, I'm sure there have been. Maybe sometimes our timing was bad in some decisions that were made."

Such as?

"Such as certain construction in the country," he conceded. "Maybe we shouldn't have built as many skyscrapers as we did, or at least controlled the building better. But as I've said, it all happened very fast. Of course we learn from our past. When you look down from here you see La Condamine, the port area, where there are a lot of old buildings that will one day have to come down. Some of them date from 60 or 70 years ago and haven't the proper sanitary installations. So we're remodeling that quarter. But we're not building high."

Building might well be a key word when it comes to his reign, and some people felt that his legacy would be that of "Le constructeur"—the builder.

He pondered that. "The builder or the constructor is a nice image and I like it. But I must explain that it hasn't been building just to please the speculators. Far from it. Fontvieille is a project that's brought a great deal to Monaco but that was a major gamble because it meant reclaiming so much land from the sea. Then again, I'm not sure if the builder or the constructor is the way I would describe my legacy. Perhaps I'd rather it read that I did good for the country. That my reign was successful. That I was right."

And that, when the time came to make unpopular decisions, he had the courage to make them. "It's not easy to take an unpopular decision but there are times when you don't have a choice. I'm open to advice. I've never wanted yes-men around me. I always tried to insist that everyone give me their point of view before I make a decision. It's generally easy to spot the yes-men because they're the ones who wait for me to say what I think. So I find that at meetings I generally don't begin by telling anyone what I think. I ask everyone in the room for their opinions before I express my views. Naturally there are times when some people are sitting there merely trying to second guess my opinion but they can't be right all the time. I've learned this through experience. Believe me, it works. Albert is now in on these cabinet meetings so he's seeing my style and hopefully learning something from it."

Albert knew only too well that he had a tough act to follow because no one could argue that Rainier hadn't done well for the Monegasques. Compare the principality with any city in the world whose population is only 30,000. Not many have an acclaimed symphony orchestra, a recognized ballet company, a world-renowned opera company, quality public gardens, a beach, a port, high-class restaurants, high-class hotels and the same kind of international sophistication.

All of this in a place that, when Rainier first took over was, decidedly, pretty dreary.

The Monegasques are prosperous and healthy and educated and safe. In fact, they might be the safest people in Europe. Monaco's police force is just about 500 strong, which translates to something like one cop for every 60 residents.

"I'm a great believer in the idea that a strong police presence is an obvious answer to crime," he said. "That and modern equipment so that the police can do their job. There is no real crime here. Nor is there a serious drug problem here. Of course, there are some petty crimes and there are young people I guess who sniff glue but there are no serious crimes here and drugs are not sold here. The only time there's been any shooting is at a get-away car when some bank robber has tried to escape. The great thing is that there are only four roads leading in or out of the principality and the police can very quickly and very efficiently shut them off. We have a system of rakes with points that can be pulled out and blow the tires of any car trying to get away. We are fortunate enough to have an easy border to defend."

Street crime in Monaco is almost unheard of. There are occasional murders of passion and burglars have been known to break into safes or steal valuable paintings.

In 1999, the banker Edmond Safra was murdered, the victim of arson. A suspect was taken into custody within a few days. Muggings are rare, prostitution is illegal—at least the street-corner variety—X-rated films are not shown and you can't even walk barefoot in the streets without risking a police warning to you to put on your shoes. Monaco is billed as one of the last places on earth where a woman can wear her jewels. That's very much by design.

And Rainier was extremely proud of that. "We have video cameras in key locations around the principality, on street corners, in passageways, and in public lifts. It's proven very dissuasive so we're extending the system. Let's face it, if a fellow sees a camera on a corner he's not going to do much because he knows that the police are watching."

But cameras on corners and cameras in lifts have brought on cries of "Big Brother."

He scoffed at the mere mention of those words. "I think that's very unfair. This isn't a police state. I've heard that comment but I don't agree with it at all. Come on, what is a police state? It's a place where the police interfere with your life, with who you see, with what you say, with what you think. That's not the case here. There are no restrictions on any of your liberties. The strength of our police force is for protective reasons, not restrictive ones. The major part of the force is in plain clothes. But let's face it, this is a small community and everybody knows everybody else. How long do you think you could be a plain clothes policeman in this place before everybody knew who you were? You know, there's a great imbalance in the world. Some people seem ashamed to show authority and discipline. Well, I don't agree that authority and discipline are a threat to liberty. Without authority and discipline there is only anarchy. And that is a threat to liberty."

He said, for example, that the state religion is Catholicism but there are all sorts of places of worship in Monaco. All the major sects and religions are accounted for, as are many small ones. "We didn't invent ecumenicalism, but I think we thought of it long before the Pope did."

Having mentioned religion, it seemed only natural to ask about the strength of his own faith. He admitted that, over the years, he had many questions but credited Father Tucker with keeping him in the Church.

"I rebelled the way many people do," he said. "I had a lot of questions and no one could give me satisfactory answers. But Father Tucker understood my rebellion from the Church and didn't overdramatize it. That's the way he got me coming back towards the Church. He explained things. He didn't force anything on me the way some other priests probably would have. Let's be honest, most of them, I suspect, would have tried to convince me that by questioning my personal relationship with the Church I'd committed a great sin. He had an important influence on my life."

Among other things, Rainier said, Father Tucker helped him see what the Church should be. "What is the Church? It's charity, tolerance, and understanding, isn't it? That's also what Father Tucker was all about. You know, I've always been appalled by those schools conducted by nuns for little kids where they have a triangle on the wall with an eye in the middle representing God and they tell the kids, that's God watching you. I don't think that's the right image of God at all. I see God with a smile. Or maybe more with the heart than with the eye."

As a Catholic royal, Rainier enjoyed a special relationship with the Vatican. They sent a representative to his marriage and together with Grace he's called on all the popes since Pius XII. "He was an extraordinary man, absolutely saintly. I always had the impression with him that he was the closest one could ever get to God. He didn't receive us around the coffee table with chummy talk. I don't want that from a pope. He received us in a little throne room. Grace and I sat on each side of him. He was affectionate and nice but deeply committed to his faith and deeply inspiring."

Their visit with John XXIII was slightly less formal not only because he, as a pope, was less formal than Pius XII, but because Rainier had known him when he was nuncio in Paris and he'd stayed at the Palace.

"He was then Monsignor Roncalli," Rainier recalled, "and came here for some official ceremony, although I can't remember which. He was a jolly, more down-to-earth man. Pius was a cerebral pope, a deeper thinker, a more reflective pope. John was probably the right pope for that time. He was social, more outgoing, and wanted much less ceremony. The style changed again with Paul VI. I always thought of him as a pope for transition. A man of ample goodwill who didn't make waves."

There wasn't much time to get to know John Paul I, but John Paul II was a man about whom Rainier had strong opinions. He said he found this pope very conscious of the media, very conscious of his image in the press. And that didn't necessarily sit well with

Grace of Monaco

Rainier, who said he'd have liked to see John Paul, "spend more time tending to the flock."

Grace's deep commitment to her faith inspired a Monaco-born, Rome-based priest to suggest within a few months of her death that she be put forward for beatification. Father Piero Pintus announced on the first anniversary of Grace's death, at a mass he held for her on that occasion at his church in Rome, "I propose to make Grace Kelly a saint. As an actress, I preferred Ingrid Bergman. But Grace of Monaco was a faithful wife and an impeccable mother. She lived in a world where it was more difficult to preserve one's faith. She was rich in temperament and rare in potential. She had the gift of grace and not only in her name."

The idea of having her mother canonized struck Caroline as a lovely thought but she wasn't sure it was possible. So she started to look into it and discover that, in fact, it is highly unlikely. "To become a saint," she found, "you need to have performed some miracles when you were alive and those miracles had to have been recorded in the church. Now, there is something in the church called 'Blessed,' which is one of the steps towards beatification. Maybe Mommy could become that."

Father Pintus claimed there are people in Europe and the United States collecting miracles attributed to Grace. There were stories about mothers with sick children praying to Grace, seeing a vision and watching as the child was cured. But until some of those claims were fully substantiated, Saint Grace would be a long way off.

Even Rainier suggested, "The priest involved with that movement made a lot of noise but I don't think it's very serious."

Caroline agreed with her father. "I'm afraid we're a little short on documented miracles."

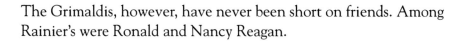

The Grimaldis, however, have never been short on friends. Among Rainier's were Ronald and Nancy Reagan.

Politically, Grace leaned more towards John Kennedy–style Democratic party politics, but if Rainier had been American, he'd almost certainly have been a Republican.

"That's been a very warm friendship," he said, "We got to know them very well and got to see their life in the White House up close."

Rainier, Caroline, Albert, and Stephanie visited the Reagans there on a couple of occasions. Rainier stayed in the Lincoln Bedroom while the others had rooms upstairs. On the night table next to the bed in everyone's room—just like those fancy hotels where they leave a piece of "sleep well" chocolate on the pillow—there was a little gift bottle of jelly beans with the presidential seal.

"The President took Albert and myself to see the Oval Office," Rainier went on, "and told us that the only time he got any exercise or any fresh air was when he went downstairs from the private apartments to the office. I thought to myself, what a change. Eisenhower had a putting green on the lawn there and he could move about pretty freely. Now the White House is like a fortress. When you look out of any window all you see are fellows in uniforms with guns patrolling the grounds with dogs. At the entrance you have a huge reinforced concrete triangle so you can't just crash through the gates and drive straight in."

Visiting the Reagan White House just after the President was shot in 1981, Rainier found security so tight that it was like a prison. "We had very nice accommodation but every time you went into the corridor some security man would pop out from behind the curtains to see what was going on. You couldn't possibly switch rooms there."

Nancy had mentioned to Rainier one evening how she loved the theatre but complained that the only theatre she and Ron could go to was the Kennedy Center because it was modern and had been planned with presidential security in mind. "Kind of sad, no? She said the only movies they ever saw were ones they showed in the White House. I thought to myself, who'd want a job where you had to live like this. It might be the worst in the world."

The Reagan-Grimaldi friendship was such that Nancy Reagan was one of the first people to arrive in Monaco when Grace's death was announced.

A gesture, Rainier said, that was very much appreciated. "Nancy was very sweet to come to Grace's funeral. We put her up in the Palace. Although the Secret Service started being a bit rude when they decided there wasn't enough security in the Palace with all the guards. We finally told them that if she stayed here she was our responsibility and they had to accept that. Frankly, I think the Secret Service just likes to show off. And maybe they could use a little dusting off because you can spot them immediately. They have wires coming out of their ears and they speak to their watches. You don't find many other folks like that."

It's interesting how, after speaking to so many people who knew Grace and Rainier as a couple for a very long time, they all mentioned the word "devoted."

It's possible, of course, that people who weren't devoted to them didn't stay around too long.

But friendship for Grace and Rainier never seemed to be a one-way street, as Rainier's old pen pal, Khalil el Khoury, testified. "When the Lebanon fell apart, we didn't have to flee our home but there was nothing more I could do for my country, unfortunately, as the odds were too great and the players were too big. So my family and I left. We didn't have any place to go until Rainier gave shelter to me and my wife and our children. He offered us passports. He gave us new roots, Mediterranean roots which are our natural roots, and the feeling of security to have this place and this nationality. It was a gesture of love and friendship."

Over the years it's a gesture often repeated for the same reasons.

King Farouk, for example, used to spend a lot of time in Monte Carlo. He'd take the entire second floor of the Hotel de Paris, some

20 rooms, because even as ex-king, he traveled with an entourage of about 40 people. Whenever he wanted to go somewhere he needed several dozen cars. Grace and Rainier got to know him and they both liked him.

"He was an interesting man," Rainier said. "I always shock people by saying I liked him. I'm not saying that I agreed with everything he did politically in his own country or how he behaved or certain decisions he made. But the times I saw him I found him to be a very nice man, although he was also a very lonely man. He was concerned about his country, about his family, about his son. He once told me, 'We have a saying that a man who has a son never dies.' I think he believed greatly in this. When he asked me to be his son's protector, of course I accepted."

Rainier admitted that another reason he liked Farouk—much the same reason he liked Onassis—was the man's flamboyance. "I like it for others but not for myself. It wouldn't fit in with my way of living."

While he was king, Farouk used to come to Monaco because he enjoyed gambling. And most of the time, he'd arrive on his yacht. "The first time I went on board," Rainier said, "I was taken back by how very obvious it was that he didn't trust anyone around him. He couldn't trust anyone, from his personal barber right down to the sailors."

When Farouk returned to Monaco after he was exiled, Rainier still received him the same way as when he was king. "That pleased him. I think it also astonished him. Don't forget how young he was when he became king and what he had to go through. I'm talking about the intrigues and the assassination plots, with the British trying to kill him I don't know how many times, and the isolation in which he found himself. Members of his own family encouraged him to perform every vice possible. He was a sad character and he had no place else to go. Of course I gave him asylum. It was the right thing to do. He didn't live here but he came here once or twice a year and carried a Monegasque passport. I'm still in touch with his son. He was married in Monaco. He's developed into a very nice man who has great respect for his father. It turned out to be quite a good family. They stayed together. They live very quietly and simply in Switzerland."

When cellist Mstislav Rostropovich needed a passport after his Soviet citizenship was revoked, Rainier made him and his wife Monegasques. Neither of them spent much time in the principality, but that's not the point. As Russian exiles, with Monegasque passports, they were able to travel. Rainier's gift of a passport was also extended to the Shah of Iran when he went into exile.

Rainier said, "I thought it was only right. I was revolted with the way the rest of the world treated him when he was down and out. Everybody at Persepolis was licking his boots, shining up to him. Remember how every country in the world tried to get money out of him? Persepolis was just the grand finale. He was the policeman of the Gulf and the best friend of the West as long as the West needed him. But as soon he went into exile everybody slammed their door on him, especially the countries that had once gotten the most use out of him."

High on that list, he continued, were the United States and France. "Tell me what they ever got from Khomeini? When I saw everyone close their to doors to him, I went to my Minister of State and said, 'Why can't we invite him here?' The Shah was pretty much alone at that point. There was just his immediate family because most of his entourage had deserted him. France not only refused to take him in but, after having given asylum to Mr. Khomeini, they allowed Khomeini to return to Iran. And the Americans were worse. They could have offered him so many possibilities. All right, don't move him to Los Angeles because there's a big Iranian population there. But how many of those Iranians now living in America went to school there thanks to the Shah's generosity? The United States is a big enough country. They could

have found somewhere he'd be safe. Sure, there was a security problem but we were assured that he was willing to handle most of that
himself. So we offered him asylum here. The Empress and the children still have Monegasque passports. Maybe the way the world
treated him brought out the boy scout in me."

Chapter 32

Rainier Revisited

In the years following Grace's death, Rainier said, his sister, Antoinette, came back into the mainstream of the principality's life. She appeared alongside him at certain functions, especially the Red Cross Ball.

But then, Antoinette's son Christian had written a book about the Grimaldis that was anything but flattering. For the most part it was dismissed as sour grapes, the nasty musings of a spoiled young man who renounced his responsibilities, defied his uncle, and subsequently saw his inheritance cut off. If Rainier blamed Antoinette for any part in that, he wasn't going to say as much.

Anyway, as Antoinette had assumed the role of elder stateswoman, and taking into account the way their lives have gone, Rainier seemed more than willing to put their past behind them.

"I went away to school when I was 11 and she stayed home," he said, "living either with my mother, my father, or with my grandfather. So from that time on there wasn't very close contact between us. We grew up, each on our own side. You say she attempted to take the throne but I wouldn't go that far. She may have criticized me. And maybe she even went further than criticism. But I've always been on fairly good terms with her. The incident at the time was grossly over-exaggerated. She's conducted her life and I've conducted mine, but the bridges have never been taken down, the conversation has never been cut off. All right, I might have been annoyed with her and she might have been annoyed with me. We've had our differences. But we've remained on speaking terms and, anyway, I don't know of any brother and sister who have never had their differences."

He wasn't particularly comfortable talking about that incident many years before when Antoinette and her then husband had tried to usurp power. Except to say that he never considered it a full-fledged attempt to take the throne.

On the other hand, there were some attempts at his throne he was happy—even amused—to speak about.

There was a fellow named George Grimaldi, who ran a pub and a garage in the south of England, who claimed to be the 13th Marquis and the rightful prince. "That never got him very far."

Then there was an Italian lawyer named Grimaldi who insisted he had a genuine, documentable claim to Rainier's throne, being a direct descendant of a Grimaldi who, in the 16th century, had the throne illegally taken away from him. "When last heard from, he was still living in Italy."

After that, someone in the German branch of the family tried their hand at pretending. But that claim to succession was so obscure, Rainier said, "It isn't entirely sure how we're related."

The thing is, he went on, "These people pop up every now and then. Grimaldi is a common name in Genoa and so there are always a few people there who pretend to be the rightful prince. Recently there was one in Corsica. There are lots of Grimaldis there, too. This chap announced that he was really the rightful heir to the throne but that he didn't particularly want to rule. He said he'd do me a favor and let me stay."

Grace of Monaco

Rainier's title as Prince of Monaco was actually only one of 142 that he had. There was a whole series of Dukes, Marquises, and Counts that made up the list. In fact, he was said to have been the most titled man in the world.

Many of those titles brought with them some sort of medal. Add various awards and honors that were bestowed on him over the years and it turned out that being so highly decorated became a real problem when he had to wear his finery at official functions.

He explained, "I must be frank and say that medals don't particularly interest me. They're given by people who are perhaps expressing a kind thought or recognize something I've done. I appreciate that and accept the medal in that spirit. But I don't attach any importance to medals and have never been anxious to get them."

Nor was he especially anxious to wear any of them.

However, because they were given in a certain spirit, he found it difficult to wear one and not others. So he usually wound up having to wear them all.

"But contrary to whatever gossip you sometimes hear around Monaco," he said, "and you already know what I think about that, I do not spend my days looking at my medals, admiring them and polishing them."

He suddenly couldn't keep a straight face. "Nor do I wear my medals on my pajamas."

After admiring some of the photos in his office, especially of his children, Rainier responded, "The hardest part of being a parent is not being able to protect your children from the pain. And to protect them from themselves, which is often a difficult thing to do. Grace and I always encouraged our children to make their own choices because in the end it's their own life."

Still, he said, it's not always easy to let a child go ahead and do that, especially when you can see that it's the wrong choice. "Caroline's first marriage wasn't a happy one. Both Grace and I knew it but we hadn't got much choice. When you have a child come to you determined to share her life with somebody, what do you say? I think it was better to go along with it than to fight it. I think the most important thing when a parent has a crisis or conflict with a child is to keep the door open all the time so they know they can always come home to find shelter and refuge."

There was hardly any doubt that when Caroline announced her engagement to Philippe Junot her parents disapproved. "He had a very bad reputation and not much of a personality. I didn't like his background. He didn't have much of a job. I didn't know what he did besides being part of a Paris clique who had some money and spent their nights out at clubs."

On one occasion before the marriage when someone asked Rainier, "What does Junot do?" The answer he got was, "Anything or nothing."

By the time word got out that the marriage was on the rocks, a story was circulating that Grace and Rainier had reassured Caroline, literally up to her first step down the aisle, that if she wanted to change her mind, if she wanted to back out of the wedding, she could and they would stand by her.

No, Rainier said, it wasn't quite like that. "I think you have to play the game as sincerely as you can. That's really the issue. You have this child who is in love. All right, we did try to stop her up to a reasonable point, at least to talk her out of it. But she was intent on doing it, so what else could we do except go along with it?"

He said he liked Stefano, appreciated him as a good husband and a good father and saw that he made Caroline happy. He also understood her grief when Stefano died. "Growing up has been difficult for our children. They've had very public lives. It hasn't been easy."

Grace's death, he recognized, was especially difficult for Stephanie.

Nevertheless, when she went off to do her own thing, Rainier conceded, he wasn't always pleased. "It sometimes hurt. But deep down, I liked to think I understood that she was merely doing what she felt she had to do. Listen, parenthood is never easy. You have to swallow a lot and let things go. But the main thing is to keep talking. To keep the door open. The child should know where home is and how to get back there, to know that no one is going to wave a wooden finger and say, I told you so."

He was concerned that Caroline, Stephanie, and Albert had grown up without a mother and that he was always trying that much more to be a good father. "But I never could be a good mother. I have tried not to shelter them too much, to help them face their own problems. And I know they are very close to each other." Although he added, somewhat cryptically, "Albert can be too indulgent."

Several years before, Stephanie had remarked to a woman's magazine, "My father is the only man who never betrayed me."

In one way it was a sad comment for the then 23-year-old to make. In another, it showed she was aware that he was there for her.

"I was very pleased about that," Rainier said. "I hope that's a result of the fact that we've never closed the door. You know, you can say, please don't do something, and give a child all the reasons in the world but if the child wants to go on doing something, there's nothing left to do but say, all right, be careful. What else can you do? I have very different relationships with my children. Albert is my son, and fathers and sons are special. With Caroline, she's a parent now, too, and she's very daughterly towards me. As for Stephanie, she has a mind of her own. I know that. I also know that she's got a tremendously strong character, maybe even the strongest of the three."

There could be no doubt that since Grace's death, the years were lonely for Rainier. Many of his friends had passed away and he, too, had slowed down. But on a visit with Caroline to the spa La Baule in France in late 1994, he suffered heart problems.

Returning to Monaco immediately, the 72-year-old Rainier went through a secret and very painful double by-pass operation.

Stories began circulating immediately afterwards that Rainier would step down.

It didn't happen.

The fact is that father and son often said they enjoyed working together and that when the time was right for a change of power, they would both know.

In 1997, Monaco celebrated the 700th year of its birth.

Two years later, the principality celebrated the 50th anniversary of Rainier coming to power.

Although he continued going to the office, taking care of his responsibilities at home, he soon stopped traveling, preferring to send Albert to do what he no longer could.

Chapter 33

The End of
the Fairy Tale

His final decade was difficult for him.

For a few years after his double by-pass, his health remained steady, at least until 1999 or so when he noticeably began to deteriorate. A chain smoker all of his life, he'd been ordered by his doctors to quit. But he didn't.

In December of that year, Rainier was back on the operating table, this time to repair an aneurysm in his abdominal aorta. The operation went smoothly and the Palace released a public statement that he was on the mend.

But his doctors knew better. They were concerned with something they'd discovered on his lung and in February 2000 they removed a small growth.

Again, according to a Palace statement, "The prince is recovering very well."

Eleven days later, on February 13, he was rushed back into the operating room to correct a condition known as pneumothorax. Air was escaping from his lung and building up in the chest cavity. The situation was repaired and he was allowed to go home.

With each visit to the hospital, speculation mounted about how much longer he would reign.

He told people he didn't know.

Close friends guessed that he would step aside once Albert married.

The best he would say about life was, "For me the future is to grow old gracefully."

But that wasn't easy for him, and in fact, at times, it was extremely painful because the "grace in gracefully" had been taken away from him.

Next, he spent three weeks in hospital recovering from what doctors described as general fatigue. He returned to hospital shortly thereafter to be treated for a coronary lesion and a damaged blood vessel. He came back again to be treated for a chest infection.

Finally, it was kidney problems, along with cumulative heart and lung problems further aggravated by more than half a century of chain smoking, that took their toll.

Rainier Louis Henri Maxence Bertrand Grimaldi, Sovereign Prince of Monaco, was an "old school" kind of man for whom manners and respect mattered. The sort of man who simply accepted responsibility for what it used to be—duty—something one had to do, like it or not.

It was not always to his liking, but he dedicated his life to his duty, and even if it appeared to outsiders as a rollicking good time, in reality, it was anything but.

Surrounded by parasites, flunkies, gold diggers, wannabees, and sycophants, it was a full-time job just deciding who to trust.

"I have hangers-on," he said without hesitation, adding that real friends were one of the main hardships in his life. "I constantly have people pretending friendship one day and suddenly asking favors the next. I think the sign of true friendship is when someone has been around for a very long time and has never asked for anything. But that's so rare. At the end of the day, I suspect I could actually name all the people around me who have never asked for anything. I think I could count them on the fingers of one hand."

Grace always said she wanted to be remembered, "As someone who accomplished useful deeds, and who was a kind and loving person. I would like to leave the memory of a human being with a correct attitude and who did her best to help others."

And he hoped that's the way she would be remembered. "As a caring person. She was. She really did care about other people. She was extremely demanding of herself."

As for himself, Rainier said he did like the idea of being remembered as "The Builder." That his legacy should be that of the man who brought the sleepy, somewhat remote statelet he'd inherited in 1949, into the late 20th century.

And that may well be what history decides.

More likely, though, he will be remembered as the man who co-wrote the fairy tale and helped orchestrate the magic.

The Monaco of Rainier's youth was a dismal place, living on past glories of some long gone golden age, way beyond its sell-by date. That changed when he met, fell in love with, and married Grace Kelly. She electrified the Riviera as only a film icon could and, along with her Hollywood friends, she delivered a cast of characters that brought Monte Carlo back as the most glamorous resort in the world.

For 26 years, Rainier and his movie star Princess sustained that magic.

And it was magic.

Grace and Rainier didn't rule a country as much as they reigned over a fairy tale. There might not have been pumpkin carriages and glass slippers, but there were Frank Sinatra and Cary Grant, huge yachts, the world's most famous casino, the most famous Grand

Prix in the world, and bejeweled ladies in evening gowns sipping champagne on terraces under the moonlight with elegant men in dinner jackets.

And, for one night every year, in the middle of the summer, during the Red Cross Ball, there was, arguably, more money under the retractable roof of the Sporting Club—in diamonds, emeralds, sapphires, and rubies—than anywhere else on the planet, with the possible exceptions of Fort Knox and the Bank of England.

Few fairy tales have ever been so enchanting.

And, yet, so few enchanting stories have ever had such a sad ending.

When Grace was killed, everything stopped.

The magic evaporated and there was nothing anyone could do to bring it back. Everyone knew it, no one more so than Rainier because, he said, "A part of me died with her."

There were, also, regrets, he confessed with typical candor. "When this kind of ending occurs, there are always regrets. You regret not having spoken enough together, not having spent enough time together, not having gotten away enough together. Not having dedicated enough time to each other. When you look back over 26 years you find moments when you think to yourself, why didn't we go on that vacation the way we always said we would? And why didn't we do this or talk about that? I regret we didn't have more time together."

Immediately after Rainier's double by-pass, stories circulated that now he would finally step down.

When he didn't, the press decided he was merely waiting until Albert married.

Truth be told, retirement had been on his mind since just after Grace died. He couldn't do anything about it then, because both he and Albert were waiting for the day when they both thought Albert was ready. But he said he was looking forward to a time when he could travel and see people he wanted to see, as opposed to people he was obliged to see.

That he didn't retire is not because Rainier was worried about Albert assuring the line of succession. If that had been the case, he could have stepped down in 2002 when he orchestrated a change in the law, putting Caroline and her sons in line after Albert.

No, he said, retirement didn't happen because he and Albert were comfortable with their working arrangement.

Anyway, Albert was gradually taking charge as Rainier's health was forcing him into the wings.

But then, this long "apprenticeship" clearly prepared Albert in such a way that he was infinitely better qualified for the job than his father ever was. Albert might not have been the only person his father trusted, but he was undoubtedly one of the very few. One of his most important jobs then became drawing up his own list of people to trust.

Unlike his father, Albert grew up in Monaco and undoubtedly knows every one of his 7,000 subjects by face, if not by name. His American college years and all those years he spent employed in the so-called "real world," gave him a different outlook, a modern outlook, something that his father couldn't have. Twenty years of on-the-job training at his father's side then equipped him with a much deeper understanding of what needs to be done and how to go about doing it.

In that final decade, Rainier cut an increasingly lonely figure. There was still joy in his family—especially the arrival of his grandchildren—but everyone could see that the light was growing dim.

During his final year, increasingly frail and weak, he was forced to spend more and more time in the hospital. He hardly ever appeared in public.

But in January 2005, he insisted on celebrating the 30th anniversary of his cherished Monaco Circus Festival.

Wrapped in a coat and a red and white circus scarf, when he walked into the big tent—with Albert and a tearful Stephanie by his side—the crowd erupted. Thousands of people jumped to their feet and greeted him with a long and emotional standing ovation.

And as the drawn and tired Prince acknowledged his people's outpouring of love, it was as if everyone there knew—the fairy tale that Grace and Rainier wrote and lived, was about to end.

On March 7, he was admitted to the Cardio-Thoracic Center in Monaco, suffering from a bronchial-pulmonary infection. A statement from the Palace noted that the infection had been brought under control. But two weeks later he was moved into intensive care—he was having problems breathing—and this time it was for the final time.

Albert rushed back to the Principality from Italy. Caroline rushed back from Paris. Stephanie was already there.

When the announcement finally came, news bulletins flashed around the world and in some countries, regular broadcasting was interrupted.

Rainier died on April 6, 2005—50 years to the day after he first met a movie actress called Grace Kelly.

Dusk

The waters turn dark.

The sun falls behind the hills.

Those buildings at the port are no longer salmon pink. They're now more of a fading strawberry red.

The souvenir shop facing the ports sells the last picture postcards of the day.

The pastry shop around the corner and down the narrow alley from City Hall on *Le Rocher* sells the last loaf of bread on the shelf.

And now there is a pause.

A small fishing boat chugs slowly back into the harbor.

Traffic comes to a halt on the roads leading out of town.

Cabana boys at the Beach Club pick up mattresses and fold umbrellas. A sign says that you can swim at your own risk after 7 P.M., and someone does. Later, the police will patrol the beaches, just in case there are any campers who think it would be sexy to sleep on the beach at Monte Carlo. It's done elsewhere along the coast, but other beaches aren't this one.

A croupier arrives late for work because he couldn't find a space in the private lot behind the casino for his bright yellow Maserati.

Four cocktail parties are about to begin, all within 500 yards of each other. They serve the same Champagne and the same canapés. Two are sponsored by jewelers. One is sponsored by an art gallery. One is sponsored by a chap who sells luxury cars privately. Everyone who shows up at the first of those parties will, inevitably, meet everyone else again at the other three.

Shops close.

Girls in white smocks struggle to pull heavy metal grills down across storefront windows covered in rose film, or yellow film, so that the sun will not spoil the bottles of perfume on display.

Men meet their mistresses.

Women meet their lovers.

The first train of the evening leaves for Paris.

A commuter train pulls in from Nice on its way to Ventigmiglia.

A stockbroker sits in front of a computer screen checking Wall Street because when it's 7 o'clock in Monte Carlo it's only one in New York.

Chefs all over town ready their kitchens.

Sommeliers all over town consider their stock of wine.

The maître d' at the Café de Paris is counting reservations when an American couple comes in to ask if gentlemen are required to wear ties, because if gentlemen are required to wear ties, they won't be able to dine there as the gentleman is tie-less. He assures the couple that they will be welcome.

The daily card game finishes at the café near the high school.

One last round of Pastis is served.

A used-to-be famous old English actor is paged at the bar in the Hotel de Paris, the way he is paged every evening at the same time, because that's what he's tipped the barman to do.

A Personal Epilogue

We each have our special memories.

Mine of Grace is of that Saturday afternoon before her last Christmas on earth. She'd spent the morning baking butter cookies cut into stars and cut into Christmas trees and cut into Santas carrying sacks of toys. Once they were ready, she walked alone from the Palace to Caroline's house, about 500 yards along a winding, narrow street, between three-story fading yellow brick houses with green shutters across the windows and freshly washed laundry hanging out of some of them.

Dressed in dark slacks with a cream cashmere sweater and a simple string of pearls around her neck, flat shoes, her hair wrapped in a scarf and large sunglasses, no one recognized her except the Palace guards in their winter uniforms who saluted smartly as she nodded to them and smiled, "Bonjour."

She let herself into the large, quiet villa.

Finding no one in the front hallway, she peeked into the kitchen. "What's for breakfast?"

I answered, "How would you like scrapple and eggs?"

She gave me a suspicious look. "Where can you get Philadelphia scrapple in Monaco?"

"Alas," I shrugged. "Will you settle for a Western omelet?"

"Sounds great," she said, placing the bag of cookies on the counter near the sink and reaching for an apron. "I'll supervise."

The years had been kind to her. She'd put on some weight but her eyes were as magical as they'd ever been and her voice was exactly the same as it was in *Mogambo* and *High Noon* and *Rear Window*.

Her face was a bit rounder now, but it was softer, more gentle than in her Hollywood days. The ice-goddess image had melted away and that once-so-beautiful movie star of 22 had become a still-so-beautiful woman of 52.

"I thought you were from New York." She started to scrub the green peppers. "How do you know about scrapple?"

"I went to school in Philadelphia. I went to Temple."

"So did I," she said. "I went to Temple." She paused, "Although I think it must have been a few years before you."

"Well," I politely suggested, "only a few," then pointed to the paper bag, "Is that for the tree?"

"I baked cookies. What did you do?"

When my pal Caroline had phoned to ask, "Want to make lunch on Saturday for my mother and me," she'd explained it was the day she was going to decorate her Christmas tree. "This year everything on the tree has to be edible. You know, cookies, candy, dried fruit, whatever you want to bring."

Her mother's butter cookies were according to the rules. But I had my own idea of edible decorations. "It's not quite the same as if I'd baked." I reached for my shopping bag. "Nevertheless," I assured her, "everything is edible."

She said, "Let's see."

I pulled out Santa-encrusted tins of tuna fish and several packages of Christmas-ribbon-wrapped pasta.

She laughed.

Grace of Monaco

And her whole face lit up.

"Your hair is a little long, isn't it?" she said, once we'd started cooking the omelets together. "Tell you what, after lunch get me a pair of scissors and I'll give you a haircut."

I turned to her. "It's a deal. But you must understand that if you cut my hair, my mother will tell everybody in Florida that Grace Kelly is my barber."

She chuckled, "You're on."

That's when Caroline appeared in the kitchen, "Hi. What's for lunch?"

Right away her mother said, "Scrapple, dear."

Caroline made a face. "What?"

Her mom and I just laughed.

When lunch was over we went into the winter garden where the tree was waiting. We hung Grace's cookies and some striped candy canes and my Christmas-wrapped tuna cans.

As the afternoon wore on, and as we only barely managed to keep Caroline's dogs from eating the decorations, all sorts of people stopped by. There was a constant stream of friends, some carrying presents to put under the tree, almost everyone bringing more food to hang on its branches. No one else brought ribbon-wrapped macaroni.

Before long Caroline's mom and I drifted off into a corner of the room, the two of us sitting Indian style on the floor. We talked of many things—of shoes and ships and sealing wax, of cabbages and Hollywood.

"It was very different in those days," she said. "Not like it is today. It was a much gentler place then."

"With gentler people?" I wondered. "Hitchcock never struck me as being particularly gentle."

"Hitch was wonderful. He was very secretive and mysterious. He was naturally shy so he was always playing hide and seek with everybody."

"But he was known to be very demanding."

"He had to be. Movies were an expensive business, even if they didn't cost anywhere near what they do today."

"He was at Paramount, wasn't he?"

"Well, *Rear Window* was at Paramount and so was *To Catch a Thief*. But *Dial M for Murder*, which was the first film we did together, was at Warner Brothers. Moving around like that always presented problems because I was on a salary at Metro. Whenever Hitch wanted me for a film he had to get me from them. MGM kept renting me out to other studios. And they made a lot of money doing it. Unfortunately I didn't. I think I actually made more money modeling in New York than I did acting in Hollywood."

"Do you miss Hollywood?"

"I miss some of the people, yes, because I was lucky enough to work with some fabulous people, like Hitch. But I never much cared for California and never really lived out there. Everything in Hollywood seems to be affected by the exaggerated importance of money. I worked out there but I always came back to New York when I wasn't working."

"Except that you worked out there a lot."

She shook her head. "I only made eleven films and don't forget I made six of the eleven in a little over a year between 1953 and 1954. And then, only one of those six was for MGM."

"Did you have the right to turn stuff down?"

"Not really." She began to giggle. "In fact, I once even got suspended for it. You could only say no when they let you say no. A director once wanted to cast me as Elizabeth Barrett Browning in a production of *The Barretts of Wimpole Street*. I was about 25 at the time and in the movie she would have been in her early 40s. He thought I'd be marvelous in the role. I told him I was much too young. And he said, 'No problem. We'll make her younger.' I couldn't believe it. I tried to explain to him that the whole beauty of her story lies in the fact that she was 40 when she had this great romance. Luckily the project was dropped. In the mean time, my reputation as a difficult young actress was greatly enhanced."

"Were you difficult?"

"Who me?" She grinned broadly. "Well, MGM thought so."

"Do you still get fan mail?"

"Yes. And I'll have you know that every letter gets an answer."

"Are the letters ever still addressed to Grace Kelly or is everything Princess Grace?"

"Of course, most of my mail is addressed to Princess Grace but, yes, I still get letters from people who say they've just seen one of my movies on television. Or they say that their mother and father were fans and ask if they could have my autograph for them. Or they ask for photos or recipes. So we send them a photo of the family or some of my favorite recipes, you know, local dishes that are cooked in Monaco. Or they ask for advice."

"What kind of advice?"

"All sorts of advice. I get questions on just about everything, from raising children to how to get into the movies. Although I stopped giving advice about how to get into the movies in about 1949 or 1950."

"Why?"

"Elia Kazan called me one afternoon to ask if I'd like to help a young actor rehearse for an audition. I said sure. I remember that the guy came up to our apartment on a Sunday afternoon. He explained that he lived somewhere outside New York, in the suburbs, and couldn't rehearse with me during the week because he was married and had a young family and had to work for his father. But he said he really wanted to be an actor. Well, the girls I lived with were home that afternoon and they had dates over and the record player was going, so the only place we could rehearse was the kitchen. Of course, it was one of those really tiny New York City kitchens so we were very cramped. He read okay. But he wasn't great. And when he asked me what I thought, I tried to find a kind way of letting him know that he wasn't going to make it. I explained how difficult it was to get work and reminded him that most actors in New York were hungry most of the time. I advised him to keep his job so that he could support his wife and child and maybe act as a hobby in amateur productions. I tried to convince him as nicely as possible to forget acting as a career."

She stopped right there and stared at me.

"Okay," I asked, "Who was it?"

And she answered, "Paul Newman."

We each have our special memories.

Mine of Rainier is that late summer afternoon sitting in his office in the Palace, the day he spoke to me about Grace's death.

He came around the side of his desk and sat next to me in a straight chair facing the coffee table. My first thought was that he seemed tired. He said he felt all right, but added that it was impossible for him to ever really get away from his job.

"I soldier on because that's the only thing I can do."

"But why do you do it alone?"

"What do you mean?"

"I mean, enough time has passed for any widower to bring someone else into his life without eyebrows being raised." He didn't answer, so I asked, "Are there any ladies in your life?"

He said he didn't want to speak about that. "I live in a fishbowl. It complicates life and puts you off doing a lot of things. I have to be extremely discreet."

Although he quickly added that, at least most of the time, he didn't worry anymore about what other people thought or what the press wrote. "Anyway, I don't interest the media so much anymore because I don't do enough that would interest them."

Except when ladies were mentioned.

He'd been hounded by a photographer in New York and made headlines, taking a page out of Frank Sinatra's book, throwing a punch at photographers.

It was the night he'd gone to see *Cats* with the wife of an American friend. Photographers swarmed him coming out of the theatre, insinuating that the "unidentified" lady on his arm might become the next Princess of Monaco.

First he asked them to leave him alone. Then he shouted at one of them. Then he let his Mediterranean temper get the better of him and hit the guy.

More photographers showed up the next day at his hotel and he took a swing at one of them.

It was clearly an episode he didn't want to discuss, so we spoke for a time about all sorts of other things, until I could bring the conversation back to him.

Now the sun began to set.

Because no lights were on in his office, the room grew darker.

He spoke about the morning of the accident, and how he'd rushed to Grace and Stephanie, and how he learned that his wife was too far gone to ever come back, and how he and Caroline and Albert had gone to say goodbye, and how then, the life support machine was turned off.

His voice grew more quiet as the room grew very dark.

Before long, he was weeping.

Tears were coming down my face, too.

After a very long time, he regained his composure and started speaking of other things, as if the moment we'd just shared was too personal.

He talked about Monaco and about pollution of the seas and the United Nations and international diplomacy. And when he'd run out of those topics, when he felt he'd moved far enough away from Grace's death, I asked him again about himself.

"Would you ever remarry?"

He shook his head. "I don't see the necessity for marrying again. I find it very difficult to even imagine. I enjoy the company of women, sure. But at this point in my life there are no thoughts of marriage. Anyway, second marriages are things I don't necessarily understand. If a marriage ends because you can't stand your wife or she can't stand you, so you split up, you separate, and go your own way. Then perhaps if you meet someone who can make you happy you might want to try again. But as it happens for me …"

He paused for a moment. "I have a wonderful family and I had a wonderful marriage. And everywhere I go is so filled with memories of Grace. We lived here together for 26 years. She's still everywhere. I couldn't have another woman here. I see Grace wherever I go. Anyway, I couldn't do it because it would be very difficult for my children. It wouldn't be fair to them."

He paused again and in his pitch dark office said softly, "So I won't."

It was a promise to her, and he kept it.

In July 2011, Albert finally married.

His bride Charlene Wittstock—now Her Serene Highness Princess Charlene of Monaco—is a tall, blond, beautiful South African woman, 20 years his junior. She'd been an Olympic swimmer and they'd met at a swimming event in Monaco in 2000, although they didn't start dating until 2006.

As of November 2013, the couple had not yet produced an heir.

Although, shortly after Rainier's death, a news story broke that Albert had an illegitimate child with a former Air France stewardess. Albert's lawyer confirmed that the story was true, acknowledging that Éric Alexandre Stéphane Coste had been born in August 2003.

A statement from the Palace quickly noted that Monaco's constitution specifies "only direct and legitimate" descendants can assume the throne.

And while his father has participated in the boy's life, spending time with him and supporting him, Alexandre is not in line for succession.

Nor is Jazmin Grace Grimaldi, Albert's daughter, born in 1992 after a liaison with a California woman.

Here, too, Albert has supported his daughter and spent time with her.

Many years before, Albert told me he wasn't sure how, when he took over as reigning prince, he could ever live up to the reputation of his parents.

I hope, by now, he understands he doesn't have to.

His sister, Stephanie, lives quietly, raising her children.

His sister, Caroline, and her third husband, Ernst, have split up.

We each have our special memories.

September 12, 1982 was an overcast and sometimes-drizzling Sunday in London, England.

All these years later it seems like only a few months ago.

My future wife, Aline, was flying out to Nice, France, on a late afternoon flight. My old pal, Caroline Grimaldi, was flying in for a week's stay at the Forest Mere health spa in Hampshire, arriving on the same plane that would take Aline back.

So I drove Aline to Heathrow Airport, said goodbye to her at Departures, walked upstairs to Arrivals, and waited for Caroline.

On the drive into London, Caroline was happy and relaxed and looking forward to her week of pampering.

"What's the food like?" I asked.

"I don't know," she said, then made a face. "British, I presume."

That wasn't particularly encouraging, so when I dropped her at Waterloo Station for the train to Hampshire, I suggested, "If the food's any good, I'll come and have a meal with you. If it's terrible, I'll smuggle good food in."

We decided that was a plan.

On Monday afternoon, Aline phoned from France to say she'd just heard on the radio that Princess Grace had been involved in a bad car accident.

I immediately rang Caroline. It took a while to get through, but when I finally did, I told her, "I'll pick you up right away and get you to the airport."

She said she'd spoken to her father, that, "Mommy had some broken ribs and lacerations and Stephie was hurt, too," and that she'd already made arrangements to fly home the next day.

Tuesday, September 14, sometime just before midnight, my phone rang. A friend woke me with the words, "I just heard that Princess Grace is dead."

These being prehistoric days before email and cellphones, I wrote Caroline immediately. Understandably, it took a long time to hear back from her. She'd moved into Stephanie's hospital room to be with her, and sat stunned and weeping next to her father, comforting him, at her mother's funeral. Then, as soon as they could, Rainier and his three children left Monaco for a long trip, to mourn, to convalesce, and like any close knit family, to help each other get through this.

It was several months before I finally spoke to Caroline again.

I found her at home. I wanted her to know that Aline and I had not stopped thinking about her and her mother and her father and her sister and her brother, and how saddened and sorry we still were that this tragedy had happened. But I never got a chance.

"Hi," she came on the line. "You know what?"

I asked, "What?"

And my old pal Caroline ... typical Caroline, forever wonderful Caroline ... announced, "Actually, the food wasn't so bad."

Acknowledgments

This book was based, almost entirely, on first hand interviews. For their help and assistance with this project I wish to thank Rupert Allan, Daniel Aubry, Pierre Berenguier, Michel Boeri, John Carroll, Dario Dell'Antonia, Julian and Phyllis Earl, Ken and Bonnie Feld, Gant Gaither, Virginia Gallico, Wilfred Groote, Robert Hausman, Khalil el Khoury, Mary Wells Lawrence, Regis L'Ecuyer, John Lehman, Andre Levasseur, Luisette Levy-Soussan, George Lukonski, Judith Mann, Francis and Josiane Merino, Jean Marie Moll, Stirling Moss, Ricardo Orizio, Richard Pasco, Prince Louis de Polignac, Francis Rosset, Marquis Livio Ruffo, Andre Saint Mleux, Francine Siri, Robert Sobra, Jackie Stewart, Clare Sychrava, Robert and Maureen Wood, and John Westbrook.

I am especially indebted to Nadia Lacoste for her kindness, affection, guidance, assistance, and so many years of friendship.

My thanks, as well, to Ruth Fecych, Christine Marra, and Amanda Murray for their work on this edition.

And, as always, La Benayoun.

However, this book could never have been written—at least not by me—without the cooperation of four very special people.

I will be forever grateful to Prince Albert, Princess Caroline, and Princess Stephanie for their time, their recollections, their secrets, their trust, and their friendship.

But I am most appreciative of all to His Serene Highness Prince Rainier III. He not only gave me his blessings to write this book, he also opened his heart to me.

I could never forget Rainier.

Nor, could I ever forget Grace.

I have been deeply touched by both of them.

Index

White House visit (1956), 119
White House visit (1981), 296
Rainier and Grace/family
    children learning to drive, 266,
        279
    humor and, 130, 174–176, 179–
        180
    music, dance, opera and, 77–78,
        128, 167
    parenting, 120, 121–122, 124–
        129, 131, 158, 266, 303–305
    private apartments, 122–123
    sailing, 120–121, 179, 275
    sweets and, 217–218
    values/rules, 125, 128
Rainier and Grace/press and
    photographers
    Allan and, 134–136
    Connaught Hotel, London, 139
    Grace and press, 134, 136, 137–
        138
    Grace at Monaco carnival, 141
    Grace on Ballet Festival, 137–
        138
    in Ireland, 139–140
    Lacoste and, 133–134, 136–138,
        139, 141, 144–145, 265
    Rainier and press, 134–135, 136,
        137, 141
    Roc Agel farm/home, 74, 75, 77,
        78, 120, 154–155, 265–266
    romance and, 55, 58, 132
    their children and, 142–143,
        145–146, 147–148
    wedding, 58, 60, 61, 62, 64, 65,
        68–69, 73, 132–133, 205

Rainier and Grace romance
    correspondence, 47–48
    engagement/announcement,
        55–57
    meeting, 6, 38–39, 45–47
    official version, 42–45
    press and, 55, 58, 132
    proposal, 45, 49, 51
    Rainier's trip to America (1955–
        1956), 40–41, 44–45, 49–52
    rumors/gossip on, 39, 40
    true story, 45–51
    See also Wedding of Rainier and
        Grace/preparations
Rainier, I, Prince, 56
Rainier III, Prince of Monaco
    ancestors history (summary), 78,
        81–83
    attempts at his throne, 97, 302
    as bachelor/matchmakers,
        25–29
    birth/full name, 88
    childhood/education, 88–89,
        91–93
    death, 312
    description/personality, 25, 28,
        46, 72, 74–75, 134, 177, 194,
        197, 285, 308
    50th anniversary of reign, 249,
        250, 306
    on friends/friendship, 308–309
    Grace's accident/death and, 268,
        269–270, 271–272, 277–278,
        279, 280, 305, 310, 321
    health problems, 257–258, 262,
        306, 307–308, 311–312

Sawyer, Diane, 260
SBM
  description/power, 86, 89, 95,
    102, 106
  Monaco's gambling franchise
    and, 86, 102, 105, 107
  Onassis and, 102–105, 106–108,
    109–110
  Rainier's changes to, 108–109,
    110
Schary, Dore, 158
Schweitzer, Albert, 184
Sea Bathing Society and
  Foreigners' Club. *See* SBM
Shah of Iran, 177–179, 299–300
Shakespeare Festival/readings,
  166, 167, 169
Sinatra, Frank, v, 70–71, 184,
  187–188, 213, 309, 320
Spellbound (movie), 6
Spencer, Diana (Diana, Princess),
  54, 64, 168–169
Spiegel, Sam, 105
Sporting Club, Monaco, 100, 101,
  190, 310
Stamps/collecting, 226–227
Stanislavski, Constantin, 18
Steinbeck, John, 6
Stephanie, Princess
  attempted kidnapping of, 221–
    222
  birth, 121
  childhood, 14, 121–122, 123,
    126–128, 158, 216–218
  children and, 260, 261, 282, 323
  children's births, 257, 261

description/personality, 146,
  214–215, 219, 257, 305
Ducruet marriage/divorce,
  257–258
education/schools, 216–218
engagement to Le Fur, 256–257
fashion courses/work, 218–219
father's death and, 312
on friends/friendship, 221
HIV/AIDS, charity work for, 282
house in America/Bloom, 255–
  256
languages and, 128–129
living in America, 223, 224–
  225, 254–256
modeling, 219–220
music career, 221, 222–223, 254,
  256–257, 258, 261
official duties, 261–262, 282
Peres marriage/end, 282
press/paparazzi, 141, 142, 145–
  147, 149, 214, 222, 224, 260,
  261, 265, 279–280, 281–282,
  287
public recognition, 223–224
romantic interests, 218, 219,
  224, 254–257, 261, 282
swimsuit business, 220–221
water skiing accident, 264–265,
  276
See also Grace, Princess of
  Monaco car accident (1982)
Stewart, Jackie, 185–186
Stewart, Jimmy, v, 6, 8, 23
Stowe school, 91–92
Strindberg, August, 19

CPSIA information can be obtained at www.ICGtesting.com
Printed in the USA
LVOW07s1347270415

436100LV00001BD/1/P